Grandchildren

of the

Pioneers

Copyright © 2004 by Marie Kramer

ISBN 0-7414-2209-3

Published by:

INFI∞ITY
PUBLISHING.COM

1094 New De Haven Street, Suite 100
West Conshohocken, PA 19428-2713
Info@buybooksontheweb.com
www.buybooksontheweb.com
Toll-free (877) BUY BOOK
Local Phone (610) 941-9999
Fax (610) 941-9959

∞

Printed in the United States of America

Printed on Recycled Paper

Published November 2004

LeRoy   Fred   John

1986

H.T. (Tom)   A.D. (Tony)   Albena   Marie

To all grandchildren of the pioneers,
especially to
my brothers and sister.

Thanks to

All the people who shared
stories and photographs
for this book,

and

Judy Krysl
for photo work as well as
for organization of parts
from my computer to the CD,

and

John Dobrovolny
for editorial suggestions.

Cover photo: Pioneer Mary (Regal) Ziska and her
grandchildren, Monica and Patricia. Atkinson,
Nebraska. 1931.

Other books by Marie Kramer

Homestead Fever

Out of Barbed Wire

Aurora: A Wartime Love Story

Heinrich to Henry

Table of Contents

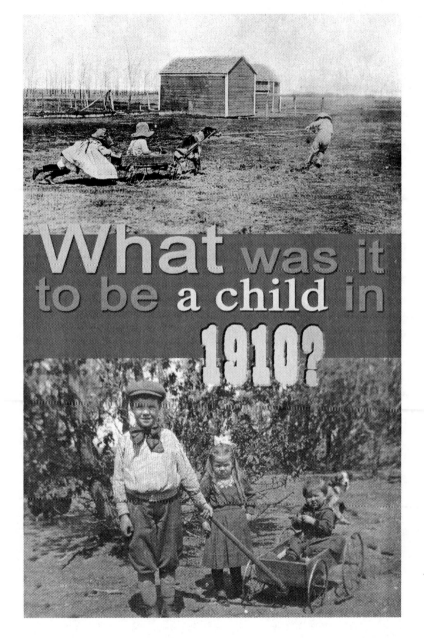

What was it to be a child in 1910?

Chapter 1

Before the Depression

The older of the grandchildren of the Nebraska pioneers were being born. The Great War, later called World War I, was fought, and President Wilson worked to establish the World Court.

The Boy Who Sat on Lincoln's Lap

Denzel McClatchey, who now in 2004 is 83 years old, tells this unique story about his pioneer grandfather who later homesteaded in Nebraska.

When my grandfather, John Brown, was a boy, his father, Robert Brown, was a shoe cobbler in Springfield, Illinois. Sometimes Abraham Lincoln came into the shoe shop. Once when Lincoln sat on a bench, waiting while his shoes were being half-soled, he lifted little John to his lap and talked to him.

John was born in 1854. Since Lincoln was born in 1809, Lincoln would have been in his late 40s when John was three or four years old.

Later, as a young man, John Brown loaded his horse and buggy on a freight car and rode the train to the end of the railroad line at Fairbury, Nebraska. He then drove his team to the York area where he met and married his wife, Katherine Hathaway. John died in 1945, and at that time surely was one of the few people in the country to have had personal contact with Abraham Lincoln.

The Titanic

Told by Bert Gissler, Osceola. 1912.

Bert is the same age as many of the Grandchildren of the Pioneers, but his mother immigrated a generation later than most settlers.

During my boyhood we rarely spoke of the Titanic, for my mother couldn't bear to hear about it. When anyone remarked about the famous ship, she shuddered, nailed us with sharp eyes, and chided us for mentioning it.

Mother's maiden name was Hanna Karlson, and she lived a meager life with her family on a small plot of rock-strewn land in southern Sweden. An older brother and sister had come to the United States, and they reported great opportunity in this sprawling land. At the age of twenty, Hanna and a cousin, Hanna Pettersson, decided to come to America.

The girls were delighted when they found tickets available on the Titanic, which was scheduled to make her maiden voyage. Even though they would have to wait a month longer to get on the magnificent ship, they purchased steerage passage on the Titanic.

Later they met two Swedish youths who also were planning to come to America. They wanted to sail on the huge Titanic, which was said to be unsinkable, and were disappointed when they found the spaces available for immigrants were taken. They proceeded to talk the girls out of their tickets. The girls sold their tickets to the boys and took a ship, the Mauritania, which was sailing earlier.

They left from Malmo, Sweden, on March 19, 1912, a month before the Titanic sailed. After stopping at Copenhagen and Liverpool, they proceeded across the Atlantic to Ellis Island. The girls went by train to Osceola, Nebraska, where their relatives lived. Hanna Karlson, in an attempt to Americanize her name, changed the spelling to Hannah Carlson, and took a job as a domestic.

We can only imagine her reaction when a few weeks after her arrival in America, she heard that the Titanic had sunk. While attempting to beat time records set by other ships, it had hit an iceberg in the dark of night, and had plunged to the bottom of the Atlantic. More than half the passengers perished in the frigid waters.

Originally, the designer of the ship had planned for more lifeboats. However, the owners vetoed the idea because they wanted the elite clientele to have easy access to the decks. More lifeboats would be a nuisance. After all, on such a sturdy ship why were lifeboats necessary?

Thus, the number of lifeboats was less than half those needed to serve the passengers if the ship were fully loaded. At some point during the discussion, the term "unsinkable" became a part of the description of the elaborate craft.

The two Hannas, after hours of terror, would have plunged down into the icy depths along with the beautiful ship. Undoubtedly, such was the fate of the two adventurous young men who used the girls' tickets.

Hannah met her husband, Rudolph Gissler in Osceola. They were married on February 25, 1914, and produced seven children. Rudolph was a blacksmith, but later rented a farm near Osceola where they spent their married life.

Is it any wonder that whenever the word Titanic was uttered by the children, Hannah shuddered, her blue eyes darkened, and she said, "Just leave that ship where it is--on the bottom of the ocean. I don't want to hear about it!"

Hannah Gissler died in 1990 at age 98.

Boom after World War I
Told by LeRoy Dobrovolny

Joe and Ella Dobrovolny were married in 1917, and were attempting to acquire a ranch. They lived on a quarter section of land about twenty-two miles southwest of Atkinson. During the boom after World War I, Joe bought a quarter section of land from Leopold Moler, which was adjacent to the south side of the quarter where they lived.

Then bad times hit, followed by the desperate Depression of the Thirties. The money Joe owed on land he bought then and more land that he bought later kept the family in dire financial straits until mid-century.

The Kiss
Told by Blanche (Freouf) Engler, Stuart. 1920s.

One day when I was about seventeen, Tillie Tasler, Clara Davis, and Frances Mlinar were visiting us. We entertained ourselves by dressing Clara and Tillie in men's clothing. Then we went outside to take a picture with our new camera.

Dad was pitching muck from the barn. From the distance across the yard, he thought Clara and Tillie were the Slaymaker boys. When I quite dramatically kissed Clara, it was too much. He called me to the barn.

"Hasn't your mother taught you anything?" he shouted. "No daughter of mine is going to behave like a street tramp and go around kissing boys. You've never seen your sisters behave like that, have you?" He glanced at a buggy whip hanging on the wall. "Big as you are, I should beat some sense into you."

The other girls pulled off their men's caps, fluffed their hair, and came running to the rescue. When Dad recognized them, he was painfully embarrassed.

"No matter what I thought I saw, I should have known better," he apologized repeatedly. "My little girl wouldn't do such a thing." I was the youngest in the family, and he always considered me "his little girl."

Dugouts
Told by Doris (Wright) Moore, Bartley. 1910s & 20s.

Everyone in our family was born in the dugout except for me. The dugout was partly a cave in the side of the canyon and partly a soddy that was connected to the front of the cave.

The older boys always slept in the dugout, even after we lived in the frame house. Paul, my youngest brother, usually slept in the house, but sometimes he got to sleep in the dugout with the others. He enjoyed being with the big boys. There were a lot of dugouts in that canyon.

4

"There must have been," said John Teter. "Our family had three dugouts. One was south of the road and two were north."

Doris' story continued:

There were seven boys in our family, and three of them, Benjamin, Harold, and Melvin, were called into the armed forces during World War I. All were sent overseas. We thought it a miracle when they came back safely!

After they were all home, Dad said, "We ought to have a dance for the boys!" That sounded good to me.

Perry Kinnison played the violin, and his wife, Elnora, played the piano or the organ.

My good friend, Marie Premer, was staying with me during the time of the dance. We got the chores done and the supper dishes put away. Then we went upstairs, laid on the bed, looked out the window, and giggled as we waited for the guests to arrive.

"Did the Moore boys come to your dances?" asked John Teter who was listening to the elderly Doris recount the story of her youth.

"Oh, yes. That's why we were watching and giggling. I had my eyes on Earl and Marie liked Lark. They sometimes arrived after others because they worked long hours and were apt to be late with chores. But they came. We could see their car lights winding down the long hill.

"Those were good days!" mused the old lady. "Yep. They might be late, but we waited for them." Then after a pause, she turned to her niece, Marva (who was the daughter of her friend, Marie, and brother-in-law, Lark Moore) and said slyly, "And we got 'em, too, didn't we?"

"You sure did!" said Marva. "You sure did."

Doris and Marie remained best friends all their lives.

Laundry in the 1920s
Told by Marie Kramer

Washing on a scrub board was back-breaking work, and was made harder by the fact that water had to be carried from the well, heated, and carried to the tub. In the summer, in addition to family laundry, our mother did the laundry for several hired men. I recall when she washed the men's greasy overalls from the hayfield, she often laid them on the scrub board and went after them with a brush.

Marie, Albena, Tony, and Ella Dobrovolny

The second picture shows a hand-run machine that was an improvement over the scrub board. We got a washer like that about 1928 or '29 when I was five or six years old. Water, soap, and the clothes were placed in the tin, cradle-shaped tub. The vertical stick on the side was pushed back and forth by hand, thus swinging the tub full of water and clothes.

On top of the machine was a wringer. The operator used one hand to turn the wringer and the other to feed the clothes into the rollers. It was a clumsy way to wring clothes, but was an improvement over twisting the water out by hand.

To wash a load of clothes was supposed to take fifteen minutes, but that time was meant for an adult. When one of us children was given the job, our rate of speed was slower, which meant we had to work longer. To us, it seemed like forever.

The Missing Ducks
Told by Joe Mlinar, Atkinson. 1912.

We had several ducks that hatched 24 ducklings. It was a wet spring and the creek was high. One day the ducks were missing. We figured they followed the creek, but we weren't able to locate them. They were gone the rest of the summer.

Each fall we made a fifty-gallon barrel of sauerkraut, which required us to have a large cabbage patch. One day my mother said, "The cabbage is big enough so we can start eating it. Go to the garden and get a head."

When I returned, I told her, "There isn't any cabbage in the patch. It's gone. Someone must have stolen it."

"Oh, that can't be!" she said. "Who would steal cabbage?" We both went to the patch. She saw that I was right, for there was no cabbage. However, this time the ducks were there, and were pecking at cabbage roots that extended from the ground.

With the coming of fall, the creek had dried up. The ducks must have decided there would be better fare at home and thus had returned. We wondered how long it took them to eat all the cabbage.

There weren't many fruits or vegetables over the winter, and sauerkraut was a main staple. We bought cabbage from the neighbors to make it that year.

Mules in World War I
Told by Charlie Mlinar, Atkinson. 1917.

My Dad sold mules to the army during the First World War. To haul baled hay to town, he hitched a well-broken mule team to the wagon, and then placed a less-experienced mule on either side. By the time the mules pulled the heavy load to town, they were tired and were glad to stand quietly during the unloading.

A government agent stationed himself by the weight scales. He'd offer to buy mules from the farmers, figuring if

7

they were using the animals to haul hay, they'd be well broken. Dad would sell the young mules and go home with our old faithful team to begin training another green pair. I think Dad got $150 per mule team, which was a pile of money in those days.

The Automobile
Told by George Hytrek, Atkinson. 1919.

Along with the arrival of the grandchildren of the pioneers came general usage of the automobile. My dad, Paul Hytrek, bought his first car, a Model T with top and side curtains, in 1919. He never learned to drive, and since I was the oldest, the job usually fell to me.

Before I cranked it, I reached under the dash and turned the key located on the coil box. Then I adjusted the spark lever on the left side of the steering wheel. If a person forgot the spark, the crank could kick him if the motor backfired, which could break an arm. Next, I went to the front of the car and spun the crank.

There was a caution for holding the crank. When you grasped the handle, you had to leave your thumb on the same side of the crank as your fingers. If you wrapped your thumb around the way a person normally grasps an object, your thumb could be torn out of joint if the motor backfired.

A wire from the carburetor came out by the radiator. The person starting the car could adjust it with his left hand while cranking with his right.

Once inside, the driver released the hand brakes while he pressed the low gear pedal toward the floor. The car crept ahead. When it reached a fair rate of speed, the driver removed his foot from the pedal, and the car was in high gear. Next, he adjusted the gas lever, which was on the right side of the steering wheel.

I remember what a hard time we had on cold nights when we went to dances. The dance would end about three o'clock and we'd go outside to start our cars. The best way was to jack up a hind wheel. One fellow would spin the hind wheel while another cranked.

Joe Dobrovolny first saw a car in 1902 when he rode on horseback into Laramie, Wyoming. Cars, invented ten years earlier, were being displayed as a novelty. They were a source of amusement, for people couldn't imagine they would ever be of much use. A car couldn't manage the rough terrain of those days, and unlike a horse, couldn't even wade a creek.

No one envisioned a network of roads. Cars didn't come into general usage until the late teens and early twenties. Joe bought his first car, a used Model T Ford, in 1921.

Chapped Hands
Told by Orval Monson, Blair. 1920s.

When I was a kid, we had to milk cows early in the morning before school and also after school at night. Milking is a cold job because a person can't wear gloves while working. One winter, due to milking in the frigid weather, my hands chapped. The rough skin turned brown and scabby, making my hands looked dirty.

"Orval," said the teacher, "You should wash your hands before you come to school. They look terrible. Go wash them right now."

I went to the wash pan, dipped some water from the bucket and washed them as well as I could. When I returned to my seat, the teacher again noticed my hands.

"Orval! I told you to wash your hands!"

"I tried," I told her. "But they're chapped. They won't come clean."

"Well, I'll get them clean!" she said as she took me back to the wash pan. "You shouldn't come to school with hands looking like that!"

She went to work on them with soap and water. Wow, did that ever hurt! I squirmed and winced. Finally, she noticed my hands were bleeding between the brown scabs, and she realized that chapped hands really couldn't look clean. She felt terrible, and apologized repeatedly.

In those days, many young girls taught as soon as they were out of high school. It was a big job with eight grades to teach, fires to build, water to carry, and janitor work to do. Considering it all, they did a wonderful job.

Invading Bees
Told by Albena Kramer, Atkinson. 1925.

In the summers, my father hired men for the hay harvest. In order to make room to expand the dining room table, our mother removed the stovepipe from the tall, Great Northern stove and shoved it back to the wall. Needing to

10

close the chimney hole in the wall, she shoved a coffee can into it. The can was slightly large, making one side of it crinkle.

One day, we discovered a huge swarm of honeybees flying around the chimney. In a short while, there were bees skittering on the dining room floor.

"They're coming in through that crinkle in the can in the chimney hole," Mom exclaimed. Climbing on a chair, she placed a cardboard over the opening. There she stood, considering what to do next.

She decided to have her eldest, LeRoy, age 6, stand on top of the stove and hold the cardboard in place while she went to the cob house to get some stovepipe. LeRoy climbed on the chair with her. She tried with one hand to help him onto the stovetop, but succeeded only in frightening him.

"Albena, take the little kids in the kitchen and close the door," instructed Mom. "I must take down the cardboard while I help LeRoy onto the stove. More bees are sure to get in." I herded Marie, 2, into the kitchen and followed with Tony in the baby buggy.

Mother took the cardboard down, and more bees came inside. She boosted LeRoy onto the stove, but the height and the angry bees frightened him. When one stung him, he screamed, stiff with fear. She took him down, sent him to the kitchen, and called me in.

She lifted me onto the stove, replaced the cardboard, and told me to hold it firmly while she went to get the stovepipe. After she put the stovepipe in place, she lit papers in the stove. Bees in the chimney soon buzzed up and out. She swatted the ones in the house. In a short while the entire swarm, intimidated by the heat and smoke, lifted in a dark cloud to look for a more suitable home.

LeRoy was embarrassed that he hadn't been able to stand on the tall stove, especially since his younger sister was able to do it. To his dismay, the story was retold many times. It may be the reason he suffered from a fear of heights all his life.

Memories from My Teen Years
Told by Earl Moore, Bartley. 1925.

Nose flies hit this country in the mid 1920's. Horses swung their heads up and down, rubbed their noses on their legs, or struck with their front feet. Finally we were able to purchase nose baskets with a fine mesh that kept the flies out.

In September, prior to corn picking, we used the baskets when we planted wheat in the cornfield. A horse pulled a small drill that fit between the rows. A man or child walked behind to drive. In addition to keeping flies from the horse's nose, the baskets kept the horse from swiping corn off the stalks.

When I was in my late teens, I could drill 40 rows a day, each one-half mile long, which means I walked 20 miles and planted eight acres. In addition, we had to fill the drill with seed each round. The horse could rest, but the man walked to the wagon, got a drink from the jug, carried seed back, and filled the drill. Thus the man didn't get any rest. Those years, a person slept well when night came, unless he was fighting allergies or leg cramps, which sometimes happened.

Another memorable experience was the moving of the graves of our father and our brother. At that time, Lark was 24 and I was 18. Our father who had been dead about 14 years and our small brother who had died of whooping cough, had been buried in the cemetery in Tryon, but Mother wanted the graves moved to Cambridge. After completing the paper work, she engaged a mortician to be present. Lark and I did the digging.

As soon as the air hit the rough wooden coffins, they disintegrated. The shoes fell into pieces. Even some of the bones, especially those of the baby, had crumbled into kind of a white ash. We collected the scraps of bone, white ash, and clothing. We reburied the remains of both bodies in one box in Cambridge.

High on a Windmill
Told by Dorothy Bunker, Milligan. 1926.

When I was two years old, I gave my mother a terrible scare by climbing the windmill. When she discovered me, I was at the top and was standing on the little platform under the turning wheel. She was frantic.

I loved bananas, and it happened she had some in the house. She coaxed me down by promising me a banana.

"Be careful! Be careful!" she cautioned gently as she stood underneath.

When I got down she gave me a half dozen hugs and the banana. Shortly after I had finished eating, the scolding began. Despite my tender age, I understood I must not climb the mill. At the end of the lecture, she spanked me.

When my father got home, he removed the lower steps from the ladder in order to make sure I never tried it again.

The Mules and the Haystacker
Told by Charley Tasler, Atkinson. 1920s.

Ornery? I think the word was invented for those two mules. Their names were Punch and Judy, and my brother Tony owned them. I never did like mules, and those two didn't do one thing to change my mind any. Tony defended them, though, and it made me disgusted the way he always babied them. He was the only one that could hook them up. If any of the rest of us tried, their hind feet flew like lightning.

One day Tony was moving the hay stacker, using those two outlaw mules. He was leaning back against the slanted boards. As they were crossing a ditch, one of the runners caught on the bank, making the stacker lurch. Tony was thrown off, and he landed on one side of the "V" chain that was pulling the stacker.

The mules, frightened by the lurch of the stacker, began to run in spite of the fact they were pulling the huge

13

piece of equipment. Tony clung to the chain desperately, but a part of his body slid under the boards of the stacker.

I was operating a four-horse sweep, and I managed to pull in front of the plunging team while a couple other fellows in the crew came running from the sides. Tony's mules stopped when they ran into my sweep. They stood in a tangle around it. Someone grabbed the lines, and I ran to Tony.

We had a difficult time rescuing him from under the stacker boards. He had been dragged in the stubbles and was bleeding from deep scrapes over his entire body. We hauled him to Atkinson, and Doctor Douglas had the tedious job of removing the spears of stubble from his chewed flesh. Tony couldn't do field work for the rest of the summer. During that time, brother Bill worked Tony's mules.

They had discovered that if they pulled to the side in opposite directions, the driver could no longer control them, and they'd run away. So Bill chained them together. Then he made a leather whip, and those two outlaws learned to work.

But still they were ornery. They were the meanest creatures that ever ate hay.

Pigs in the Ditch
By the Herricks about the Hytreks, Stuart, 1920s.

After people began using cars, their children often used the old buggies to drive to school. The Hytrek children and the Krobot children both drove one-horse buggies. There was a barn in the schoolyard in which the horses were stabled during the day.

The children were told to come directly home after school, but sometimes the Hytreks took the long way home and drove around the section past the Krobot place. The horses were too old for racing, and the trip past their friend's house made their journey two miles longer. However, the children of the two families enjoyed switching seats in order to pair up with their friends.

Once some of Herrick's pigs, in an attempt to stay cool, burrowed into a muddy ditch. In those days, pigs were

14

often not confined. As the Hytrek buggy rumbled by, a huge sow rose out of the mud and emitted a loud grunt. The startled horse shied and began to run. Rita Hytrek fell head first into the mire, landing among the hogs.

The old horse didn't run far. The other children caught him and waited for their limping sister to catch up. Scuffed and muddy, she climbed back into the buggy.

Dough on the Floor
Told by Mary Tenopir, St. Paul. Early 1920s.

When Carrie Kramer, Stuart, was in the hospital having her tonsils removed, her teen-age niece, Mary Kramer, came to look after the house and the three small children. Mary was determined to manage all the work well. She mixed the bread dough and placed it on the cupboard to rise. She set the laundry tub and the washboard in the kitchen, and while keeping an eye on the three tots, she worked at the laundry.

"I'm going out to hang some clothes," she told them. "You kids can watch me from the window."

The children didn't watch for long. Looking around the kitchen, they spied the dough on the cupboard. One of the little girls stepped on a lower shelf and reached a hand up to grasp the edge of the bowl. It was soon on the floor.

Punching and pulling at the dough was even more fun than she had supposed. The other two children joined her, and they all had a wonderful time until Mary returned. Then the fun was over, for she was, she said later, livid with anger.

"I didn't spank them," she said, "but I sure felt like it. I had to discard the dough and mix a new batch."

Orphan Train
About Mary Tenopir, St. Paul, and Toni Weiler, York. Early 1900s.

Since New York City was full of immigrants who often couldn't get jobs, children sometimes had to be left at

15

orphanages. The overflowing foundling homes were somewhat alleviated when many of the children were sent on trains to the Midwest in an effort to find homes for them.

Mary (Kramer) Tenopir came at age two from New York City to Nebraska on an orphan train in 1912. John and Mary Kramer of Stuart, Nebraska, adopted her. At the time, there was a small boy, Leo, in the family. Later, four more brothers, Joe, Lawrence, Bernard, and Louis, were born.

Once a year a social worker came to see the Kramers. The visits were extremely upsetting to Mary for she feared she might be sent back to New York. When she was ten, she had been told to pick up a basket of cobs. She hadn't yet gone when the social worker arrived.

"Mom met him at the kitchen door and he asked if I had been a good girl," said Mary. "As soon as possible, I slipped into the living room and out the side door. I hurried to the pigpen and the cobs were soon flying into the basket. When I returned with the cobs, the worker talked to me for a while. I was scared half to death. But when he left, he gave me a dime."

After considerable research, Mary discovered her original name had been Rogers. Her mother had died soon after she was born, but she was able to find other relatives in New York.

Five other families in Stuart adopted children from the same orphan train.

The mother of Bob Weiler, Antoinette (Martin) Weiler, lived most of her life in Hastings. She came from New York City from a foundling home when she was about three years old. She was one of thousands who came on orphan trains. George and Millie Martin who lived in McCook, Nebraska, adopted her. They were in their late forties.

George worked as a conductor for the *Chicago, Burlington, and Quincy Railroad* and thus was gone from home much of the time. Millie was reluctant to take in a child, but George thought it would be company for her, and also would be a help to them in their old age. Millie finally consented.

Antoinette (Toni) had a forlorn childhood. She later vowed that when she had children, no child in the world would be more loved than her own. She kept her word, and was a loving mother to her eight children, three boys followed by five girls.

Toni searched for information about her birth parents. She learned that she was Irish, her father's name was Murphy, and she had a brother or sister. One of her great sorrows was that she was not able to find any information about her sibling.

In their elder years, both Mary Tenopir and Toni Weiler were active in the annual Orphan Train Reunions. They knew each other well.

Toni lived to be 85, dying in 1996. Mary lived to be 92 and died in 2003.

From Hired Girl to Marriage
Told by Mabel Werner Bogue, Atkinson. 1920s.

I began working for mothers with new babies when I was fifteen. If I arrived before the baby was born, I helped Doctor McKee deliver the baby. Then I cleaned the newcomer with olive oil. We didn't use water on a new baby for about three days.

The baby was fed boiled water with a little sugar until the time when the mother had milk. In addition to caring for mother and baby, I did the cooking, cleaning, bread baking, churning, and laundry, as well as took care of the other children.

One of the first babies I helped Doc McKee deliver was for Mrs. Roy Hipke. It was a little girl. I don't recall if it was Goldie Fern or Sylvia. I liked working there because the older kids were such good help.

After I married, we had no cellar, and the flowing well that served the house was near the creek, several blocks beyond the barn. My husband put a barrel over the well, drilled holes in the sides to let the water out, and made a lid out of wood. On top was an iron wheel to keep the lid in place. Unhandy as it was, I could keep butter, milk, cheese and vegetables cool by storing them in the barrel. I beat a worn path to the well.

Once when we had threshers, a downpour of rain stopped the work. The men came in for supper early, putting a rush on me. Milton Andrus offered to help by going to the well to bring in the milk and butter. He had to wade water because the low ground near the creek was flooded

"If ever there's another flash flood like this," he said later, "we will go without milk and butter for supper."

Ghost Lights
Emmet, Nebraska. 1920s and early '30s.

Some people called the strange lights of the 1920s and 30s "ghost lights" and some called them "earth lights." People northeast of Atkinson or about ten miles north of Emmet often reported seeing them. In those days the prairie was dark at night except for the occasional appearance of ghost lights.

Some thought fumes from rotting vegetation near Eagle Creek caused the phenomenon. Another theory was that the lights indicated oil deposits, a thought that initiated the formation of an oil district. A drilling outfit was hired, but no oil was found.

Rose Goeke said, "The lights would float around. Sometimes they were so bright you could take out your watch and see the time. They sure did cause a stir!"

George Albrecht said, "Once my folks saw a spook light by the windmill. It was so bright it lit up the side of the barn. This one was not moving, but usually the lights moved along on the prairie. Some people chased them with a horse, but couldn't catch them."

Ted Braun said: "We lived north of Emmet. One hot day my brother and I decided we would shock grain after sundown when it was cooler. We were hard at work when suddenly a light lit up the field.

"We stood still, stiff with surprise. In a couple seconds the light went out. Frightened, we ran home. Our folks said the lights were common in this area and weren't dangerous. But we were scared anyway.

"We had a mule that sometimes jumped the fence and ran south. One night the neighbors saw a light north of their place, and thought it probably was us, using a lantern to look for our mule. The trouble was, our mule wasn't out that night and neither were we. We figured it was a ghost light."

Dorothy Janzing said: "We were married in 1927. One winter when the snow was deep, the earthlights were especially bright. If they came out of the earth the way people said they did, how did they get through all that snow?

"We hatched chicks in an incubator, and I usually got up at two-thirty in the night to check on it. I had to go from our bedroom, through the kitchen and front room, and into the spare bedroom where we had the incubator. Some nights it was so light that I didn't have to light a lamp. I think I could have read a newspaper.

"Scared? Not really. We worked hard and I was short of sleep. I just went back to bed."

Roy Goeke said: "Once I pulled a joke on a fellow. I knew he would be coming home from town in the night. We had an old railroad lantern and I polished it and lit it. I turned the shield so it couldn't be seen from the road.

"The old fellow was driving a Model A. When I heard him coming, I turned the lantern toward him. He stopped. When I bounced the lantern up and down, he took off with a roar. I think he had his foot all the way into the carburetor. He went home a-tearin' and didn't stop for a second look."

19

Ralph Ries said: "Fortunately, the lights never set anything afire. One night a fellow was driving a team of mules. A light came rolling over the prairie and scared the mules so bad they ran away. The fellow went home fast that particular night.

"The lights appeared in both cold weather and hot, and were more apt to be seen after midnight."

Melvin Riley, Speeder *My uncle*
Late 1920s. Atkinson. *& Mother*

As a young man, Melvin Riley worked during haying season on the Hookstra Ranch about 21 miles southwest of Atkinson. His sister, Olive Riley, worked as a hired girl on the Joe Dobrovolny Ranch about three miles north of Hookstras. Melvin was paid six dollars a week and Olive got two-fifty. Each Monday, Melvin brought Olive to work and then proceeded to his own job. He drove an old flivver, which was little more than wheels and running gears with a box behind. It seemed to be made mostly of rattle and noise.

Joe always chugged slowly into the ranch yard, driving his old Model T Ford, but Melvin came swinging in at a brisk rate. The dog barked, the cats fled, while chickens squawked and flew every direction.

One day Joe was home when Melvin wheeled merrily into the long driveway.

"Don't you come into this yard at that speed again," he told the youth. "There are small children living here. The speed limit in Atkinson is twelve miles an hour, and that's fast enough out here, too."

Thereafter, Melvin reduced speed when he drove into the ranch yard.

Duck Hunting in the Pasture
Told by Lawrence Kramer, Atkinson. Early 30s.

When Lawrence was a kid, he loved to hunt ducks. There was no thrill greater than that of getting a duck and having it appear, roasted with dressing, on the supper table. As long as he could get home by chore time, no walking distance was too great, and no weather was too cold. The marksmanship of this new hunter was less than perfect, but he enjoyed trying.

One day while crossing a pasture, he heard a thundering sound. He turned and was startled to see a herd of steers running toward him. He also noticed their wild rampage had scared up a couple ducks.

He didn't know whether to run from the steers or shoot at the ducks, and there was no time to debate the question. Oh, how he wanted to get a duck! These were big, plump mallards and were flying low.

He raised the gun to his shoulder and fired, then pivoted to face the steers. He was surprised to see the frightened animals turning to run in the opposite direction. His story didn't reveal whether or not he got a duck, but the odds are against it. Probably he didn't.

Vaclav's War with New Styles
Told by Albert and Mary Ziska, Stuart. 1925.

Pioneer Vaclav Krysl stomped and roared concerning the indecent styles worn by his younger daughters. As the older girls, born in the late 1800s, grew up and married, they wore respectable clothes. Skirts reached to the ankles, bodices were fitted, and waists, with the benefit of corsets, were nipped in. The narrow, pointed, high-topped shoes, fastened with many buttons, were extremely confining and uncomfortable, but it had been so for many decades. Vaclav was proud to present his children.

But two decades later, he scolded his younger daughters for "going about in rags." Dresses hung loosely from shoulders to hems. Worst of all, legs were revealed almost to the knees. Disgraceful!

"You could cut neck and arm holes in a gunny sack, and wear it," Vaclav roared. "You would look as good."

21

Christina, V.J., Mary, Joe, Agnes

Mid 1920's

Early 1900's

Styles changed from older children to younger ones.

Also the delicate shoes had disappeared, and in their place, low-cut, round-toed footwear became popular.

One night when Mary Krysl and Albert Ziska were "keeping company," Albert's Model T stopped when they were on the way home from a party. By the dim light of a kerosene lantern, Albert worked frantically but could not restart the machine. Mary would obviously miss her curfew, and Vaclav was famous for his rages.

Finally, in desperation, they walked to a nearby farm where Albert asked for assistance in getting Mary home. More time elapsed while they drove horses into the barn, harnessed them, and hitched them to a buggy. It was nearly dawn, but Mary hoped to slip into the girls' bedroom, unnoticed.

Vaclav rose from his chair as she opened the door.

"Where have you been?" he roared in Czech. "I told you when to be home! Can't you tell time?"

22

Albert, a tall but slight man, stepped to Mary's side and cleared his throat. "I'm sorry," he said in his thin voice. "We had car trouble."

"Car trouble!" Vaclav boomed, and added some vulgar words. "You could have walked home and arrived before this. That party was over three hours ago. Three hours ago! What were you doing all that time?"

"We-l-ll, I tried to fix the car, and then we had to walk for help--and harness horses--"

Vaclav ranted on and on. Finally he turned back to Mary and ended his tirade with, "and if you ever do this again, I'll throw you out of the house, and all your shameful rags with you!"

The Bronco Named Bob
Told by Lawrence Dobrovolny, O'Neill. Late 1920s.

A cousin who lived in Norfolk raised some purebred goats. They milked them and made butter and cheese. We thought the baby goats were cute, which prompted our cousins to crate some newborns and send them to us. After several batches of goats arrived, we had seven goats.

Those little rascals got into everything: chicken feed, cattle bunks, hog troughs, the garden. They even nibbled on Mom's homemade soap. They ate the little trees that we were tenderly caring for in the hope of getting some shade and shelter on the barren prairie. One day the goats upset a can of cream, and when Pa saw them lapping it up, he swore he'd shoot all seven of them.

"Let me get rid of them," I told Pa. "I'll trade them to Charlie Massey." Charlie was a Sioux Indian who lived in a shack a few miles north of us and raised horses and goats. He had a sorrel horse he considered too ornery to be of any use. He had never broken him to ride and hadn't even named him. He simply called him "the bronc".

"Well, those worthless goats better be off the place by tomorrow," said Pa darkly.

We kids had a horse named Molly, too old to be of any use to the men. She took me to Charley's place, and I managed to make a deal with him: for the seven goats he traded me the ornery bronc.

I named my horse Bob. At first he was a mean one. He'd buck and kick like a mule, but I didn't give up on him. It took a long time and much patience to tame him and train him to ride, but eventually, he became a trusted, faithful animal. I kept him all his life.

Later I lived on the O'Donald place, which was several miles away from my parent's ranch. I'd get on old Bob early in the morning and go coyote hunting by Holt Creek. I shot several coyotes from Bob's back. I'd drape a dead coyote behind the saddle and take it home. I could get three dollars apiece for the hides.

Chicken Thieves
Told by Marie Kramer, Atkinson. 1928.

When I was four years old, I was suddenly awakened by Mom's insistent whisper as she shook my dad awake.

"Joe! Joe! Someone's stealing our chickens."

Outside, hens were squawking and flapping their wings. Dad slipped out of bed and went to the storage space under the stairs to get his shotgun. Even though he was having trouble loading it in the dark, he cautioned Mom not to strike a match as it might warn the thieves. I covered my head with blankets and trembled with fear.

After loading the gun, he quietly crept out the door and slipped around the corner of the house. He aimed at the treetops and fired. The house shook with the mighty blast that was followed by loud popping sounds in the grove. I think the popping must have been the sound of the shot hitting tree branches.

Soon we heard a Model T car roar away from the backside of the grove. Dad returned and put his gun under the stairs. He struck a match to look at the clock.

"It's midnight," he said.

24

I trembled through the long hours until morning. At that time our house had no closets, and clothes were hung on nails along one side of the wall. Faint light from the moon allowed me a dim view of the garments of varying colors, and my imagination turned them into sinister forms.

The next day my mother found that about a third of her laying flock was gone.

Lost in a Fog
Told by Bernard Kaup, Bassett. Late 1920s.

We always got up long before dawn. Our dad made sure of that. The idea was to get the milking chores done and our breakfast eaten in time to be ready to go to work at dawn. One morning there was more than the darkness to obstruct our view, for a dense fog hemmed us in. We needed to bring in the horses, which prompted three of us boys to head into the pasture.

Since we wouldn't be able to see a horse unless we bumped into it, we decided to separate so as to cover more ground. Soon afterward, I became disoriented in the milk-like fog. I wandered about.

Eventually I came upon the horses, but how would I get them home since I had no idea which way to drive them? I pushed them ahead aimlessly, hoping to come upon something that would indicate our position. There was nothing visible except the grass and weeds under our feet and the darkness and the thick fog around us.

Finally I decided to startle the horses, hoping they would then head for home. I leaped into their midst, shouting, and waving my arms. They struck out across the pasture, and I had no idea whether they were stubbornly going the opposite direction or were going toward the barn.

Eventually, the corrals rose out of the fog. The horses had led me home.

Turkey Roundup
Told by Orval Monson, Blair. 1920s.

We always raised turkeys on our Iowa farm. In the spring we watched where the turkeys nested and then placed a wooden barrel on its side on that spot for the hens to use for protection while they brooded the eggs. After the eggs hatched, we'd care for the hatchlings for a while, but soon some wild instinct seemed to call. The old turkeys lifted their heads, looked this way and that, and headed for the sloughs. The young turks went with them.

When fall came, we had a turkey roundup. Mother, Dad, and all we kids scattered along one edge of the farm. We walked toward the opposite side, shooing the turkeys ahead.

When they squatted in the grass to hide, we made a gobbling sound, and they lifted their heads to investigate. Then we'd continue to drive them. The turkey roundup was always an exciting time for us. When we reached the yard we had a big noisy flock that we penned in the barn.

We slaughtered them and dressed them for the holiday market. Mother and Dad were fast at dressing turkeys. They could do sixty in one day.

Long Underwear
Told by Hazel Strope.

I grew up on a farm between Tobias and Ohiowa. During the winter we wore long, black stockings, held up by hated garter belts with over-the-shoulder straps. Worse still, our family was required to wear long underwear.

At that time, and for many years to come, girls wore dresses to school, which meant their legs were visible. There was no way to make stockings look smooth since the underwear legs ended at the ankles and produced bulges. I begged my mother to let me wear shorter underwear, but she was firm. She didn't want me to catch pneumonia, after all!

My brother and I walked a mile across a field to get to school. We paused in a low spot in the middle of the field where I unfastened my stockings, and after rolling up my underwear legs, refastened them. On the way home, I reversed the operation.

We had water in a stone jar, with one dipper to serve all, usually about a dozen pupils. Since we burned coal in an old stove, there was no way to keep fire overnight. The jar had to be emptied, or the water would freeze and break the jar. Looking back, the common drinking dipper probably initiated more colds than the absence of winter underwear would have.

The Horse and the Bicycle
Told by Derrel Hutchens, Geneva. 1920s.

When I was young, I rode a horse named Pet about five and a half miles to Geneva High School. I envied another boy who wheeled merrily to school on a bicycle. I thought it a more modern way to travel and wished I had a bike, but there was no way we could afford one.

One day I told him how I admired his bicycle and was surprised to learn that he wished for a horse. We decided we'd trade for a few days.

I felt quite stylish, up with the times, riding the bicycle home. When I got home, I parked it and went directly to do my evening chores.

I grinned. How easy! I had no horse to stable or water or feed. One less chore! In addition, when Saturday came, I wouldn't have to clean a horse stall. I was sure it was a good trade and hoped my friend would want to make it permanent.

The next morning there was a strong, cold, north wind blowing. Facing into the howling gale, I pedaled courageously, but by the time I had struggled against it for five and a half miles, I was exhausted. I was glad to reverse the deal and repossess my sturdy pony.

Jesse Dobrovolny and his horse, Molly.

Horse Stories
Told by Catherine Hamilton, Stuart. Early 1930s.

Lincoln Hamilton came home with a team of horses who were tired and thirsty from an afternoon of fieldwork. He took them into the barn, leaving the barn door open. He unharnessed the first one and turned him loose to go outside. Just as the horse headed for the door, Linc's small son, Alvon, appeared in the doorway. The child's mother, Catherine, was near, but did not see the approaching horse in time to snatch Alvon out of harm's way.

The horse, anxious to get outside, trotted purposefully toward the opening. The small tot wasn't enough to dissuade the thirsty animal from his desire to reach the water tank in the corral. Gathering his muscles, he gave a leap. More than half a ton of horseflesh lifted into the air, sailed over the doorsill, and over the head of the little boy. Alvon was frightened, but probably not half as scared as were his parents at the thought of what could have happened.

When corn had to be picked and husked by hand, it was difficult for people to get the job completed before winter commenced in earnest. Children, probably from third grade on, helped pick after school and on Saturdays. Wives helped their husbands whenever they could.

When Lincoln and Catherine Hamilton picked corn, they placed their two small children, Luella and Alvon, in the front of the wagon box. They made sure they threw the ears of corn in the back part of the box so they wouldn't strike one of the children. As was usual in cornpicking, no one drove the horses. The animals moved down the cornrows by themselves, starting and stopping according to the directions given by a picker.

Catherine was a careful mother and warned the children of all the dangers she could think of.

"Don't throw kernels of corn at each other. You could put someone's eye out. Be sure not to stuff corn in your nose. One of the Gans kids put a bean in his nose, and he choked to death on it. Don't climb on the corn in the back of the wagon. You could get hit by a flying ear."

Luella didn't take her doll along, for it was the only toy she possessed. She was careful with it. The children were bored, penned in that tiny enclosure for an extended period of time.

One day Luella leaned over the side of the wagon box, and as Linc clucked to the horses as a signal for them to move forward, she tumbled out. She landed ahead of the front wheel, and it ran over her. Her mother was picking the row nearest the wagon. She grabbed the child and pulled her out before the back wheel, which bore the main weight of the load, passed over her.

Luella was stiff and bruised for some time, but miraculously, she suffered no broken bones.

Polio
By Pauline (Teter) Phillips, Cambridge. 1930s.

I had a headache on Tuesday night, September 30, 1930. When I had to miss school on Wednesday, I took it in stride, but was upset when I had to miss a second day, then a third. I was in the fifth grade.

Friday morning I started across the kitchen, planning to make the usual morning trip to the outhouse, but I fell. I'm sure, with as much polio as there was during those years, my parents were alerted. They took me to the doctor where I was immediately given a spinal tap.

It came back positive. I had polio. By that time, all I could move was my arms.

Our family was immediately quarantined in our own home. No one could visit us, and people from our household couldn't leave. Ordinarily, we sold cream, but now Dad had to feed the milk to the hogs. When people brought us groceries, they left them in the yard.

The doctor prescribed medication with eight ounces of water every four hours. The medicine had a wintergreen flavor, and to this day, I can't stand to taste wintergreen.

We had a telephone, and when neighbors or relatives called, I could hear everything that was said about me. Since the news was usually not good, I didn't feel very encouraged about my condition.

I looked forward to the mail. A neighbor had my name announced over the radio, and requested mail for me. I enjoyed the letters and cards. Our mailbox was by the schoolhouse, but while we were quarantined, the mailman brought the mail to our farm.

Also, many people brought flowers. Every flat surface in my room was occupied by a vase of flowers. Each morning, Dad changed the water on them.

My brother Don was two years old. He didn't understand why he couldn't come into my room to see me. They had to watch him because he often tried to sneak in. My sister, Elma, three years my senior, was barred from school. She slept in the dining room on the spring couch while we were quarantined.

Mother changed my bedding and did the laundry every day. It was long before the time of electricity in rural areas, so the laundry was no small job, especially since Mother was waiting for a child (John) to be born. The lack of electricity meant no refrigeration, and the farm homemaker usually killed, plucked, and dressed a chicken each day. Now Dad took over that task for Mother.

After three weeks, the quarantine was lifted. Then we had to fumigate. My parents placed a boiler on the stove, filled it with water, and heated it to boiling. Then they added a medication and we left the house. We stayed with an uncle and aunt that night.

Dad carried me everywhere I went. My legs were drawn up and my back was weak. The most painful part came later. My legs had to be stretched. Dad was the one who pulled and stretched them. I cried with the intense pain, and everyone else cried with me. Mother rubbed my legs and back with cocoa butter to help strengthen, straighten, and exercise them.

It took about two months of torturous exercises to get my limbs so they would stretch out, but since they were paralyzed, I couldn't move them.

The braces came next. Doctor Paul Rodwell made them for me. First we got high-topped shoes. Then the doctor drilled holes in the heels. Iron rods went from the heels up my legs to bands that were both above and below my knees. When they were ready, we went to his office. He fitted them on me.

I still couldn't stand up. It was no wonder since I hadn't been on my feet for about two months. I was disappointed, but the doctor told me I should take the braces home and keep trying.

There was a little space between my bed and the wall. I could wiggle off the bed into that space. Using the bed and the wall to hold me up, I kept trying. I was determined. Finally I was able to walk a little. It was a real treat after being carried everywhere for months.

The folks got me a tricycle, thinking it would help me exercise, but I couldn't ride it. I was too big for it. The next summer they got me an old bike and put a frame under the back wheel. It worked better.

Mom's mother, Grandma Mayo, died in October. Grandpa died the following March, and John was born in July. It was quite a year for Mom.

Crawmers had a store in Bartley. They had ramps, probably for carting groceries into the store. They also had a step. I was able to get up and down the ramp, but had to practice on the step for a long time. It was an exciting day that summer when I could navigate that step.

The next fall I returned to school. I had missed an entire year. I had discarded my braces and crutches in May or June of 1931, and now walked three fourths of a mile to school. When I fell, I crawled into the ditch and used the slope on the side of the road to get back on my feet.

The summer of 1934, I went to Lincoln to Dr. Thompson and Dr. Ferciot (pronounced fur-see-o). They put me in a body cast to help straighten my back. That first trip to the hospital, I was in traction with weights on both legs and on my head. They straightened my back about four inches. I was four inches taller when I came home. I was still in a body cast.

The casts were changed every six weeks, and my back was slowly getting straighter. Then in the fall of 1935 I was told they couldn't straighten any more. I had two choices: I could wear a brace all my life, or I could have spinal fusion surgery.

In the fall of 1935 after my first semester of tenth grade, I decided to have surgery. I was told I'd have to stay in Lincoln for eight weeks afterward. My parents took me from Bartley to Lincoln in a Model A, driving over graveled roads. The car traveled about 35 MPH, which made it an all day trip.

The doctor suggested I go to a movie during the departure of my parents. That decision was a wise one, because I was excited about the movie and there were no tears when they took leave. I got out of the car to go to the movie and they left for home. After the movie I took a bus to the hospital. I had to walk the last two blocks.

I was in traction for five weeks. My spinal fusion surgery took place the day before Valentine's Day. In an effort to straighten my back, the doctor took bone from one of my shins and fused it to my spine. In the area where the bone was spliced, my back is stiff.

After surgery I was placed in a cast and lay on my stomach for a week. Later I was allowed to change position a part of the time. The cast enclosed my body, and also there was a cast on the leg from which they had taken the bone.

I was allowed to stay in the children's ward even though I was actually too old. It cost ten dollars a week. I was in Lincoln for thirteen weeks.

My back remained curved. All my life, I have had to wear padding on one side of my body to make my clothing fit. My legs turned out all right, but one heel won't reach the floor.

I came home from Lincoln in a brace. Dad had taken the passenger seat out of the Model A and had installed an ambulance cart that extended from front to back. We made many trips and wore that old car out. I recall that once the rods went out on the way, and the car had to be overhauled en route.

I had worked hard to keep up with my school lessons, but barely had credits enough to graduate. In fact, I had to take a semester of typing to get a credit I needed. I was the only one in that typing class.

I had taken Normal Training, and had received good grades in it. I applied for a teaching position in Freedom School, and signed a contract. I taught there three years.

For a time, I was going with Junior Housley who lived south of Freedom. In August, my sister Elma got a letter from Walter Phillips asking her for a date. She refused him. When county fair time came, Walter drove into our yard. Elma went out, but in a short time she returned.

"It's you he wants to see," she said to me. I went out and he asked me to go to McCook to the fair. I went. It was our first date.

He said he hadn't been interested in Elma to begin with, but he thought I was off limits because I was going with Junior Housley who was his friend. He was reluctant to interfere.

We went together for about a year and a half. We were married in the front room of my parents' little house. In the years that followed we had two children, Margaret and Steve.

Up the Windmill!
Told by Marva (Moore) Teter, Holdrege. Early 1930s.

Donna was an active child. She was like a little flea, quick of movement and into one bit of mischief after another. She learned to walk young and was a handful for Mother, especially since Mother was expecting mc to be born soon. I arrived seventeen days before Donna was a year old.

When Donna was ten months old, she climbed the ladder on the windmill. Once she was high in the air, she couldn't, or wouldn't come down. Daddy was in the field, and there was no one except mother, who was in a clumsy state, to climb up and get her.

Since we were so close in age, we were great playmates as children. We made paper dolls and mud pies and played with kittens.

Our mother cats always had two kittens, one for Donna and one for me. We grew up thinking that cats always had only two kittens. We didn't know that Daddy found the kittens first, and that he, in an effort to hold the cat population down, made sure there were only two kittens per litter by the time we found them.

One time we had two, white, longhaired kittens. We were thrilled over them, and were devastated when a tomcat killed them.

We put them in shoeboxes, and with the help of our cousin, Norma Moore, prepared to bury them. We grieved for our pets, prayed over them, and finally buried them.

After it seemed we were finished, one of us would get a different idea about where they should be buried, and we'd dig them up and do it all over again. We had an entire afternoon of funerals. As adults, we've talked about that day. We've decided the reason we buried the kittens several times was so each of us could have a turn being in charge.

Burned Baby
Told by Marva (Moore) Teter, Holdrege. 1930s.

We lived in a small house, one that now, more than seventy years later, is used as a garage. I was born on the kitchen table. My grandmother, Mary Etta Moore, and a neighbor lady, Josie Weylan, delivered me, and had also delivered my sister, Donna. Grandmother was a pro, as she had given birth to thirteen children of her own.

When I was about ten months old, Mother was doing the laundry. She had filled the washing machine with scalding water. I was toddling around, probably getting in the way. I pulled a plug out of the washer tub, and the hot water spewed out on me.

Mother grabbed me and began pulling my clothes off. I had on a cotton flannel diaper that was soaked with the scalding water. The pin was stuck, probably because the thick cloth was wet. By the time she got the pin out, I was deeply burned.

Mother didn't know how to pick me up to carry me because of my severe injuries. She had some cotton that she meant to use to fill a quilt. She rolled me in the cotton and took me to the doctor.

Since my skin was pulled off in places, I stuck to the cotton. More skin came off as they unwrapped me. It took a long time for me to recover because I got infection, and there were no antibiotics then. I still have scars on my hip. I had to learn to walk all over again.

Mules on a Hay Sled
Told by Aloys Kaup, Stuart. Late 1920s.

When I worked for Karos, I used six mules to cable hay. We used a drag sled with straight runners, and the only place for me to stand when the sled was loaded was on the evener behind the mules. Since I was close behind the team, I had a tangle of lines doubled up in my hands.

One day I dropped a line and the sled ran onto it.

"Whoa!" I yelled.

The team stopped suddenly, but the momentum of the load carried the sled forward, and I was pinned between the load and the rumps of the mules. Since the line was under the runner, I couldn't urge the mules to move ahead to release me.

The animals weren't "broke to ride", but the only way for me to get out was to climb over them. Believe me, there was a prayer in my heart when I started clambering over them. Fortunately, they were tired and were glad to stand still for a while.

Once out, I went to the head of the team, unfastened the snared line, and led the mules forward until they pulled the sled over it. I walked behind, picked up the line, and brought it to the front. After reattaching it, I got on the evener, and we continued.

Mules have small hooves and can't walk on ice. Karo had a team of mules that was shod so that in an emergency on an icy day, he would have a way to get around. He didn't dare turn them out with the other animals because the iron shoes were lethal weapons. When a shod mule kicked, he could rip the hide of another animal wide open.

High Kicker
Told by Max II and Luella Karo, Stuart. 1930s.

Like most boys in ranch country, Max Karo II was given a job in the hayfield at an early age. He was about seven when he began driving the stacker team.

One day the crew hitched up the wagon for the trip to the field. They used a well-broken horse and a skittish one that needed extra training. Little Max was crouched on the floor in the front of the wagon box. The skittish horse stepped around nervously and got a foot over a tug. Frightened, he began to kick violently, his hoof flying high and wide. He struck the front of the wagon box with such force that he split a hole about eight inches long and two inches wide. Small Max narrowly missed being struck in the face.

"When I think back," said Max in 2002, "I wonder how any of us ever grew up. We all experienced so many near misses." He considered for a moment. "But then, all of us didn't grow up. A neighbor boy, Andy Miksch, was killed by a kicking horse."

The Carbide Explosion
Told by Ray Kramer, York. 1930s.

Before rural electrification, we used carbide to light the house. It came in granules that were combined with water to produce the necessary combustible gas. The vat where this transformation took place was located outside about fifteen feet from the house.

One night the carbide supply ran low, making the lights dim. Dad (August Kramer) decided to go outside and shake the carbide hopper, hoping to get enough gas to last the evening. He removed his pipe from his mouth and tucked it into his vest pocket. He lit a lantern, which he handed to me.

"Don't get too close with that lantern," he cautioned. "The fire from it could ignite the gas."

I stood back a bit and tipped the lantern so as to shine more light in Dad's direction. As he bent down to shake the hopper, his pipe, which had some sparks in it, fell into the vat. There was a mighty explosion, blowing us both into the air.

I was a ball of fire when I landed. The burning carbide granules were powdery and clung to my skin and clothes. Terrified, I jumped to my feet and ran. Finally, I remembered to fall to the ground where I rolled. I rubbed dirt onto my face to smother the flames.

Once the fire had been extinguished, we went to the house. It was obvious we needed a doctor's care. We got in the car and drove to Stuart. The doctor smeared us with some yellow salve and bandaged our injuries.

He told us to drink soda water when we got home, but we forgot. In addition to the pain of my burns, I was sick to the stomach the next day.

When I finally got new skin on my hands and face, it was delicate. I had to be careful not to get it rubbed, torn, or cold. I missed a considerable amount of school, and fell far behind in my class work.

My parents decided, even though I was only in the seventh grade, for me to quit school and study "practical subjects" at home. They ordered several different mechanical books for me, which I found interesting. I spent many an evening poring over them. During most days, I did farm work outside.

Eighth Grade Examinations
Told by Lela (Hall) Hutchins, Geneva.

Rural children had to pass Eighth Grade Examinations in 14 subjects before they could enter high school. All grades had to be at least 70%, and the average must be at least 75%. These exams were composed by the state and were administered at the high schools.

I got up early the morning of the exams and immediately complained to my mother that I was sick.

"I'm sure you feel sick," she said. "But you aren't really. You're just scared. Once you get there you'll feel better."

Of course, she was right. But why wouldn't I be scared? We went to a one-room country school with only a few pupils. The kids in a town school looked like a multitude! Besides, I worried I'd get lost in the huge building.

Tests for four of the fourteen subjects were given in the seventh grade. If a student passed them, that left only ten for the eighth grade. The test scores were sent out in March. If an eighth grader's scores were high, he could quit school. Those not passing were required to continue classes and were given a second test later.

I was glad I passed in March.

"I have a job for you," Dad said. He outfitted me with a sulky plow (a plow with a seat for the rider and two blades) and a team of horses and put me to work plowing. Contrary to what you might think, I enjoyed plowing.

Fourteen subjects seem like a considerable number, but separate tests were given for English composition and grammar, and also for history, geography, and civics. There were three math tests: arithmetic, mental arithmetic and bookkeeping. The other tests were reading, physiology, penmanship, spelling, agriculture, and drawing.

Preparation for the tests focused the attention of the students. Seventh and eighth graders were dead serious about their class work. Spare minutes were used to review material from former lessons or from a large book that printed test questions from previous years. No one thought of goofing off.

Brief Flashes from the Times

During the 1920s and early '30s, livery barns went out of style and were replaced by automobile service stations. There was a horse-drawn livery wagon that operated in Atkinson through the Thirties, however. It hauled coal, lumber, or any other heavy object from the depot or lumberyard to individual homes.

39

The neighborhood icehouse was a going business during the summers of the 1920s into the '50s. Celebrations such as community picnics on the last day of school, church picnics, and Fourth of July celebrations all called for ice cream and lemonade. Ice was cut from ponds and lakes, and stored in icehouses where it was packed in sawdust. After rural electrification, which took place mid-century, the icehouse fell into disuse. Refrigerators made cold drinks and ice cream common.

Before refrigeration was available, every farm family had a water tank or a well curbing where they placed perishable items to keep them cool. If the family milked cows and sold cream, the cream can sat in the water tank. Going to the well house before and after each meal was one more chore for the busy housewife.

Watermelon rinds were saved to make pickles, and corncobs could be used to make jelly. Corncobs were also used inside the fingers of gloves when the gloves were being patched or darned. The main use of cobs was for stove fuel, and picking up cobs from the pigpen or chicken yard was a daily chore for children.

Dishwater and water used to rinse milk pails was saved and later fed to the pigs. Also, the "windfalls" under apple trees and the weeds pulled in field or garden were fed to the pigs.

Because trees were precious, a branch of a tree was often used for a Christmas tree instead of a whole tree. Decorations were home made. Sometimes people decorated tumbleweeds instead of trees.

To save on matches, men, especially the grandfathers, often used a straw or a twig to light their pipes. They inserted the twig into the front of the cookstove to ignite the end of it.

Gathering new-fallen snow, placing it in bowls, and pouring cream and sugar over it could make a substitute for ice cream. (This practice should not be continued today because of the impurities gathered by the snow when it passes through polluted air.)

Prune pits were cracked for the bits of nutmeat inside.

When the teakettle began to pop and produce a tinny smell, it had boiled dry. It was an uneasy moment for a wife when a farmer hurried into the house to wash up and shave prior to a quick trip to town and found the teakettle empty and the fire out. Shaving was done with a sharp, straight-edged razor, and a warm, soapy lather was a necessity.

When an old hen emerged with a brood of chicks she had hatched in a hidden nest, children were given the chore of grinding some corn in a small coffee grinder. Otherwise, the chicks were fed a handful of oatmeal, cornmeal, or breadcrumbs in order for them to learn to peck and eat. Later, the hen scratched for bugs and worms for her family.

Older pupils opened the lunch buckets for younger ones. The tin syrup buckets that were commonly used for packing lunches were difficult for small fingers to open.

Cornhusks must be perfectly dry before being piled into ticking for mattresses, or they will mold. The husks were spread in a wagon box to dry in the sun prior to the stuffing. There was noisy crickling and crackling when a person climbed onto a husk mattress.

People dangled a tin cup from a nail in their wagon or from a button on the dashboard of their car. Thus they could avoid drinking from the common cup that hung by the hand pump in the town square.

When people cleaned their barns in winter, they were apt to toss the muck out a window and into a pile. By spring, there was a sizeable manure pile by the barn.

Joe Mlinar reported, "There were no trees on the plains except along the larger rivers such as the Niobrara. About 1912 I cut and peeled cottonwood fenceposts for a penny each. Working from morning chores until time for evening chores, I could earn about 35 cents a day, and I was really proud to get it."

Most farm families did not have a sewer system for draining used water. People usually approached the porch of their house from one side, so water that had been used for washing hands was tossed to the other side. Over the winter, layers of frozen water were apt to form an icy mound.

The shipping tags sent out by cream companies had lengths of soft wire to be used to tie the tags to the handle of a cream can. There were other uses for this fine, soft wire in addition to its original one. It was handy to poke out a fuel line, make stems for home-made flowers, hang pictures, tie sets of buttons together, fashion a usable sacking needle, repair holes in screens, make key rings, clean out the generator on a gas lamp, and to secure the flapping sole of a shoe.

Sometimes when people couldn't afford axle grease, they tried to locate pitch from a pine tree and used it. In this treeless country, people might use tallow.

Charley Massey never used grease on his wagon wheels. He said it collected sand, which would grind rather than lubricate. He used kerosene. "We could tell when he was coming by the squeak of his wheels," reported a neighbor.

To grease a wagon wheel, a person took the burr off the outside end of the axle, pulled the wheel outward a little, and applied grease behind the wheel around the axle. After shoving the wheel back, he placed some grease in front of it. Then he screwed the burr back on.

Black Blizzard or Panhandle Dust Storm Apr 14-35 Wilson Studio Texhoma Okla

Chapter 2

The Depression

Many of the Grandchildren of the Pioneers were in grade school. Others were toddlers. The Depression began with the collapse of the stock market in 1929. Farmers could have survived it, except for the following drought.

My Pony Rex
Told by Elsie Dickerson, York. 1930s.

When my parents, William and Mary Anderson, lost their land near Bradshaw during the Thirties, it must have been a devastating catastrophe. However, they shielded us children from the true force of the blow.

"We'll rent some land and start over," said Dad. "We still have machinery and our livestock."

I felt secure. At that point in my life, about all that mattered to me was my pony, Rex. My brothers and sisters had cats and dogs for pets, but Rex was my special companion. When it was time for the milking chores, I'd jump on his back.

"Go get the cows!" I'd tell him, and off we'd go. Our family was too penniless to have a saddle, and often I didn't bother to put a bridle on him. No matter. He headed to the place where the cows were grazing and took them home. I felt like a queen riding on his back.

We were poor, but so was everyone else in our farming community. We had a cousin in Grand Island who had better clothes than we did. When she got new things, her family sent us her cast-offs. Mother did the best she could to make them over to fit me.

After the bank had claimed our land, my father rented a farm near Bradshaw and mortgaged the livestock and machinery to get money to plant the crops. Ordinarily, all would have gone well. Who would think that, after two dry years, we would be visited by continued drought?

The corn came up, but soon was shriveled by the scorching sun and hot winds. Using a cream can and a wheelbarrow, we kids hauled water from the windmill to the garden in an effort, only partly successful, to save the scrawny vegetables. We struggled and sweat and puffed in the sweltering heat.

With scant produce from our garden and the mortgage on the animals, which prevented us from butchering any of them, we had a limited diet. My brothers hunted rabbits to put occasional meat on the table.

After additional drought, the bank foreclosed on our personal holdings. All the farm animals became the property of the bank. Imagine my grief when I found that Rex must be included in the foreclosure sale. I burst into tears.

"No point in blubbering," my mother said. "All the animals have to go. Every cow, calf, and horse. The rest of us could cry, too, but it wouldn't help a thing."

I swallowed my sobs until I got inside the chicken house where I could cry in private. On the sale day I waited. The other animals were sold first. To the men, the Shetland was of scant value, a mere after-thought. Rex brought ten dollars, money that went to the bank, of course.

I hid in the chicken house and sobbed as the new owner led him away. I was positive it was the worst day of my life.

I wish this was the conclusion of the story, but there was more disaster. Rex was turned into a pasture with workhorses. For some reason, they refused to accept this small newcomer and ganged up on him. Biting and kicking, they kept him away from food and water.

Since the days were scorching hot, he was soon dead. By the time I heard about it, we had moved to Bradshaw and Dad had secured work on the WPA.

When word of Rex's torturous death reached me, I thought it was the end of the world. I've had other bad times in my long life, but nothing has ever put me into such a state of despair as the needless death of that gentle, obedient pet.

But that was the way of the Thirties. Just when you seemed to be at rock bottom, where you thought your situation couldn't possibly get worse, another tragedy sneaked up on you and clubbed you on the head.

Haying Accident
About Bert Garwood, Atkinson. July 22, 1932.

Bert Garwood's crew, working about 14 miles southwest of Atkinson, was finishing a stack of hay. There was one more load to go up. Bert was in the stack and was in the process of rounding out the top. Then for some reason, he lost his footing and plunged to the ground.

He was badly injured in his upper back and neck area, and a doctor from Stuart was immediately summoned. The doctor did what he could, but needed to have him in the hospital for X-rays. At that time there were no ambulances in the area.

His older sons put a mattress in the back of a truck and carefully lifted their father onto it. Bert's wife, Cecelia, rode with him and did what she could to support his neck.

After a couple miles of dirt roads, they came to the boggy section around Wright's Lake. The truck crept over it, rocking in and out of the ruts. After another half mile of dirt road, they reached the graveled county road. Fifteen more miles brought them to the hospital.

X-rays showed that his broken neck could not be repaired. The entire community grieved when he died.

Ray Greenfield and Lauril Martin TOPPED OFF the stack.

Photo courtesy of Rachel Greenfield

The Chickens in the Potato Patch
Told by Frank Johnson, Newport. Early 1930s.

After a couple of dry years, we feared another and planted some potatoes in a low spot. A patch we put on higher ground soon dried up, but the potatoes on the low ground clung to life in spite of the heat. Then a bumper crop of grasshoppers hatched.

We had a hen with some young chicks. I built a crate to house the hen and put her and her chicks in the garden. The slats of the crate were spaced so the chicks could get in and out, but the hen was confined. The idea was to pen the hen so she wouldn't scratch out the potatoes, and also to keep her in the garden so the chicks would stay nearby.

The chicks ran about in the potato patch and dined on hoppers. When we dug the potatoes, they were small but welcome, for there wasn't much else to eat that year.

Skittish Horse
Told by Albena Kramer, Atkinson. 1932.

Our father, Joe Dobrovolny, was in the barn, getting the extra horses ready for haying. Some had been in the pasture all winter, and needed taming. As Dad worked, a horse that was temperamental began kicking.

We youngsters were in the yard and heard the sharp drumming of hooves striking the sides of the stall followed by Dad's loud commands meant to control him. Next was Dad's pained cry, and we knew the horse had kicked him. For a while all was silent.

We ran to the barn. Hearing moans, we peaked through a crack. "Dad? Dad? Are you all right?"

"Stay out! Stay away! A green horse is loose!"

The animal had run to a back stall. We could see the whites of his wild eyes as he tossed his head above the partition. Dad was lying on the ground between the horse and the door.

We moved back, muttering in low, worried tones. We had no idea how badly he was hurt.

By then, someone had alerted Mom, and she came to worry with us. None of us dared ignore Dad's commands to stay out of the barn. His words were always law.

Finally he was able to drag himself on hands and knees to the door and over the high sill. He lay beside the building for long minutes until the worst of the pain subsided, then limped, with the help of our mother, to the house. There was no thought, in those penniless days, of calling a doctor.

Haying preparations were delayed until his injuries healed enough for him to continue work.

Loaned Cows
About Buzz Herrick, by Anna Krysl, Stuart. 1934.

During the depth of the Depression, everyone ran out of feed. The government bought our starving cows for twelve dollars each, hauled them to a blowout, and shot

49

them. The men went there afterwards and saw that they had poured oil over the carcasses. We assumed it was to control insects.

We had enough feed to keep a few milk cows.

A neighbor, Mr. Brown, had a patch of weeds that he thought was too poor to bale and sell. He told Buzz Herrick he could have the weeds.

"I would hay them," said Buzz, "but I don't have any cows."

We thought about it. Everyone was flat broke. We were all desperate for feed, but who had money to buy hay-- or weeds? Finally we had an idea.

"I'm forced to sell most of my herd," V.J. told Buzz. "But the government hasn't come for them yet. You stack those weeds, and I'll hold back a few extra cows and loan them to you. You feed them the weeds, milk them, and keep the cream checks. When we get better years with more feed, we'll take the cows back, but you can keep the calves they produce while you have them."

It was a bargain for both families. Herricks often told us they didn't know how they could have survived without those little cream checks.

Eventually the rains did come. In 1935 we had good crops and plenty of hay. Our herd was depleted because we had relinquished about three-fourths of our cattle during the bad years. Now we needed to reclaim the few cows we had loaned to Herricks.

It was hard to do. We knew how they depended on the cream checks. I thought perhaps we should leave them a couple cows. I really felt bad for them.

But V.J. said, "A deal is a deal. After all, they get to keep the calves. We told them we would take the cows back when we had enough feed."

We brought the cows home. I felt heartsick, and did all I could to help Mrs. Herrick with garden produce and the like. Men don't realize how hard it is to feed a family when food is scarce. But the women dealt with that problem three times a day.

More about Buzz by Don Krysl:

Buzz had very few tools, but he was inventive. He used his car for such chores as sawing wood and grinding feed. He'd jack up the back of the car and place a homemade contraption under it. Two pulleys went under the back tires and a third, located in the middle, turned a belt.

While the car was running and in gear, he lowered the back wheels to touch the pulleys. The wheels turned them and also the belted pulley in the middle, which powered the saw or the grinder.

"It had an amazing amount of power, especially in low gear," reported Don. "The motor was worn out and leaked oil. Buzz placed a pan underneath to catch it, and every little while, he'd pull it out and pour the oil back into the engine."

The Still at Milligan
Told by Leonard Kassik, Milligan. 1930s.

My uncle was a mortician. One day in 1934 when I was about ten years old, I was helping him set up a tent in the cemetery in preparation for a funeral. He pointed to a barn south of town.

"Ya' know, Leonard, something funny is going on in that barn," he said. "It used to have an ordinary ventilator, but now it's topped with that huge, fancy one. No farmer needs a barn ventilator like that."

I've thought about it, and I figure he probably knew why the barn had the unusual ventilator. Probably most people in town knew there was a huge still in the barn that was producing a thousand gallons of "moonshine" per day, but of course, no one would tell a kid.

At that time, Prohibition was coming to an end, but most states continued to set up their own guidelines on how to regulate alcohol consumption. Nebraska allowed a weak beer called three-two beer. The title came from the fact that only 3.2% alcohol was legal in it.

Later I found out that prior to the still in the barn, there were a couple stills in the basements of two Milligan farmhouses. One was in a house between the big barn and town, and the other was in a house west of the cemetery. Business was good, causing the moonshiners to enlarge their operation.

I slept in an upstairs room that overlooked a vacant lot in the middle of town. Sometimes semi trucks, their loads covered with canvas, came into town during the night and parked there. Excited about the huge trucks, I'd get up and look out the window. By morning they were gone. Later I found that it had been equipment for constructing the huge still.

The still was in operation twenty-four hours a day. The finished product was shipped in five-gallon cans to the large cities of the Midwest.

Federal agents raided the operation on Saturday, September 29, 1934. The agents had spent a good part of the day in the yard of a local country school. During the night, trucks loaded with supplies for the still began to trickle into the farmyard. The agents followed a load of sugar to a place near the location.

A wooden gate was opened, the sugar truck entered, but the gate was immediately closed. The truck stopped near the barn, and workers began to unload the sugar. Then the agents suddenly zoomed their vehicle into the yard, smashed through the wooden gate, and proceeded to arrest the moonshiners.

Some escaped through a tunnel that extended from the back of the barn into a wooded area. As two workers exited the tunnel, police fired at them, wounding one.

Two trucks loaded with cans of alcohol were parked that night in a garage in Milligan. They were not discovered, and after the raid the drivers were able to deliver their product.

The way I remember it, one fellow took the rap for engineering the whole thing even though he wasn't one of the top men. Some of the employees, also, got jail sentences.

News spreads fast in a small town, and the next morning, people in the area went to the farm to see what was going on. The agents had opened the spigots on the bottoms of the huge vats, and alcohol was streaming down into a draw east of the barn, making a little pond of booze. The odor was sharp. There was a considerable amount of yeast stored in the barn, and each person that came was given a portion. The Milligan grocer, Charlie Kotas, said he didn't sell any yeast for quite some time after the raid.

While the still was in operation, a druggist in town ran a second business. He bought bottled three-two beer, opened it, and spiked it with alcohol from the still. "It sold fast on dance nights," he reported.

Disappearing Stacker
Told by Tony Dobrovolny, Atkinson. Early 1930s.

It was evening and we kids were supposed to watch to the southeast for sight of the stacker. The hay crew was moving the equipment home that day. Once it appeared in the distance, we were to tell Mom and she would put the potatoes on to fry, get the butter from the well house, and the like.

They were coming home from the portion of the ranch referred to as the Long Land. Stackers were too wide to travel on roads, and thus went across country. The place where they crossed Holt Creek was southeast of us.

Finally we saw it, tall and stately, with the slanting boards gleaming in the evening sun. It looked tiny, for it was about a mile away. We gave the alarm and stood watching it as it crept slowly north. Then in the blink of an eye, it disappeared. We ran into the house.

"Mom! We saw it. We did! But now it's gone."

Mom came out to look. "You must have imagined you saw it," she told us. "There's no sign of it. A stacker can't evaporate into thin air. Keep watching, though, and let me know when it appears."

Perplexed, we stood in the yard, muttering to each other. Finally we saw a team and wagon coming around Wright's Lake.

"They're coming, Mom. They're riding in the wagon. They're already north of the lake."

The wagon arrived, and the mystery was solved. When the men were crossing Holt Creek, a runner on the stacker caught on the edge of the bank. The old stacker twisted, and the braces popped loose. In the blink of an eye, the tall structure tumbled down, becoming a mere pile of boards.

The Snake under the Milk House
Told by Marie Kramer, Atkinson. 1933.

About mid-forenoon on a particular day, my brother Tony and I, 8 and 10 respectively, were sent to the milk house to churn butter. Our older sister, Albena, who was washing the cream separator, was in the milk house, too. Originally, the building had been the homestead cabin of Frank Rosenberry, but he had vacated his land and had moved to Canada. The floor of the cabin rotted because it rested on the ground.

Our crank churn was about two and a half feet tall, and it turned easily. At first we worked earnestly, but were soon distracted by the dismal cries of a frog under the rotting floor of the building. We knew without seeing the frog what his problem was.

We lived near Wright's Lake, and often had seen frogs caught by garter snakes. The frog suffered a slow death, for it took long minutes for the snake to suck it down its throat. We always tried to rescue the frog.

The drama under the floor was much more interesting than churning butter. We did take turns, slowly, very slowly, turning the crank, but mostly we peered between floorboards and poked sticks down into the soft earth below. Our mother came to the door.

"You kids stop fooling around and get that butter churned. We need it for dinner." (The noon meal was called dinner, and the evening meal was supper.) She took the churn handle, gave it a few fast spins, and gave it back to me. After getting some milk that was cooling in the water tank in a corner of the building, she returned to her work in the house.

Her pep talk helped momentarily, but soon the pitiful croaking of the frog again distracted us. However, all our efforts failed to rescue the doomed creature. We were ashamed when our dad chided our mother at dinnertime because there was no butter for his bread.

Jokes from the Thirties

As grim as life was during the Depression, people found reasons to laugh. Years later, one humorist remembered these jokes.

My calves are so small this year that I have to watch so the garter snakes don't swallow them.

I knew a fellow who hitched a cart to a tumbleweed and took off for the Gulf of Mexico. He had heard there was water in the gulf.

Our neighbor ate so many dandelion greens that he had to wrap his legs with rags soaked in kerosene. Otherwise, the cutworms would cut him down.

We ran out of feed for our hogs and decided to sell them. We loaded them in a wagon and headed for town. We lost all the hogs on the way because they fell through the cracks in the bottom of the wagon. We hurried back to see if we could locate them, and found one that the ants had dragged half way down their hole.

Remembering back to Sod Houses
A group of Thedford citizens were seated around a table in the year 1999. Also present was Marie Kramer, York. All were "Grandchildren of the Pioneers".

Robert Miles offered, "In the 1930s, my brothers, sisters, and I were jumping on a bed. My sister, Eldora, lost her balance and fell backwards through a window. That was when we were living in a soddy."

"Living in a soddy!" exclaimed Marie. "I didn't know there was anyone alive today who had lived in a soddy. In our part of Nebraska, soddies went out of existence around the beginning of the 1900s."

"Oh, we had soddies for a long time after that," said Robert. "This area was too poor to afford lumber for housing. Quite a few of us lived in soddies when we were kids."

A poll of the eight people around the table revealed that Robert Miles, Maxine Ayers, Gene Lesher, and Morell Ayers had all lived in soddies.

"Tell me an interesting event that happened when you lived in a soddy," said Marie.

"We moved out," said Gene.

After the laughter died down, Morell said, "During my early married years, my wife and I lived in a soddy. Our first son was born there."

"My sister, Lois, married Grant Figard in 1947, and they lived in a soddy on the bank of the Dismal River," said Alice Dubry. "They built a frame house in 1961. The soddy is still there, but a tree has fallen on it."

"This sandy area wasn't homesteaded until all the other ground in Nebraska had been taken," continued Alice. "After it was settled, most homesteaders starved out and abandoned their land. Those who stayed lived in soddies and saved every penny they earned to slowly enlarge their acreages. Only the extremely thrifty managed to hang on. You have to have a good-sized spread to make a living in this area. Maybe five or ten thousand acres."

"We had an earthquake tremor when I was a child," said Robert. "It was in the Thirties. It shook our sod house and a lot of dirt fell. Mother had a terrible cleaning job."

"Soddy walls were about two and a half feet thick," Morell remembered. "After we moved out, my wife missed the wide window sills. She always set potted flowers on them."

Herding Cattle
Told by Robert Schrup, Burwell. Early 30s.

By the Early Thirties, most of the homesteaders had abandoned their land and had moved away. People were penniless, and fences were poor or non-existent. The children of the remaining families herded cattle, hunting for bunches of grass scattered in the parched, sandy hills.

I herded mostly on the abandoned land of people who had starved out. In this dry, sandy country, it takes more acres to make a living than were allowed in a homestead.

There was a pump left on a vacant place, and I often got a drink there. From the hilltops I could see our yard in the distance. I gazed at it longingly, wishing for the day to finally end.

If my mother wanted me to come home, she hung a sheet on the clothesline as a signal. It was boring out on the prairie all day, especially on blistering hot days. The sheet rarely appeared, but when it did, it was a welcome sight. It meant home and some degree of relief from the sun.

I recall I once helped a neighbor look for his milk cows that had wandered away. We rode ponies. The hills have vegetation on them now, but in the Thirties, they were bare sand. When we went uphill, we had to get off the horses because our added weight made it impossible for them to climb up. The sand slid under their hooves.

We walked and led the horses to get to the top. Without riders, they could lunge and manage to climb up. Then we could mount and ride again. We found the cows about two miles from home.

Robert's Cowboy Hat
Told by Robert Schrup, Burwell. Early 1930s.

As soon as my mother thought I was old enough, I rode a horse to school. My parents bought me a cowboy hat. It was a cheap one, but it had a wide brim, and I imagined myself to be quite a cowboy. Every time I went out of the house, the hat was on my head.

One day when I was about twelve years old, a neighbor, Bert Shaffer, asked me to come to his place and help him change bands in the transmission of his Model T. Since I was fascinated by the mechanical make-up of a car, I was happy to go. Not wanting to risk getting grease spots on my precious hat, I laid it aside on a patch of clean sand.

We gave the job our full attention. I was surprised at how much I could understand about the mechanics of the transmission.

Chickens idled around, snapping up bugs or chasing grasshoppers. Pigs grunted as they went about their hoggish business. In those days no one confined their barnyard fowl and often let their pigs run loose. Ranchsteads were far enough apart so people had to tolerate only their own animals.

When the job was finished, I wiped my hands on a piece of gunnysack and glanced around.

"What became of my hat?" I asked. "I laid it there." We soon found it in two jagged parts. The pigs had apparently played tug-of-war with it.

About thirty years later, I was a County Commissioner. The members were all cattlemen, and they arrived at the meetings attired in proper western garb, including wide-brimmed hats.

Once a seed corn salesman gave me a cap that advertised his product. On a windy day I was doing ranch chores and decided that, rather than fight to keep a hat on my head, I would wear that little cap. It so happened that a cattle feed salesman came that day.

"Robert," he said, "I want a picture of you in that puny, little cap. I'm going to show it to the other commissioners so they can see what kind of a cowboy you are."

Planting and Cultivating Corn
Told by Don Krysl, Stuart. 1930s.

When we were kids, we hated spring. First of all came corn planting. The blackbirds discovered they could walk down the row of sprouting corn, pull a plant, and eat the kernel at the root.

Early 1930's

Bill, Bill Stroda, DON

To solve the problem, Dad made replanting tools out of leaf springs from a wagon box. Bill and I were each given a tool and a carpenter's apron full of seed corn. Our job was to walk down the corn rows, locate the places where plants were missing, poke a hole in the ground with the spring, drop in a kernel, and close the hole by stepping on it. He placed a sack of Indian corn on one side of the field so we could replenish our apron pouches when we ran out. We used Indian corn because its growing season is shorter, and it would catch up with the corn that was first planted.

Back and forth we trudged, hot and sweaty, backs tired. The long rows seemed endless, and when one was finished, another awaited. What a boring way for boys to spend the springtime.

One year we got an idea. If we planted more than one kernel in each hole, we could finish the job faster and be free to play. For a while, we dropped two kernels in each hole, then three--or four. The sack of corn disappeared.

Hurrah! Now we could play. The swimming hole held our interest for the rest of the day. The corn told on us, however, for it came up in clumps. You can guess Dad was not happy, and we were soundly scolded in his thunderous voice.

Cultivating came next. Dad ran one cultivator and our brother, Leo, a second one. Neither Bill nor I was large enough to manage a third machine. So Dad fixed an old walking cultivator so two boys could manage it. He placed a seat on the tongue of the machine, and Bill, who was 8 or 9, sat on it and drove the horses. Being 10 or 11, I walked behind and guided the cultivator.

It would have been a tedious job for adults. Bill, not seeing how the cultivator was following the furrow, couldn't guide the horses properly, and I on the machine couldn't steer straight if the driver erred. We were told to stop and rescue any plant we covered, and you may be sure there were plenty of stops. When one of us got disgusted with the performance of the other, we threw dirt clods at each other. This conflict didn't improve our farming skills.

Continued by Alvin Krysl. Atkinson:

Before we were old enough to manage a cultivator by ourselves, Dad borrowed Uncle V.J.'s cultivator that could be manned by two kids.

Oh, I got tired of sitting on that iron seat and driving. There were no springs on it, and my backside took a beating. The hours were endless and a day was forever. I envied my older brother, Bob, who got to walk behind and steer the cultivator.

Finally the year came when I graduated to the job of machine operator and one of my smaller brothers became the driver. I was elated at the promotion. No longer would I have to take a beating on that iron seat.

I soon found that walking behind a cultivator was no picnic, either. The handles of the cultivator were made for a person the height of a man, which meant I had to reach higher than was comfortable. This gave me less strength, which made me work harder. My legs got so tired I could hardly keep moving them.

When it comes to the English language, "walking cultivator" is a term that still makes me shudder.

Old King and the Runaway
Told by Don Krysl, Stuart. About 1936.

I was about thirteen at the time, and was helping move our hay equipment from one quarter to another. I was driving three head of horses and pulling a two-hitch rake. Our rat terrier, Jiggs, was riding at my feet. The middle horse, named King, was an ornery rascal.

I don't recall how the horses were hitched, but I know the lines were fastened only to King. The driver guided him and the others followed his lead.

On this particular day, King's bit broke, allowing him to do as he pleased.

"Whoa! Whoa!" I yelled.

He knew when he had the advantage and took off on a dead run. The other two horses followed his lead. Since pulling on the lines did no good, I was at their mercy.

They were headed straight for a grove. Not wanting to be wrapped around a tree trunk, I knew I should attempt to bail out. If I leaped, I must avoid the rakes, which extended far to either side, for the teeth were bouncing wildly up and down and would be lethal if they hit me.

The rakes were fastened to a timber that extended to the middle of each rake. I ran on this timber and gave a mighty leap toward the outside wheel. My foot brushed its rim, but I landed beyond the snapping teeth.

The horses broke free when the machinery hit the trees. Jiggs came crawling out of the grove, head and tail down. He looked embarrassed, as if the accident were his fault. The rakes were both bent into Vs.

Hay harvest stopped for several days while the crew worked at repairing the rakes. They tied them to sturdy trees and used the tractor to straighten the long bars that held the rake teeth.

Dust and Grasshoppers
Told by Homer Brauning, Geneva. 1930s.

Even though I was a small boy of about six, I remember the dust storms clearly. One day it was too dark to see in our rural schoolhouse. The dim light was eerie; different from any I've ever seen. Since there was no artificial light available, the teacher ushered my sister and me across the road.

"If you follow this fence, you will come to your house," she told us.

When we arrived home, Mother was frustrated because of the drifts of dust on the windowsills. Oddly, in the strange darkness, the chickens had gone to roost and the cows had come home to be milked.

I also remember seeing the sun clouded when the grasshoppers flew in. They covered the ground and devoured everything. There was a slick covering of bug juice on the roads because car tires smashed the hoppers. Drivers had to be careful or cars would skid.

Camping in the Hayfield
About Tony Dobrovolny, Atkinson. 1935.

While 1934 was a dry year and was the depth of the Depression, rains came in '35. Ranchers in north central Nebraska had good hay crops, but everyone was without money. Hay wasn't worth much because there was no demand for it. Ranchers had cut their herds during the prior years because they lacked feed for them.

Tony's father, Joe, had bought land during the Depression, but it was "all on paper." He hadn't as yet begun to pay for it. With a huge crop and no funds to hire help for the harvest, he decided if he took Tony, age 10, into the crew, he could manage with one hired man.

Joe, himself, did two jobs. He mowed evenings and mornings, using his 1929 Farmall tractor. When a portion of the hay was dry enough, he dropped the trail mower, raised the bar on the power mower, and employed the tractor to do the sweeping.

LeRoy, his oldest son, age 16, raked, and also did such odd jobs as sharpening sickles and caring for the horses. Tony drove the stacker team, pulling the loads of hay over the stacker and dropping them onto the stack. The hired man, Ray Waldo, stacked the hay and did what cooking was necessary when the crew camped on far parts of the ranch. Ray was paid the ordinary wage for hard labor, a dollar a day.

LeRoy drove a four-horse team on the rakes, and Tony had two large horses, King and Bill, on the stacker.

"I can hear Dad yet," said Tony sixty-five years later. "Whenever he brought in an extra heavy load, he'd yell at me, 'Stay away from the double tree!'"

His worry was that the hard pull might cause the double tree to break, thus allowing it to fly back and hit Tony with the deadly force of the falling load.

Load going **on**...

Load going **up**...

Camp Shack

Because Joe's land was scattered, he had built a "camp shack" on wheels for the crew to live in while they were working on the more distant meadows. It was probably eight by fourteen feet in size.

In the forenoons, Tony had spare time. He picked sand cherries in the Sandhills. When his stomach was full, he put more in his hat, an old gray felt he had inherited from LeRoy, and took them to camp for the others.

Afternoons were hot and long, especially since they often worked into the long summer evenings in order to get all the hay into stacks. Tony ran out of energy, and watched the lowering sun. Only when darkness arrived could he be sure of a reprieve from his job.

At night, the little shack with small, high windows was heavy with heat. The men left the door open to get more air. This was a worry to Tony, for coyotes howled in the hills. His imagination sometimes gave him the feeling the animals were lurking at the open door. As desperate as he was for rest, some nights were nearly sleepless with worry.

"But I guess I was safe enough," he said years later. "I never got eaten."

A Bird in the Hay field
About Tony Dobrovolny, Atkinson. 1936.

It was Tony's second year in the hay field, and on a sweltering afternoon, the crew was haying on the South Place located on Holt Creek. Suddenly, someone saw smoke rising to the southeast. Joe yelled at Tony and Ray Waldo, the man stacking.

"Get in the truck!"

Once in the old, Ford truck, Joe swung it around to the stacker and loaded the ten gallon cream can full of water they kept there. He collected the other crewmembers, and they headed over the hills to the fire.

It was farther away than it looked, and by the time they arrived, closer hay crews had extinguished it. Now the men were sitting in the scant shade of their vehicles, watching lest the fire rekindle itself. They were chatting about the weather, the size of the hay crop, the performance of their equipment, and also about how the fire, far away from all humans, could have ignited. Had the hot sun on a bit of glass caused the dry meadow to smolder and burst into flame?

Presently a tiny bird flew into the group, and lit in the stubbles. The bird was panting from the heat. The men were fascinated by the fact that it was completely unafraid. It would hop onto an extended hand and peck at a ring or a cuff button.

"He's thirsty," said Joe. "Those shiny metal buttons look like water to him. Tony, get him a drink."

Tony opened the can and dipped some water into the lid. The tiny bird drank gratefully. The recess was short, for mown hay awaited the attention of the various crews. The men soon departed, leaving the tiny, mysterious bird to rule the vast meadows.

Lost Underwear
Told by Alice Dubry, Thedford.

When I was a child, flour and chicken feed came in cotton sacks that were printed in a variety of designs. Since times were hard, our mothers made many of our clothes, including our underwear, from those sacks.

One day in school, I was writing at the blackboard when the elastic in the band of my underwear came untied. The garment dropped to the floor. I stood frozen, shocked, confused. I had no idea what I should do next.

The teacher was gracious. She came forward and put a hand on my shoulder.

"Just step aside," she said quietly.

She picked up my undies, and class continued as if nothing had happened.

A little later, she retied the elastic. I can't remember where she sent me to put on the repaired garment, but it was probably into the hall or to the outside toilet. Those details are blocked from my mind by my humiliation.

Learning to Rope
Told by Morell Ayers, Thedford.

As you can imagine, it takes endless practice for boys to learn to rope a critter, a necessary skill for a real cowboy. Many begin tossing a rope as soon as they are able to walk, probably throwing it over chair backs, pets, and wastebaskets inside the house. As soon as they can go outside, they rope anything that stands up: posts, milk buckets, machinery levers, calves, dogs, and each other.

When I was a small boy in school, one of the older boys enjoyed working on his roping skills during recess. At his direction, I'd run by, and he'd swing his rope. Nearly always I'd end up in the loop. He had fairly well mastered throwing the rope over my head and needed more challenge.

Once when I ran by, he roped me by the foot, and I was thrown headlong to the ground. My new, sharp, front teeth went completely through my tongue. I had a sore mouth, which made eating difficult for quite some time.

Our School Chariot
Told by Alice Dubry, Thedford. Mid 30s.

My dad, Lloyd Hamilton, removed the hood and engine of an old car body, enclosed what was left, and mounted it on a wagon chassis. We hitched a team to it and drove it to Antelope Valley School, which was north of Thedford.

Once when we were goofing around on the way home, we broke a window. It was a cold day and the team, traveling at plug-horse speed, would take a considerable amount of time to get the five miles home. The older kids considered how best to close the huge, drafty hole.

We had a blanket inside the "cab", but there was no way to fasten it over the window. Then one of them conceived the perfect idea. Anyway, it was a perfect solution for everyone except me.

They rolled me, the smallest member, inside the blanket, then poked me, backside first, into the gaping window. The trail road was rough and long which means I remember that ride to this day. When we arrived home, our mother was less than happy.

Don and His Wheeled Vehicles
Told by Don and Bill Krysl, Stuart. 1936.

Children in the Thirties had to find ways of entertaining themselves, for people couldn't afford toys. Don Krysl, from boyhood on, had an intense interest in mechanical devices, and was especially fascinated by wheeled vehicles. He scrounged the junk pile for castaway parts and attempted to assemble them into machines that would roll.

When he was about thirteen, he spent days making a "carriage" out of some discarded buggy wheels from horse and buggy days. The sun beat down mercilessly those dry years, but he pursued his goal to completion. He fixed a seat for the driver and made a harness, using twine and strips of gunnysack. When the "inventor" had finished, he became a "horse". His eleven-year-old brother, Bill, small and wiry, was pressed into service as the driver.

All went well in spite of the blazing sun. The horse whinnied, perspired, tossed his head, trotted, perspired some more, and turned a deep shade of red from exertion. For a time the driver rode grandly, but his interest waned. Finally, he decided to call it a day and hunt some shade.

He drove to the stock tank, and while the horse immersed his face as if he were drinking, the driver climbed out of the carriage and trotted toward the yard.

"Hey!" said the horse. "You can't quit. I need a driver."

"It's too hot. I'm going to find some shade."

"What do you mean--too hot? I'm the one doing the work. All you have to do is sit."

"I don't care. I quit." Bill walked toward the yard.

Don ran behind him, grabbed him around the waist, turned him about, and began forcing him toward the carriage. Bill pretended to accept his older brother's decree until Don's arms loosened. Then he pulled away and whirled toward the house, his bare feet pounding the hot sand. Don ran after him.

When Bill sensed Don had gained until he was immediately behind him, he suddenly dropped to the ground in a tight ball. Don stumbled and fell headlong into the sand. Before Don could collect himself, Bill leaped up and darted for the house. Don had no driver for the rest of the day.

Little Brock
Told by Tony Dobrovolny, Atkinson. 1932.

One day when Dad wasn't home, LeRoy, six years my senior, was doing the chores. He suggested that I, at age seven, should try milking our tamest cow, Little Brock. My hands were small and inexperienced, but I managed to get her milked even though it took me a long while.

When Dad came home, I bragged, "Dad! Guess what! I milked Little Brock all by myself."

"That's great!" Dad said. "From now on, that will be your job. Each night and morning you can milk Little Brock."

There were some cold, dark mornings when I wished I had kept my mouth shut about my new accomplishment.

Years later, the father often said, "Tony started milking when he was so small he could hardly see over the rim of the bucket. But he was always on the job. No matter how bad the weather, I could depend on him."

The Christmas Catalog in the Outhouse
Told by Marian Discoe, York.

When the Christmas catalog arrived in the mail, my mother sent my sister, June, to the outhouse with it.

"Take that catalog where it can be of some use," she told her. "We don't have enough money for essentials, and for sure can't afford toys."

Once in the outhouse, June seated herself on the wooden seat and proceeded to look at the catalog. The dolls, dressed in ruffles and lace, held her attention for some time. Before she had finished the doll section, darkness began to creep into the windowless building.

"Drat!" she exclaimed. "I have only a few pages left." Then she remembered the matches in her apron pocket. She rolled an old newspaper from the "toilet paper box" and set one end afire to make a torch.

While she was engrossed in the contents of the catalog, a wisp of burning paper fell from the torch down into the papers in the box. Suddenly fire was shooting upward.

June looked around for something to beat out the flames. She recalled her mother slowed a fire under the soap kettle by throwing sand on it. She leaped outside and clawed at the earth, but the ground was frozen as hard as cement.

Screaming for help, she ran to the well house for a bucket of water. Her mother arrived, and they managed to extinguish the flames. They saved the building, but a hole had been burned in the floor.

Goat Wagon and Wind Sailing
Told by Alvin Krysl, Stuart. Mid 1930s.

My older brother, Bob Krysl, and my cousin, Don, rigged up a two-wheeled cart, using a trailer Don's dad had made to haul cabbages to town. They made a harness for a pet goat, and fastened him to the cart. Either of them was too heavy for the goat to pull, a fact that made me eligible as the rider because I was of slighter build and was much younger.

They installed me in the cart.

"Giddap!" they both shouted. "Giddap!"

But the goat was stubborn and wouldn't cooperate.

"I know how to get some action out of him," said Don. "Let's light a firecracker and throw it behind him."

It wasn't the first time the goat had heard a firecracker, and he was aware it was a good idea to put some distance between himself and the sputtering noisemaker. He ran for as long as the fuse crackled, but stopped dead at the explosion. That was no problem. The boys had more firecrackers.

Needless to say, the driver and the goat both tired of the sport long before Don and Bob did.

Another time Don, his brother, Bill, and my brother, Bob, decided to put a sail on a four-wheeled cart to see if it would go across the meadow in the wind. They used a large bed sheet for the sail.

After the machine was constructed, they waited for a windy day, and anyone who knows Nebraska can believe they were soon supplied with one. Again, because of my size, I was elected to be the passenger, but remembering the goat ride, I was reluctant.

"Oh, this is different," said Don in cajoling tones. "The wind will give you a smooth ride. It will be like sailing on a pond."

Deciding he was probably right, I walked boldly across the meadow, glad to be included in the activities of the older boys. They shoved the invention ahead of us. Of course, the sail was tied securely to the mast.

We got to Karo's fence. Because of the south wind, we turned the machine to the north. They put me in the trailer, unfurled the sail, and I took off!

I hung on for dear life, scared half to death. The cart bounced over the rough ground, veering this way or that in the wind. The other boys were running full speed, but they couldn't keep up. I was totally on my own.

Most of the meadow was now behind me, and I was heading for the pigpen fence east of Uncle V.J.'s place. I braced myself, hoping not to get tangled in the barbed wire that was strung above the woven wire. The machine hit, rolled over the fence, and collapsed in the pigpen.

My howls were sailing forth on the winds when the older boys arrived. They untangled me and got me on my feet. I'm sure they were relieved to discover I was more frightened than hurt. Thereafter, I was wary of riding in their homemade contraptions.

1983: Decades later, as an EMT, I was called to the West Holt Memorial Hospital in Atkinson to transport a patient home by ambulance. As we pulled up to the hospital, the attendants wheeled a gurney toward us. On it was sixty-year-old Cousin Don, now in his final illness. I had avoided visiting my once-sturdy, muscular relative, knowing that he was now wasted and immobilized by a brain tumor.

As I took a deep breath and stepped forward into a strong, March wind, I was struck by the fact that he was stretched out on an easy-rolling vehicle. The words I needed to break an awkward silence came to me.

"Why, we don't need an ambulance to haul this fellow home," I said, mustering a chuckle. "Let's just tie a bed

sheet to this gurney and let the wind blow him home. I know it will work. I've had experience."
Don laughed.

From Horses to Tractor
Told by Jim Barth, York. 1932.

When I was twelve years old, my father, Harry Barth, traded six horses and six mules for our first tractor. I imagine the dealer immediately took the animals to the sale barn and turned them into cash. Buying fuel for a tractor was a new expense, but my father figured that the only time he had to burn fuel was when he was using the tractor. Horses had to be fed and cared for year-round whether you used them or not.

In our area, we had a fair corn crop in 1933, but times were depressed, and corn was only about eight or ten cents a bushel. Then 1934 was hot, dry, and windy. The corn dried up before ears set on. Dad worried about what we would use for feed that winter.

He decided to bale some straw, but it was too short to hold together well enough to be contained by the baling wire. So the crew went in the cornfield and cut the short, dry cornstalks that had never matured. They put some of those stalks at the beginning and at the end of each bale. That way the bales were firm enough to hold together inside the wire.

Our only income was from the cream and eggs we took to town each week. The trouble was, we were so short of feed that the cows and the hens didn't produce much cream and eggs. Thus our income was pathetically skimpy. Those were mighty slim times.

A Length of Rope
Told by Vaughn Fulton, Geneva. Mid 1930s.

Times were grim, but my father, Alva Fulton, had a sense of humor and enjoyed joking around in spite of the desperate situation. Before we moved from the tiny town of

Colome, South Dakota, to Geneva, Nebraska, he ran a store. One day a farmer came in and requested a length of rope. When he asked the price, Dad jokingly said,

"To anyone planning to hang himself, I give it free. Otherwise, I sell it for a penny a foot."

The man paid for the rope and departed. A short time later, the man did hang himself. For years, Dad was heartsick about his crude remark.

Vaughn added these comments:
I recall that when a barrel of peanut butter came into the local grocery store in Colome, we tried to get our jar refilled soon afterward. The peanut butter at the top of the barrel was creamy, while that at the bottom was thick and dry.

Carrying More Than Mail
Thedford, 1930s.

Because of the poverty of the region and the great distances between ranches and towns, Abe Carter, the Brownlee-Thedford mail carrier, often hauled boxes of groceries, machinery parts, and passengers in his mail truck. One time Pete Boeh asked Abe for a ride to town.

"Hop in," invited Abe.

Pete got into the back of the truck and settled himself on the spare tire that lay in the truck box. The old vehicle chugged down the rough trail road. Abe's attention was engaged in the task of placing the correct mail in the various boxes along the way.

When they reached Thedford, Abe found Pete's inert form in the truck box. Further examination revealed that he was dead. He had suffered a heart attack.

Skunk Grease
Told by Morell Ayers, Thedford. 1930s & 40s.

Some people used Vicks Vapo-rub to put on their chests when they had a bad cold, but most families in our area couldn't afford it. Instead, our mothers rubbed skunk grease on our chests. We hated it.

Of course, it was easy to obtain. Trapping and skinning skunks was an activity that brought in a few dollars of income. Whenever my mother ran low on skunk grease, she told my father to save her some more. He pulled the fat from the inside of the skunk carcasses, and she rendered it in an old pan.

We hated getting a cold because we despised Mother's skunk grease. It didn't smell skunky, but the thought of it being smeared on our bodies was repulsive.

Mules in the Hayfield
Told by Bernard Kaup, Stuart. Mid 1930s

My brother, Bill Kaup, and I were raking hay. I was driving a team of mules, Mabel and Henry, and he was using horses. The flies were bad, and the mules were switching their tails and stomping their feet in an effort to get some relief from them.

Then while switching at flies, Henry caught one of the lines under his tail. He leaped and ran, and Mabel ran also. I tried to yank the line from under his tail, but the harder I yanked, the harder he clamped his tail and the faster they ran.

I was afraid we would hit a hole, which, at the rate we were going, might unseat me and throw me into the bouncing rake teeth. I decided to try to leap free. I let go of one line, and hanging on the other, I managed to throw myself over the rake teeth where I hit the stubbles behind them.

I landed on my knees. Because of the speed, I couldn't regain my footing. Pulling on only one line made the team travel in a circle, and round and round we went.

I hoped Bill would come to help get the mules under control, but he continued to rake hay as if nothing else was happening. It seemed to take forever for the mules to exhaust themselves to the point of giving up.

My overalls were in shreds and my knees were like raw beefsteak, but the rakes were saved.

"You could see I was in trouble," I said to Bill later. "Why didn't you come and help?"

"I thought after all the years you've worked in the hay field, you ought to be able to drive a team," he told me unremorsefully. "And after all, I was sent to the field to rake hay, not to chase mules."

Bumblebee Attack
Told by Darlene Heyne, Stuart.

My father, Joy Greenfield, liked mules and had more mules than horses. When it was time to harness them, they weren't popular with the hired hands because they sometimes kicked. But Dad crooned to them and petted them, and they'd tolerate him.

It was haying time, and one day Dad wasn't feeling well. I offered to mow in his place. He harnessed the mules, Tom and Joe, and I drove them confidently to the field. I was proud to help, and the clacking of the mowers was a peaceful sound.

All went well until we hit a bumblebee's nest. The bees came zooming out, attacking us like dive-bombers. The noisy, painful siege sent the mules into a dead run.

Yelling commands and pulling on the lines had no effect. The animals tore across the meadow, the machinery bouncing behind. When I realized I couldn't control them, I jumped off on the side opposite the mower. Luckily I received only bruises.

Other members of the hay crew caught the mules. My job for the day was over, for the mowers were badly damaged. I sat in the shade under the wagon until the crew was ready to go home.

Forbidden Words!
By Marie Kramer, York. 1920s and 30s.

· During the first half of the Twentieth Century, people were careful of their speech to a degree that would astonish their children and grandchildren. Most families permitted such words as heck and gosh, but stronger words were not spoken by women and children or by most men in the presence of women and children.

The telephone companies insisted on polite language, and if someone was reported for using vulgar terms, the company chastised him. He was warned that more reports could result in the loss of telephone service.

Most men knew a variety of cuss words, and when out on the range, they might vent their wrath on some hapless, stubborn critter, but when they were in mixed company, they watched their language. Children who overheard and imitated the forbidden words were punished in order to teach them what was acceptable and what wasn't.

Youngsters on farms and ranches were apt to see kittens or puppies being born and thus knew that mother animals gave birth. However, the part played by the male of the species was hidden from them.

The word *stallion* was not used on farms and ranches. In our area, if a rancher had the need to identify such an animal, he called him *the horse*, and in order to distinguish him from other horses, he spoke the word with a special inflection. I was shocked, when children's books began coming out with such titles as *The Black Stallion.*

On farms and ranches, children knew the cows were the girls of the species, and steers were the boys. The bull, called *the animal,* was a creature that lazed around the pastures or corrals. Children were cautioned to be careful around *the animal* because he sometimes was mean. When Roland Hall told me that as a child his sister, Treva (Hall) Perkins, was shut in the cellar for using the forbidden word *bull* I called her on the telephone.

"What were you supposed to call the bull when you were a child?" I asked her.

"We called him the booie-cow."

"Booie-cow?" I questioned.

"Yes. *Booie*, as in *scary* or *spooky*. We needed to realize he was sometimes mean, and thus he was called the booie-cow.

"When I was small, maybe about five, I picked up the term *bull*. I probably heard the men talking out in the corral or pasture. Anyway, I once referred to *the animal* as a bull, and promptly I thought the world was coming to an end. My mother scolded me severely for using a bad word and locked me in the cellar."

"Was it dark in the cellar?"

"Oh, yes, and spooky, too."

"Did you scream and hammer on the closed door?"

"Oh, no. I knew that I was supposed to be quiet and consider my misdeed. I suppose I was released in a couple of minutes, but they were long minutes."

"The bull was referred to as *the animal* in our area," I told her. "The men used the term *bull* in the wide open spaces, but around the house they called him *the animal*. But by the 1940s and '50s, I think we were using the term *bull*. Does that seem right to you?"

"Well, possibly other people were, but I wasn't because of my early punishment."

"Would you use the word *bull* now in 2003? If you called the neighbors to say their bull was out, would you use the term?"

"Oh, yes. It 's a common word now"

"Would you use the term *sex* now?"

"Probably not. It is plastered on magazine covers, and used regularly on TV, but I wouldn't use it."

I'm sure that most women her age have the same reticence about sexual terms. In the 1920s and 30s, instead of using the word *pregnant*, adults, in hushed tones, might say to each other, "She is 'in the family way.'" Possibly they might say quietly, "She doesn't feel well in the mornings." Thus they conveyed the message that an acquaintance was pregnant without using words that made them uncomfortable. If a child overheard and asked questions, he was told, "Never mind."

In portraying cowboys on the cattle trail rides, which took place earlier in the twentieth century, modern authors make a mistake. Knowing that, in the sparse towns along the trail, there were "dance hall girls" whose morals were lacking, they allow the cowboys to josh about them. It is true that ladies of ill repute did exist. However, the cowboys did not joke about them.

Actually, the men held to a stern code when speaking of "the fairer half of the population." If anyone made crude or off-color comments about any woman, he was warned that his remarks were offensive. If he continued, the other cowboys would, on signal, attack him. They held him down, stripped off his trousers, and whipped him with a pair of leather chaps.

Joe Dobrovolny, who trailed cattle from Montana to Mobridge, South Dakota, spoke of such an incident.

"When they finally turned him loose," he said, "his backside was as red as a barn."

In *Dakota Cowboy*, Ike Blasingame, who was on a trail drive from Texas to Dakota, told of a similar incident. Andy Adams, in *The Log of a Cowboy*, wrote of his trip as a trail hand from Texas to Montana. In describing the population of the cow towns, he mentioned dance hall girls. However, the cowboys didn't joke about them, and anyone who visited them did so secretively.

It was a different time.

Buffalo Horns
Told by Marie Kramer, York.

By the time the pioneers arrived in the late 1800s, most of the buffalo had been shot. Their bones were strewn about the prairie. Over the years the bones were picked up and sold for fertilizer and bone meal. By the time the grandchildren of the pioneers were frolicking on the prairies, the bones were gone.

One day the Joe Dobrovolny children were examining a part of a horn they had found, and showed it to their father.

They assumed it was a cow horn, but wondered about its unusual ridges and color.

"How come it is split and curled on the one end?" asked one of them. Joe examined it.

"This is the tip of a buffalo horn," he told them. "The sun and the weather cause them to split and curl at the base. As years go by, they disintegrate from that end. They continue to split and curl until finally there is nothing left. In a few more years, this one will be gone."

He looked across the pasture.

"It's a scrap from the past," he finally said. "A past that wasn't that long ago. It seems like only yesterday when there were buffalo bones all over the prairie."

In later times, some of the ranchers began acquiring a few buffalo, thinking the animals should be preserved. They proved to be unusually hardy during snowstorms and interest in raising them is slowly spreading. A market for their meat has begun to grow.

Constructing Highway 11
Told by Pete Weber (in Atkinson Good Samaritan Center).

Pete Weber lived on a farm during the thirties, but he also worked on the WPA for three years. He helped build Highway 11, using a slip. A slip was a large scoop that was pulled by a team of horses.

"I tell you, it was an exhausting job those hot days," said Pete. "Sometimes it was over a hundred degrees in the shade. You got to the point where you'd give a whole lot for a breath of cool air. But I was glad to have the work. I didn't once complain."

A worker walked behind a slip, and when it was in the correct spot for loading, he raised the back of the scoop, which forced the front edge to dig into the dirt. When the scoop was full, the worker pressed down on the back so the loaded scoop slid on top of the ground.

Upon reaching the loading site, the team walked up a ramp. There was a hole in the center of the ramp. One horse walked on one side of the hole, and the other horse on the opposite side. When the slip was in the right position, the driver dumped it.

Some dirt tumbled down through the hole and into a wagon underneath, but some remained on the outside of the hole. It had to be shoveled down by hand. Once a wagon was loaded, it was pulled to the roadbed and another wagon took the place under the ramp. The wagons had "belly dumps" which the driver opened and closed with a ratchet.

"We had bought a quarter of land and had already paid $3000 on it," said Pete. "Then during the Depression, in spite of my WPA job, we couldn't make payments and lost it."

Breaking a Horse
Told by Earl Moore, Bartley. 1933.

After working with a green horse, I was unhitching. My wife, Doris had parked the baby in the baby buggy near the house, and had come to the corral gate to help me. She was holding the bridle of the trained horse so I could concentrate all my attention on the horse I was breaking to the harness.

Suddenly there was a great thunder of hooves. A driverless four-horse team pounded toward our yard. I recognized them as the horses of an elderly neighbor. Apparently, they had become frightened and had gotten away from him.

Since we had no yard fence, Doris was terrified for the baby, but there was no time for her to get to him. I did manage to open the gate and get our team in the corral. They, frightened by the approach of the plunging horses, galloped excitedly in circles.

The wild-eyed team ran through our yard, hooves thundering. As soon as they had gone by, Doris went to the baby who was terrified by the noise but not injured. We had a cross fence behind our buildings, and the horses turned to follow it. I managed to catch them and hold them until the neighbor arrived.

Scattered Groceries
Told by Charlie Mlinar, Atkinson.

One bad winter in the late thirties we ran low on groceries. Every kind of sweetener, sugar as well as honey and syrup, was gone, and the flour bin was nearly empty. My wife Ella was distressed. We boarded the teacher and Ella liked to present decent meals.

Mahlon Shearer and I decided to attempt a trip to town. There was no way a car could travel through the deep snow, so I set out early in the morning on my horse, Marco. From Mahlon's place, we took a team. We wound around on high ground, wherever the snow was less deep.

When the horses bogged down in the drifts, we had to shovel them out. Finally we got to town. We shopped and by mid afternoon were back at Shearers. But how could I get our groceries home on my horse? We tied the fifty-pound sack of flour behind the saddle, a twenty-five pound bag of sugar on one side, and a gunnysack containing other items on the opposite side. I walked and led Marco.

The groceries, unevenly distributed, kept sliding to one side. Mahlon suggested I use his children's small sled. So I put the groceries, except for the flour, on the sled. The flour remained behind the saddle. I got on Marco and we tried it again. However, every clod of snow upset the sled and spilled the groceries.

I decided the horse would go home without guidance. Dismounting, I walked beside the sled, steadying it so it wouldn't upset. I talked quietly to Marco in encouraging tones. All went well until we were about a quarter mile from home. Then a jackrabbit bounded out of a sheltered niche in the snow and startled the horse.

When Marco took off, he left me behind in a swirl of flying snow. The bouncing sled upset, and the groceries spilled. My calls to the horse were of no avail, and he didn't stop until he was floundering in the snowdrifts in the cornfield near our house. The saddle had slipped, and the sack of flour was now under his belly. The sled was broken, and food items were strewn about.

I collected the groceries except for some scattered rice and macaroni. The precious bags of flour, sugar, and salt as well as the carton of matches and a tin of coffee were still intact. Thus the excursion was a success.

Boy in Orbit
Told by Bob Dobrovolny, North Dakota.

There were about thirty kids in our one-room country school. The teacher was overworked and was glad to usher us outside for recess. She had a thousand things to do, not counting overseeing the playground.

We boys played around an old shed located near the school ground. We discovered if we stuck a pole under the shed, put a rock under the pole for a fulcrum, and employed every boy at pushing down on the opposite end of the pole, we could lift the side of the shed. It was great fun.

The larger boys engineered the project. My brother, George, was an eighth grader, as were Adolph Pocta and John Hermanson. My brothers Harry and Fred were also in the upper grades.

When we got the shed as high as we could, our leader counted to three and we simultaneously let go and leapt back. The shed would fall to the ground with a whoof and a bang. We spent our recesses rearranging the pole and fulcrum, trying to lift the building higher.

One day a wise guy among us devised a plan. We would play a trick on a member of the group, Raymond Tomes. Our leader instructed us to let go of the pole on the count of two instead of three. That action would leave Raymond, uninformed of our plan, alone on the pole when the shed fell.

It worked better than we had anticipated. As the shed fell, Raymond was zoomed up into the air and over the roof of the shed. We were all pale with fright as we ran to the other side.

Would he have broken bones? Would he be dead? That was a herd of worried boys!

When we reached the other side, we found Raymond bruised and scratched, but all in one piece. We knew we had lucked out, and we didn't try it again.

An Introduction to Tooth Paste
Told by Olga Peterson, N.Dak. 1930s.

When we were in country school, our teacher passed out some toothbrushes and sample tubes of toothpaste, which were provided by a toothpaste company. We had always brushed our teeth with salt or soda, and had never seen or tasted toothpaste.

On the way home from school, we opened the tiny tubes of toothpaste and found the contents tasted like peppermint candy. This business of brushing teeth took on added glamour!

But by the time we had reached home, we had eaten all the toothpaste. Needless to say, children in those times had numerous cavities in their teeth and most of them were forced to get false teeth in adulthood.

Cattle Drive to the Sale Barn
Told by Lawrence Dobrovolny, O'Neill. Late 1930s.

Once I helped Charlie Freouf drive some cattle to the Atkinson sale barn. He was a kindly fellow, but never got very excited about anything. It was a long drive--I suppose about 30 miles. On the way we both ran out of smoking tobacco.

Charlie had an old, dried plug of chewing tobacco. I managed to carve off a little with my pocketknife and chewed it. He shaved at it until he got enough to fill his pipe. I recall the smoke was blue.

When we got to within six or eight miles of town, we came upon a fellow who was trying to take a bull to town. He was driving a team and hayrack with hay on it. The idea was to coax the bull along with the hay, but it wasn't working.

Also there was a kid on an old plug horse, but the bull didn't pay any attention to him. In order to try to control the bull, the farmer had tied him to a skinny cow. Whenever that bull decided to go someplace, he'd simply drag the exhausted cow along.

"Why, he'll never get to town with that set-up," Charlie said to me. "The bull will drag that cow to death. You hold the herd and I'll go help him."

They got the bull under control and put him, still tethered to the cow, into our herd. The old fellow was really appreciative, and when he found we were out of smoking material, he pulled a can of Prince Albert tobacco from his pocket. Charlie filled his pipe and I rolled a cigarette. We both felt amply repaid.

More People Remember the Depression

Ruth Barnes, Atkinson, worked at the Nite and Day Cafe from 4:00PM until 4:00AM for nine cents an hour. "It wasn't much, but it kept us from starving," she said.

Winnie (Bogue) Hupp worked at the same cafe one summer. It was during the time the government was buying starving cattle. The cows that weren't killed locally and buried in blowouts were shipped to the cities. There were many trains coming through.

"The railroad crews called their food orders from down the line," said Winnie. "We fixed the plates and set them in the warming oven or on the reservoir. When they arrived, we served fast. They had to get back on the job, switching cars."

A reservoir was an oblong water container on the back end of a kitchen range. Anytime the stove was in use, the water in it was lukewarm.

George Vinzenz got a summer job at Stolte Brothers south of Atkinson. He made 75 cents a day stacking hay.

"The machinery had to cover the usual amount of ground, but we did well to get a stack or two a day," said George. "The grass was thin and wispy. Much of it slipped through the rake tines and was lost."

"We had four horses and three cows. We were worried we'd have to sell them because we had no hay. But I made enough during the summer to buy a little commercial feed and we were able to keep them."

Viola Naber and her sister wanted to learn to crochet. The family had a crochet hook, but no thread or yarn. They ripped string from cattle feed bags and flour sacks and used it to crochet dishcloths.

When Edward and Christine Gall of South Dakota married, Ed's neighbors felt sorry for him because his new wife, a schoolteacher, didn't know anything about farm life, not even how to milk a cow.

"I didn't marry you to be a hired hand," he told her. "I don't expect you to do farm work."

During the Depression, everyone was desperate for a way to get some cash. Christine went back to teaching school, and the neighbors stopped making negative comments.

"Louis Allgayer of Avoca found himself in a bad predicament in the Thirties because his well went dry," said Bud Peck. "So that he wouldn't have to sell the last of his cattle, he purchased an old horse-drawn water wagon to haul water from Weeping Water Creek. The wagon had originally been used to haul water to operate a steam-powered threshing machine.

"Louis hired me, a teenager, to haul the water. I had to pump it from the creek by hand, after which it was pulled by a team to the Allgayer farm and unloaded into a tank. I hauled load after load all day long. My wages were fifty cents a day."

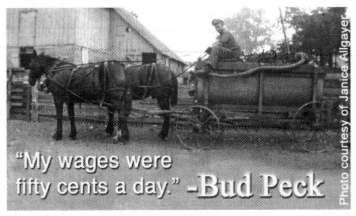

"My wages were fifty cents a day." -Bud Peck

Photo courtesy of Janice Allgayer

In 1934, Swan Lake, located in the hills between Atkinson and Burwell, dried to a point where it would no longer support fish life. The State sent men to move as many of the fish as possible to other lakes.

Rains came in 1935, and by the following spring, Swan Lake held enough water so that 10,000 bullheads were trucked from a hatchery to the lake in order to reseed it.

Henry and Margie (Masters) Dobrovolny had a large family. Most of the children were born on the ranch southwest of Atkinson. Both a doctor and a midwife attended the birth.

Margie told how she sterilized the bedding and other articles that would be needed at the time of the birth. After collecting all the items, she wrapped them in a sheet and baked them in a slow oven to kill the germs. The bundle was stored unopened until needed.

At the end of World War I, Joe Disterhaupt borrowed money from Gib Morgan and built a beautiful house in south Atkinson. During the depression, he couldn't make interest payments. He lost the house to Morgan.

Amelia Kaup was in high school during the dry thirties. In order to have something to wear, she sewed her own blouses and smocks. She wore her hair in a home-cut short bob. To buy her class ring, her mother let her sell some of their hens for thirty-five cents each.

"When the dust came rolling in," said Ora Whipple, who lived far in the hills southwest of Atkinson, "it settled on everything, but especially collected in lower, more sheltered areas. Since we lived by Whipple Lake, it was lower ground, and the dust really piled up. I remember red dust and tan dust, but most of it was gray.

"It seems like the house was its favorite place," continued Ora. "It was fine like flour, and when you tried to wash it off, it turned to paste.

"We were lucky since we had a flow well. We planted a garden near it. Also, there were springs in the hills where we planted more vegetables. But we had to bucket the water from its source to the rows of plants. It was just too blistering hot, and we didn't get very much in the way of vegetables. Just got the exercise."

"I especially remember dust coming in from the Dakotas," said Frank Johnson, Bassett. "We thought we had a well-built house, and was amazed how dust worked itself into the building. It piled up deep along fence lines. I remember swirls and rivulets of dust that had been whipped into patterns in protected areas outside.

"One afternoon I went in our car to get our daughter from school which was a mile and a half across the prairie. Visibility was poor because the car lights couldn't penetrate the thick, flying dust. There was only one blowout along the way, but we got stuck in it and had to walk home.

1995

Bill Krysl
watching the grandkids in a blowout.

"The strong winds blew us off course, and also we were blinded by the dust. I'm embarrassed to admit it, but right by our own place, I got lost! Finally we came to a fence I recognized. We followed it and got home."

"We didn't have range cows," said Mary Fallon of O'Neill, "but we had twelve milk cows, six horses, geese, chickens, and ducks. Our corn dried up before it made ears, and Dad cut it. We piled it up in the field. Then in the winter, dad would go to the field and bring in some to feed the cows.

"We didn't have a hay stacker. We pitched the hay into a hayrack, hauled it home, and pitched it into a huge, long stack behind the barn. The terribly long workdays out in the heat were the worst part. Sometimes I thought I couldn't take another step, couldn't pitch another forkful, or I'd be sure to pass out. Late at night after milking, we almost groaned out loud when Dad said:

"'You kids unload that hay tonight. We need to get in the field early in the morning.'

"Sometimes we worked until midnight, but still had to start early the next morning. There wasn't any dew to speak of, and the hay would be dry soon after it was cut.

"I know what hard times are. We only had one cow when we came to O'Neill. Our meals were simple and tiresome. We had oatmeal every day for breakfast and again for supper. At noon, we had bread and butter and a little of whatever else we could scare up."

"Some of our kittens got sick," said Marie Kramer, who grew up southwest of Atkinson. "Looking back, I'm sure they had dust pneumonia. They were a sorry sight, for water from their eyes and noses ran down their faces, and the dust caught in it. They sat by the cob house, sick and miserable. We children wanted to comfort them, but our mother worried they might have distemper.

"'People can catch it from animals,' she said. 'And everyone who gets it dies. There isn't any cure. So don't touch them.'

"Overnight, they disappeared. I imagine some of the adults 'helped' them leave this world."

"Even though we lived 18 miles from town, hobos often appeared at our door," said Albena Kramer. "They were looking for work. I was 12 the year my mother was sick in bed, and I was doing the cooking for seven family members and two hired men. It was nearly time for the noon meal when a hobo arrived.

"Dad invited him in for the meal. He repeatedly asked for more bread, and finally the plate was empty. I went to the cupboard for more, but the breadbox was empty. Over and over, the man apologized for eating so much bread when our mother was sick in bed.

"Of course, I mixed a new batch in the afternoon, but I was clumsy at all the work, and the bread was late getting baked. We had a late supper."

"We had recently built a new house," said John Herrington, O'Neill. "We considered it to be airtight. But the fine, beige-colored dust came in anyway. It seemed to go through steel and wood. Everyone stayed inside because of the dirt and the wind.

"Afterward, outside we found piles and swirls and ridges of dust collected in protected areas. Tumbleweeds that had caught in the fences now, in turn, caught the dust, and it piled up along the fence lines. Later, I had occasion to climb to the roof of the house. Oddly the rain gutters were completely filled with dust."

"People salvaged anything they could for feed," said Charlie Skopec who then lived near Wilbur. "They cut weeds at the edges of fields. Farmers used corn knives to cut the small, dry, earless cornstalks.

"My dad lived southwest of Lincoln. He cut corn with a grain binder, shocked it, and ran it through a threshing machine to pulverize it. He thought he'd get more benefit from it because the animals would eat more of it when it was ground.

"Something else we tried was to spill a little molasses over rough feed to make it more palatable for the livestock. It worked to a certain extent."

June Gilman said, "We had some little pigs but didn't have feed for them. One day a magazine salesman came. Of course, there was not a penny to be had for a luxury like a magazine. But I told him I'd trade him a little pig for the magazine. He put a pig in a gunnysack, and we got a farm magazine.

"A neighbor, Lee Sammons, gave him two guinea hens for the magazine."

Margaret Henning, who lived in South Dakota at the time, said she remembered drinking cold water to try to get some relief from the terrible heat. She drank so much she got sick, but was still thirsty. Adding a bit of lemon to the water helped to quench thirst, she said.

George Hytrek had a Model A Ford truck, which, in those days, didn't have an air cleaner. He was delivering free food from the county welfare station. Lesser roads were trails, and he had to leave the main road between towns.

"Now that land is a grassy pasture, but then it was just sand and dust. The intake on the carburetor sucked up dirt and the motor stopped. I had to clean out the bowl of the carburetor before the truck would run again. We wore out motors fast in those days. No one can imagine how those dust and sand storms were."

Lawrence Ziska, Atkinson, stayed with relatives in town while he attended high school during his ninth and tenth grades. By the time he was in the eleventh, he was permitted to drive an old Model T to school. It was a good arrangement for his dad because Lawrence could then help with farm work nights and mornings.

"I was really excited. I thought I had a Cadillac!" he later reported, chuckling.

One day he was plagued with flat tires. The first tire went flat while he was parked at school. He fixed it, but after he started out, the tire went down once more. He patched the tire again--and again.

The problem was, the older Model Ts had wooden wheels, and the rims were riveted on the wood. The wood had dried and shrunk causing the rivets to loosen. When he started to drive, a loose rivet would poke another hole in the tire.

They replaced the wheels with newer metal ones that needed no rivets. The problem was finally solved.

During the Thirties, Joy Greenfield, Stuart, didn't have enough feed for his livestock. He butchered small pigs, took them to town, and sold them for a dollar apiece.

When Charlie and Ella Mlinar were talking about the Depression, Charlie said, "We should tell what we did with the little pigs when we ran out of feed."

His wife looked up. "Don't say another word about those pigs!" she said emphatically. He didn't tell.

"When farmers ran out of hay," said Rose Hoffman, Stuart, "they butchered some of the baby animals that weren't yet listed on a mortgage. They ground some of the meat with hand grinders, fried it in patties, and packed it in stone jars. While it was still hot, they poured boiling grease over it, effectively preserving it.

"They dried some of the meat. To keep it from molding, they stored it in shelled corn in the granary."

Boyd Young, McCool Junction, said much of their grain was too short to cut with a binder. So they mowed it, bunched it up, and stacked it. The corn dried up before it made ears and they mowed and stacked it, also.

Cora Jeffers said they were living near Aurora. West of their place, the dust was so deep they couldn't travel the road. In some places it covered fence posts. The next year her father hired a road maintainer to move the dirt back on the land.

Ralph Ries reported the government bought cows for twelve dollars. The thinner ones were shot and buried, but the better ones were butchered and given to people on relief. "I sold forty pigs to Guy Cole in Emmet for two dollars and fifty cents each," he said.

"The fields were barren, a sea of sand," said Beulah Miksch, Stuart. "You couldn't believe it even when you saw it. My sister didn't even raise enough feed for the chickens. There was nothing growing in most places and only sandburs and thistles in other isolated spots."

George Hitchcock, Atkinson, said, "I recall when those dark clouds appeared. People were relieved, hopeful. They thought it was rain clouds. But it was fine, dirty dust riding on a brisk wind. Some animals--cattle, horses, and pets--got dust pneumonia and died.

"You can still see where the ridges blew up along the fence rows. Tumble weeds caught in the fences, and the dust caught in the tumble weeds."

"My sister and I were on the way home from school," said Roy Goeke. "We had passed Anthony O'Donnell's when the choking dust came rolling over the prairie. There was a howling wind with it. A person could hardly breathe because it got in your nose and eyes.

"When that dust hit, Anthony O'Donnell came in his Model A to give us a ride home. Inside the house, Mother had lit the kerosene lamp because it was so dark."

"When I was a kid, I liked to read the ads in the magazines," said Lawrence Kramer, Atkinson. "Sometimes I'd get excited about one that sounded like a good deal, and I'd take it to my mother.

"She'd recite a German proverb: 'Paper is patient.'

"She'd go on to explain that paper will take anything you write on it, no matter whether it's true or not. Then she'd add, 'And mostly, it's malarkey!'"

"I remember having a dry, parched throat when we kids shocked grain on hot days," said Paul Kaup, Stuart. "It was hot enough, I think, to have baked potatoes in the sand. Besides, there was a certain amount of dust in the bundles, and when we piled them in shocks, it made the air more choking yet. My tongue got so dry I couldn't even move it. We had our water jugs at the end of the field and had to make a full round before we could have a drink.

"From planting in the spring through corn picking time in the fall, we worked long hours, but ate five times a day. In addition to our regular meals, we had a lunch in mid forenoon and another in the afternoon. Lunches usually consisted of corn bread spread with lard."

"In the Depression when the grasshoppers were bad," said Dorothy Schaaf, Atkinson, "the outside of the house was covered with them. When they attacked the garden, it looked like it had been mowed. We had to be careful when we went in and out the door because they came in the house at every opportunity. They chewed holes in curtains and clothes."

"Our family was especially good at training horses," said Orval Monson, Blair. "That's how we got through the Depression. People were short of feed and got rid of their ill-trained horses. We bought them cheap, sometimes got them for free. With patient handling, we turned outlaw horses into faithful workers and sold them at a profit."

Steve Papiernik of Ord said when he was in high school, he had one pair of school pants each year. By the time school was out, they were worn so thin the seat almost looked like window screen. Girls often had only one or two dresses each for the entire term.

"My dad had a 50-gallon barrel that he used to slop the hogs," said Kenneth Ziska. "He had it rigged between two buggy wheels and had a big handle on the back for pushing it. During those dry years we kids were sent to water the garden with it.

"First we had to pump the water into a bucket and dump it into the barrel. Then we shoved it through the sand to the garden. Oh, how we grunted and sweat in the hot sun. People made good use of 'kid power' in those days. When we got to the garden, we bucketed the water from the barrel to the plants. I can feel the burning sand on my feet yet."

"The government bought most of our hungry cows," said Philip Wintek, Elyria. "Even then, the remaining animals almost starved. They ate the leaves off the trees as high as they could reach. They licked the pasture down to bare dirt. Farmers bought old slough grass, rushes, and rotted hay. The cows nosed it around and searched for something edible, then looked at us accusingly and bawled. It was sad to see them starving and not be able to do anything about it."

"My wife's family, the Christensons, were out of food," said Ralph Ries. "They got some corn that was sent from Iowa. They shelled it by hand and ground it in a tiny coffee grinder. All winter they lived on corn bread and corn meal mush. The milk cow was dry, but the corn bread was made more palatable by dipping it in hot water. Oh, the kids got tired of corn bread and water, but it was all they had."

John and Fred Dobrovolny

1940

Mlinar Children

From the Barbara Mlinar Collection

Chapter 3

After the Depression

Most of the Grandchildren of the Pioneers were in school or were entering the work force. *Gone with the Wind* **was a best seller. The Empire State Building and the Golden Gate Bridge had been built.**

Cattle, Buffalo, and *Dances with Wolves*
Told by John Ziska III, Atkinson. 1936-37.

The drought ended sooner in northern Nebraska than it did in South Dakota. In 1935 and '36, our area of Nebraska had moisture to spare, bringing bumper hay crops. Since cattle numbers had been severely reduced during the dry years, there was an excess of hay. But the Dakotas continued to be plagued with drought.

In the fall of '36, several desperate ranchers from South Dakota came to Holt County, NE, and rented hay land with the right to winter their cattle on it. Two such families, the Roy Houcks and the Jay Lakes, unable to raise money for trucking, drove their cattle from north central South Dakota to land located about ten miles south of Atkinson, Nebraska. There the two families lived together in a small house on the Matousek place, and their children attended a local rural school, District 77. They had roughly a thousand head of cattle.

They baled some of the hay, trucked it to South Dakota and sold it. These funds then allowed them to send their cattle, along with the newly born calves, back by rail.

Finally, fortune smiled on the Houcks, and with hard work, they rebuilt their herds and prospered. During the Blizzard of '49, Roy was surprised to see that a small herd of buffalo survived the severe storms unaided, even though many of his hand-fed cattle were lost. In addition to his cattle herd, he began raising buffalo.

When Hollywood was looking for a large herd of buffalo in order to film them for the movie, *Dances with Wolves*, they chose Roy's buffalo herd and also used his ranch lands for the setting of the movie.

Haying Mishaps
Told by Bernard Kaup, Newport. Late 1930s.

When a storm was approaching, V.J. Krysl was reluctant to have hay get wet. He pushed to get as much hay in the stack as possible before rain began to fall. All six of his children worked in the field, and being intimidated by the lightning, were anxious to get off the iron machinery. But not V.J., and he was the boss.

One day when they had hayed until rain began to fall, the order to quit finally came in the form of hand signals and V.J.'s mighty bellow. They scattered the machinery so if one piece of equipment got hit by lightning, the others would not be near enough to be affected. Then they unhooked the horses and hurried toward the wagon that was their transportation home. They hooked one team to it, and led the others behind.

Josephine, in her teens, was running in front of her trotting horses as she led them toward the wagon. Suddenly, she tripped and fell, but the horses continued on. They stepped over her and miraculously missed her with all eight hooves. They knew where they were supposed to go and continued until they reached the wagon. Josephine jumped to her feet and followed.

Another time, Don Krysl, probably 16 or 17, was stacking hay. The load hadn't dumped well, and the stacker driver, a young cousin, left the buck up so Don could pitch the hay from it onto the stack. Just as Don got the load leveled, a friend stopped by to visit for a few minutes. Don, not noticing the buck was still high on the stacker arms, leaned over the top of the boards to talk with him. Suddenly the stacker driver saw that the sweep was approaching with another load of hay. He yanked on the lines and shouted.

"Back! Back up!"

The heavy buck started down, pinching Don between it and the stacker boards.

"Hey!" gasped Don. "Lift--the buck."

One glance told the driver what needed to be done.

"Giddap!" he shouted, slapping the lines. "Giddap!"

The horses went forward, releasing Don. He was a sturdy young man, and escaped with only bruises. The hay harvest proceeded as usual.

Model A Trip to the Coast
Told by Jim Schippert, Republican City. 1936-39.

Discouraged by the drought of the previous years, my parents, Eugene and Beatrice Schippert, decided to move our family from Republican City, Nebraska, to the state of Washington. I was ten, my sister Vera was six, and Joyce was three. Dad drove a 1931 Model A car.

Because Mother would not give up her wood-burning kitchen range, Dad made a four-wheeled trailer from an old Model T car and loaded the stove on it. The stove had a blue enamel finish, a warming oven over the top, and a water reservoir on the end opposite the firebox. (When the stove was in use, the water in the reservoir would be heated to lukewarm.) Around the stove, they packed other household furnishings. I recall that it was difficult for the car to pull the heavy trailer over the mountains and through the deserts because the motor kept heating.

Our family of five rode in the Model A. Along the way, we slept in motels, which were then called cabins. Most nights it cost us about fifty cents to get a cabin, but in Mother's journal she recorded that one night we had to pay the exorbitant price of an entire dollar!

The cabins each had a pot-bellied stove to use for heat and for cooking. The motel furnished a little tub of wood for fuel. Once I found some small, thin slabs of wood like the ones used to make cheese boxes at that time. I took some of them along and used them to corral my imaginary livestock, which were merely spools from my mother's sewing projects.

My uncle continually wrote us letters, telling us that conditions were improving in Nebraska and that we should return. Finally in 1939, my parents decided to come back.

Remembering how difficult it was to get over the mountains, Dad built a smaller, two-wheeled trailer. Again, Mother's range was the main article on it, and again, it was a struggle to get over the mountains with the Model A. After being accustomed to the lush greenery on the coast, Nebraska looked desolate.

"If it hadn't been that we were waiting for more articles to arrive by parcel post," my father often said, "we'd have gone back without unloading."

As it was, by the time our parcels arrived, we were unpacked and were getting settled. We didn't feel like reloading and making that long trip across prairie and mountains and desert. Eventually conditions improved in Nebraska, and we were happy we had stayed.

"How You Gonna Keep 'em Down on the Farm"
Told by Homer Brauning, Geneva.

I recall when I was small, often when Dad harnessed the horses and went to the field, my oldest brother, Oliver, struggled to start the old tractor. He'd finally get it running, and go out to help plow. In a short time he'd be back, again trying to fix the tractor.

Oliver saw no future in farming, and in 1936, he left for Omaha where he did clerical work at Dun and Bradstreet. Later he did office work at Eaton Metal.

In an effort to keep my second brother, Wilbert, on the farm, Dad borrowed money from the banker in Grafton to buy a John Deere tractor. It cost $825, which was a huge amount of money in those depressed times. It was driven out from Sutton on steel wheels, and lugs were installed after it was in our yard.

Wilbert was interested in being a welder. When Oliver found such an opening at Eaton Metal, Wilbert left. I was ten, and immediately my responsibilities and my work load on the farm increased.

My father's health was poor, probably because of the stress of the Depression. By the time I was 11, I was working in the field whenever I wasn't in school, doing tractor work, helping to pick corn, and the like.

On stormy nights, we awoke to find snow on the windowsills, and sometimes even on our quilts. We didn't have storm windows, and wind and snow sifted through the cracks. Overnight, the water in the teakettle on the kitchen stove froze. We hated to crawl from under our quilts and dress, shivering in the icy air.

Before hybrid seeds, sometimes there was a freak ear of corn that was red. You might pick for days without finding one, but occasionally one appeared. An old saying proclaimed, that if a young fellow found a red ear, it meant he'd get a kiss from his sweetheart. I was too young for girlfriends, but I saved the red ears anyway.

We had a good crop of corn when I was in the tenth grade. In October, I left school and my mother and I picked corn until stormy winter weather shut us down. If an ear of corn happened to fly over the bang board, I had to go around the wagon and pick it up.

The following year, I reentered tenth grade and graduated in 1946. I continued to work full time on the farm, but I didn't yet have a share.

Dad asked, "Are you going to be the farmer?"

"I'll farm," I told him, "if we can get a cornpicker." He agreed.

In 1949, I rented a quarter and got more serious about farming, but after a couple years, Uncle Sam called me to the service. My stint as a soldier was a short one. After eleven weeks of basic training, I spent two months in the hospital, and then was given a medical discharge.

I married in 1955, my parents moved to Sutton, and my wife and I took over the farm.

Spot Livingston, Atkinson's Big Man

The Nebraska Farmer, once listed Spot Livingston as the biggest man in the state. Not only was he big in size, but he also was big of heart, making him everyone's friend. People in north central Nebraska each had favorite stories about Spot.

C. C. Raymer: I ordered Spot's clothes, special-made. When he was in the meat market in Atkinson, he wore trousers and white shirts. I always worried his pants would fall down, for he had a huge stomach. After he moved to the farm, he wore bib overalls with a 72" waist and 36" inseam.

Fred Braun: My dad, Gottlieb Braun, sold Spot a cow. Spot went to the farm and butchered it. After he had it dressed, he picked up an entire side of it and flopped it into the back of his pickup. Then he grabbed the other side and slapped it on top.

You know, a quarter of beef is a big load for a man. I've never before heard of anyone who handled beef by carrying a half carcass at a time. After he covered the meat, he signaled to the boy who was driving, and the pickup pulled away. Spot got in his car and drove off.

Fred continued: In spite of his weight, Spot was a wonderful dancer. One time a scrappy little fellow named Fritz, kept bumping into Spot on the dance floor. Spot took it good naturedly until it became apparent the fellow was purposely colliding with him.

"Hey, there! Stop that!" Spot said.

Fritz answered, "Who's gonna make me?" and bumped Spot again.

Spot let go of his partner, and grabbed Fritz with two big hands, pinning the feisty fellow's arms to his body. He lifted him straight up and carried him to the door. As soon as Spot set him down and unpinned his arms, Fritz swung a fist.

Spot held him back with a long, thick arm. He lifted his other arm and let his huge hand, as big as a stove lid, fall straight down on Fritz's head. Fritz staggered and immediately found business elsewhere.

Winnie Hupp: Spot loved to dance, and was amazingly light on his feet. The girls, young and old, were pleased to dance with him. He taught a lot of young girls to dance.

Ed Bouska: Once I was at a dance in Stuart. A big fellow who ran a beer truck arrived, and as he came in, I said, "Hi, ya, Kid!"

He bristled. "If I'm a kid, where do you have your men?"

As fate would have it, just then Spot came in, bowing his head to get under the top of the doorframe, and wedging his huge body through the opening.

"I said to him, 'Hi ya, Kid!'"

"Hi, ya, Eddie!" he boomed back.

The beer salesman simmered down.

Freddie Ziska: After Spot moved to the farm and was our neighbor, he came over on a cold day to help us butcher. He was sitting on a steel barrel in order to be the right height to work, and also to take that enormous load off his feet. He reached up, slashed the critter, and soon had him butchered.

I said, "You probably shouldn't be sitting on a steel barrel in this cold weather. You'll catch cold."

Spot answered, "I never did get a cold in that part of my body."

Roy Goeke: When the Livingston car came down the road, you could tell from a distance whether Spot was in it or not. If he was in it, the car was lop-sided.

During warm weather, Spot carried a can of ice cubes in his car. He'd put a couple in a washcloth and apply them to his wrists to cool himself.

Melba Dvorak: Spot was visiting us, and I said, "The only time I feel small is when I'm beside you, Spot. I'd like to have my picture taken with you." Afterward, she loved to show the picture because, standing next to Spot, she felt like a small person. *went to school with gene*

Mabel Bogue: I worked for Livingstons at the time their son, Gene, was born. Spot was in the butcher shop then and lived west of the grade school. I didn't enjoy ironing his huge white shirts, which were as big as bed sheets. I put chairs along the ironing board to keep them from dragging on the floor. Then we hung them on a hook above the door, and they filled the whole doorway.

One of Spot's favorite breakfasts was a plate of baking powder biscuits and about four pork chops. After the chops were fried, we poured a cup or so of water over them and removed them to a plate. We stirred the water, lard, and pan-fryings together, poured them over the biscuits, and called Spot to his breakfast.

One of Spot's favorite breakfasts was a plate of baking powder biscuits and about four pork chops...

John Ziska III: Dad and I were at Livingstons when Spot and Ferne were selling some turkeys. The cream man carried a chicken crate along and was picking them up. After the turkeys had been weighed, someone suggested Spot get on the scales.

"Yes, do," said Ferne. "You've been telling me you're losing weight. Let me see for myself."

Spot got on and tipped the scales at 535 pounds.

"You have lost," she said. "About 75 pounds."

That meant he once weighed 610 pounds.

Clarence Tasler: We needed some cash to pay for the delivery of our first child. We sold Spot a calf for $35. He came to the farm, butchered it, and hauled it away. Alice was born at her Grandma Kissinger's house, so we had no hospital bill. The $35 from Spot paid the doctor.

Mrs. Fred Braun: When my nephew was small, he was standing with his arm around a barber pole and was pivoting around it. Suddenly he stopped and stared. I followed his gaze and saw Spot had appeared on the street. The boy was transfixed, motionless as Spot crossed the street and disappeared behind the bank. The child was riveted, amazed that he had just seen a real giant. It was several minutes before he resumed his trip around the barber pole.

Ira (Spot) Livingston died on September 19, 1949, at the age of 52.

The Easter Rabbit
Told by Marie Kramer. Late 1930s.

During the childhood of the five older children in our family, the Easter bunny never managed to make it to our house. I'm sure the Depression was the culprit. I can't say I minded his absence. He was a fairy tale and, like the three bears or Goldilocks, he had never come, and there was no reason to expect that he ever would. But by the time my two youngest brothers were toddlers, I was old enough to prepare an Easter surprise for them.

"Now you shouldn't do that," my mother chided. "If you do it one year, they will expect it every year. It's better not to get it started."

"I don't care if they expect it every year," I said. "I like to do things like this, and I will fix something every year."

We had Rhode Island Red hens that laid brown eggs. It was hard to color them, and I had only crayons and watercolors. Neither gave satisfactory results. Finally I glued a band of colored paper around them, which, since the two little boys had never seen brightly colored eggs, was acceptable.

We learned in school how to make baskets from folded paper. My baskets, fashioned from wallpaper with hand-drawn bunnies on the side, were a success. For grass, I cut green paper in fine strips. It was too stiff to work well, but the recipients were not fussy.

I think at that first celebration, there was no candy or anything else sweet, but nevertheless, the little boys were surprised and delighted with my efforts. After that, for as long as the boys were small, the Easter Bunny came.

The Child Orator
Told by Marie Kramer, Atkinson. Late 1930s.

Since toys were rare, it was a time when children invented their own activities. The ingenuity that went into their play was a learning experience as well as a means of recreation.

The Dobrovolny family kept a bench under an elm tree in the yard. In the summer, a bucket of sun-warmed water, a wash pan, and a bar of soap were placed on it. A towel hung on a nail driven into the tree, and a comb rested in a crotch between two branches. The hay crew used these items to "wash up" at mealtime.

When John, one of the young members of the family, was about five or six, he piled apple boxes and orange crates on and around the bench in order to make a stage. Then he climbed on the stage, and went through the motions of giving an oration to an invisible audience. There was no television at the time, but he had the opportunity to observe speakers at Memorial Day services and to hear presidential speakers on radio.

Sometimes he spoke words and sentences, but other times, he babbled. His voice rose and fell persuasively, and he punctuated his arguments with appropriate hand gestures.

Apparently his practice bore fruit, for when he was in high school, he was one of the students who went to state speech contests. Later, after attending Creighton University, he taught speech in high schools, and later in colleges.

Halloween Prank
Told by Tony Mescher, Petersburg.

Tony Mescher and a companion we will call Abner were celebrating Halloween. In their wake they left a trail of laughter and upset privies. The usual pattern was for them to get on opposite sides of a building, rock it left, right, left, right, and then slam it down on its side.

107

In Petersburg, they came to an unusually large out-house. Unbeknownst to them, the owner had hidden inside the building with a loaded shotgun.

"This must be a three-holer," said Abner, chuckling.

"We may have to teeter it a few more times to get it to fall," whispered Tony.

"Let's get it rocking," suggested Abner, "and when I think it is teetering enough to fall, I'll say 'Timber!' Then you leap out of the way and I'll shove it over."

The two young men positioned themselves and began the rocking motion. Suddenly the door flew open, and a gun barrel pointed skyward. A flash of light and an ear-shattering explosion split the night air.

The terrorized culprits fled, pounding the ground with mighty steps. In the dark they ran into a barbed wire fence with such force that they were slammed to the ground. Abner knew that his clothes and his hide had been ripped, but was up as quickly as Tony. They sped away.

The fun was over, and the two were glad to head for home. Upon arriving, Abner discovered that both his legs had gapping slashes above the knees. They should have been stitched but weren't. Healing was slow, and he carried inch-wide scars for the rest of his life.

"That was the last time we upset privies," said Tony. "Somehow, it just wasn't fun anymore."

Scarlet Fever
Marva (Moore) Teter, Holdrege. 1936 or 37.

Childhood diseases continued to be serious during the nineteen twenties and thirties. Whooping cough was a threat, as was small pox, scarlet fever, diphtheria, measles, and of course, polio.

I was about six and Donna was about seven when we got scarlet fever. We had a bad case of it, and missed six or eight weeks of school. We were miserable with the itching and the fever. I recall that Aunt Doris came over sometimes and held one of us while Mother held the other. I don't know who took care of her children during that time.

Mother washed us with mild soda water and used a light lotion on us. We were kept in a semi-darkened room, because light was said to be harmful to the eyes of anyone who had a disease such as measles or scarlet fever. When the fever left us, our skin pealed off.

Donna and Marva Moore

Afterward, we had to fumigate. We strung lines across the room and hung objects on them so the antiseptic fumes could circulate around them. We draped the books over the lines and spread the pages. We had to discard some things that couldn't be fumigated.

Mother heated a boiler full of water on the kitchen range. She added more wood to the fire and sent us to the car before she dumped the medication into the water. Then we went to Uncle Earl and Aunt Doris' house for the night.

The Development of 4-H Clubs
Told by Tom Dobrovolny, Stuart. Late 1930s.

I don't recall what the driving force was behind the organization of 4-H Clubs in Holt County, but I imagine it was the work of an energetic County Agricultural Agent. I was probably nine years old when I, along with some of my brothers and sisters, joined.

The object of the clubs was to teach young people farm, ranch, bookkeeping, and homemaking skills. First projects for my brother Tony and me were stocker-feeder calves. Dad let us choose calves from his herd. He discussed with us the price he expected us to pay when eventually they were sold, and helped us get organized for feeding them.

At that time, ranchers preferred compact critters. They should have blocky bodies, short legs, and broad heads. Being ignorant of the fine points of judging, I had chosen a calf that was a little taller than Tony's. I figured I had a head start.

When we appeared at the county fair with our animals, Tony's compact critter won a ribbon. The judges ignored mine because of its rangier body and longer legs.

Some decades later the cattle industry changed to meet the needs of a public that preferred leaner meats. Then the accent was on a taller, rangier critter.

"If our two calves could be judged now," Tony told me, "probably yours would be considered the better of the two."

Putting the Boys to Work
Told by Don Krysl, Stuart. Late '30s.

Toward the end of the Depression, when Don was eleven and Bill was nine, their father, V.J. Krysl, bought some old hay storage barns and hauled them home in sections. The boys were directed to take them apart and sort the boards and the two-by-fours according to length. Every nail had to be pulled, including the shingle nails which were in the roof boards by the thousands.

"Oh, we got sick of it," said Don. "It seemed to take forever! The pile of boards was like a mountain. We could work all day and not see any progress. And Dad was so-o-o fussy. Everything had to be done according to his pattern."

From the lumber, they built the machine shed, garage, shop, calf shed, milk house, and a part of the big cattle shed. About that time they also rebuilt the pig house, brooder house, and hen house.

V.J. saw to it that everything was well painted, barn-red with white trim. At the end of the six-year project, the boys admitted they were proud of the farm buildings.

Water Fountain
Told by Tony Dobrovolny, Atkinson. 1938.

Our family had traveled to Nebraska City where we were visiting Gladys Parks, the landlady of a part of the Holt County ranch where our family lived. I was about twelve or thirteen years old, and Leroy Parks was perhaps sixteen. We were downtown, and had stopped at a street corner water fountain to get a drink. At that time, we didn't have water fountains in our town. We used a hand operated pump located on a street corner.

After quenching my thirst at the fountain, I continued to examine the unfamiliar mechanism, testing the force of the stream it produced. A passerby stopped to scold me.

"Get away from that fountain!" he demanded in belligerent tones. "That's not a toy!"

I backed away, embarrassed to be caught in a childish act. In those days, country kids were meek, and in the strange environment of a town, they tended to be unsure of themselves. However, I was amazed at the reaction of my city friend, Leroy.

"And just who are you?" he demanded of the man, a note of defiance in his voice.

The man turned toward him and snapped, "If you're his family, all right. Otherwise, mind your own business." He walked away.

This incident gave me cause to ponder the differences between country kids and city kids.

Harvesting in Minnesota
Told by Roland Naber, Utica. 1939.

In most parts of Nebraska, the drought was over in the mid 1930s but debts were so large that it was years before people crept out of depressed times. I graduated in 1939, and after we had finished our harvest, three of us, Carl Weimer, Harvey Robinson, Melvin Naber, and I, went to Minnesota to help with the harvest there. A neighbor fellow, Fred Gierhan, had gone the year before, and knew that we could find jobs on farms in the Big Stone area.

We bought a worn-out Model T Ford for ten dollars and set out. We got as far as Wahoo before the car quit. We managed to fix it and went on

Farmers in Minnesota were short of labor during harvest season, and we had no trouble finding jobs. At that time, they used binders to cut the grain and threshing machines to thresh it. Our job was to follow the binders, pick up the bundles, and pile them into shocks. We received twenty-five cents an hour, which was good wages at that time.

Even though farming was about the same there as it was here, the trip was a good learning experience. I was away from home and was associating with different people. One thing I remember is that they really fed the hired hands well.

Armistice Day Storm
Atkinson, 1940.

John Ziska III, then a boy, said that his elderly grandfather, John Ziska (who, as a young man, had guided the Ziska Wagon train from Iowa to Atkinson, Nebraska) came in from chores on Saturday night, and stated:

"It's going to storm in the next day or two. The geese are pouring south across the sky. Usually geese settle down in the evening to rest. When they fly in large numbers at night, you know they are rushing to stay ahead of a storm."

True to his warning, a severe storm moved in the next afternoon, Sunday, November 10th. The snow was driven by strong winds, and temperatures dropped.

Disterhaupt's cattle were behind a grove, and possibly would have survived the blizzard unattended. However, Joe and Ed Disterhaupt decided to feed them. They cabled a load of hay on the underslung and drove across the meadow. It happened they hadn't yet changed the tractor from steel wheels to rubber tires, and it bogged down in a drift of snow. There was nothing for the men to do except walk home in the blinding storm.

Unfortunately, the hungry cattle heard the tractor and thinking food was on the way, left the protection of the grove. They strung across the meadow toward the sound of the tractor. If they had stayed behind the grove, they probably all would have survived. As it was, about fifty head froze.

That same Sunday, continued John, Charlie Ziska set out to take his daughter, Viola, to the Frank Dobrovolny ranch where she boarded while teaching school. His young sons, Kenny and Marvin, rode along. Charlie got stuck near the John Ziska place. While attempting to open the trunk to get his tire chains, he dropped the car keys in the snow. Blinded by the storm, he couldn't find them. They walked to the Ziska place.

Charlie and his three children were forced to stay there for the duration of the storm. Finally someone came to pick them up, but they left the car stalled on the road for some time.

Tillie Kaup was teaching District 205, said Anna Krysl, and boarding at our place. Her parents, Mr. and Mrs. Aloys Kaup, brought her Sunday afternoon and got snowed in. They were forced to stay for a couple days. Aloys was a nervous person. He paced the floors, looked out the windows, and worried that they were a nuisance to their hosts.

Joe Dobrovolny had gone to Sioux City in the caboose of a freight train, taking cattle he was planning to sell there. His son LeRoy, age twenty-one, was left in charge of the ranch. Usually on Sunday afternoons or evenings, Joe or LeRoy took Albena to the boarding place where she lived while she taught a rural school. They continued on to deliver Marie and Tony, high school students, to their boarding places in Atkinson.

On this particular Sunday afternoon, the storm, later to be called the Armistice Day Storm, came in with immediate force. Their mother, Ella, thought it a good idea for people to stay home and forget about school, but the younger ones were confident. In addition, LeRoy was anxious to do everything as well as his dad would have done it. They tossed the suitcases in the car and set out.

Heading north, the snow was blinding. Drifts were forming on the roads, and whenever the car bogged down, it was necessary for the boys to shovel and push. The girls made a move to help, but the boys over-ruled them. In their particular family, it was the men's place to do such things.

One unfortunate result was that the girls did not realize the power of the storm.

After battling the way into the driveway of Albena's boarding place close to where she taught, they unloaded her. The boys helped her carry her books and suitcase through the howling storm, and then returned to the car.

The trip to town continued, and once the two high school students were dropped at their boarding house, LeRoy headed for home. Since he was alone on the twenty-mile return trip the others wondered how he managed to get home.

Somehow, he did.

When Joe returned, he was not happy that the young people had gone to town during the storm. In hindsight, all could see it had been the wrong thing to do. They knew that, with all the people stranded in the storm, their guardian angels had worked overtime that day to see them through.

A check for Albena's monthly room and board. Her salary was probably about $45. In her family, grown children kept their funds in their father's account, each initialing his own checks.

A Trio of Tricksters

A man named Willis was on a bus traveling across Nebraska, and told this story to fellow passengers. He asked that his last name not be recorded.

When I, Willis, was only a few weeks old, my mother discovered she was again expecting a child.

"Children this close together will be almost like twins," she said. "If our new baby is a boy, we should name him William, which will go nicely with Willis."

It turned out we were more like triplets, for when I was about ten months old, she gave birth to twin boys. They were named William and Willard.

We lived on a farm, and we boys kept the place lively. We had a neighbor who complained about the mischief of his only child. My dad always told him: "Well, just multiply that by three and you will know what real mischief is."

We weren't really naughty, but we did enjoy playing tricks, and with three of us putting our heads together, we had a lively time. For instance, I recall an incident when our dad was threshing grain.

The threshing machine was pulled into a field of wheat, and was stationed near a pond. It was a breezy day, and chaff from the straw soon covered the pond. In a short while, there was so much chaff floating on the water as well as lying on the field around it that a person couldn't see where the field ended and the pond began.

A neighbor and his son, Ted, stopped by. Ted was a little bigger than we were. After we played awhile, Willard had an idea.

"See that tree over there," he said. "I can beat you to it."

"Bet you can't," said Ted. He didn't know there was a pond between the tree and us, but William and I caught on to what Willard was planning.

"I'll be the judge," I said "You have to run to the tree, go around it, and come back. Now get in line."

Willard, William and Ted lined up.

"Go!" I shouted. They took off, Ted's long legs easily putting him in the lead.

When he reached the invisible pond, he tumbled headlong into it. Willard and William stopped on the bank. The drenched Ted crawled out to the hoots of three boys.

Willis continues: The year we were all about four or five years old, a couple men came in from the field to fill jugs at the stock tank. The water was for the machinery, but I thought it was for drinking.

"Do you drink that tank water?" I asked in surprise.

"Oh, sure," teased one of them.

"There're bugs in it!"

"We don't pay any attention to a few bugs. Besides, they give the water a good flavor."

After they left, I approached the tank. There was a mossy scum floating on the top. I brushed it aside and peered into the water. Except for the moss on the bottom of the tank and clinging to the sides, the water looked clean. There were only a few bugs. The mill wasn't running that still day, and I decided I was thirsty.

I got the can that hung from a wire on the tower. It was meant to catch water when the mill was running, but now I used it to dip water from the tank. If the men could drink tank water, so could I.

It was a hot day, and the water was cool and inviting. I called to my brothers.

"Hey, you guys. D'ya want a drink?"

They came on the run. I assured them the men drank water from the tank, and we could, too. We took turns and drank our fill. We messed around catching water bugs until our mother saw us and yelled:

"Get away from that tank! Someone will drown."

That night, all of us were sick. I was old enough to figure out it was the dirty tank water that upset our stomachs. After that, we drank from a cleaner source.

A Tragic Coincidence
Told by Rita Miller Hanus, Katherine Kemp, & Bill Looby.
1940.

Leo Miller, a young man of twenty years who lived in Atkinson, developed a marked interest and a great talent for baton twirling. He threw back his head, lifted his feet high, and marched about twirling his baton.

Another inducement that led Leo to practice constantly could have been that during practice, he was not plagued by an annoying tic that had troubled him for some years. He could toss his baton hour after hour and never feel a single spasm.

He didn't receive the nickname, Duke Miller, until a few years later, when he was hailed as the national champion drum major and was leading bands in Buffalo, New York, and in Toronto, Canada. But the title "Duke" fit him perfectly from the day he first picked up a baton.

Many families at that time were poor, but the Millers had fewer worldly possessions than most. The father, Andy, was a night watchman in the small town of Atkinson. The wage he received was scarcely adequate for supporting his wife, Millie, and the six children.

The family had no indoor plumbing, no auto, and not even a horse. They walked to church and school, and frequented the shops in nearby Atkinson. For them, that small area was the circle of the world.

The John and Marie Kemp family lived a couple hundred miles to the northwest in Martin, South Dakota. Marie Kemp and Millie Miller were sisters, but they had not seen each other for some years because of hard times.

On July 4th, 1940, Millie's brother, Emil Freouf, arrived in Atkinson and said: "I'm on my way to visit the Kemps. Would any of you care to ride along?"

Immediately, Millie and five of her children, Leo, Arthur, Rita, Jimmy, and Charles, were in a state of great excitement. Early the next day, July 5th, they set out. Though the Kemps were expecting a visit from Emil, they would be greatly surprised to see the Millers also.

In Martin, South Dakota, that same afternoon, some of teenager Johnny Kemp's young friends stopped at the mercantile store where he worked. They were Bob and Bill Looby, the owner's sons, and Iris Mowell. They were on their way to swim at the Allen Dam in an effort to get relief from the intense heat.

"When you get off work, come on out," they told Johnny. "Most of us probably will still be swimming."

But Mr. Looby said, "When it gets this blazing hot, business is slow. Run along, John. Go cool off with the other kids."

About the same time, the Millers had turned north from Merriman, Nebraska, and were chugging toward Martin, the first town beyond the state border. Eyes were shining with anticipation, and the children were playfully elbowing each other in the hot, crowded car.

Back at the dam, the young people piled out of the Looby car and ran for the cool, spring-fed pond.

"Jump in!" said Bill. "I'm going over the hill. I'll be back in a minute." He needed to make a nature call.

He was on the opposite side of the hill when he heard Bob's frenzied shouts. He ran for the dam.

"Johnny jumped in and disappeared," said Bob. "We can't find him."

Bill leaped into the water and thrashed about. When he couldn't locate his friend, he sent Bob for help, then continued to search frantically for John.

The fire department arrived, but by the time they found John's body, it was too late. He was dead.

Within moments, the news blanketed the little town. In the mercantile store, Mr. Looby sat on a stool behind the counter.

"If only I hadn't given him the afternoon off," he moaned, "he'd still be alive."

Weighted with grief, he propped his elbows on the counter and supported his head in his hands.

Outside, Emil Freouf's car stopped at the curb near Looby's Mercantile Store, and Leo soon entered.

"Does Johnny Kemp work here?" asked Leo.

The man thought, "What ill-advised jerk is asking about John? Everyone knows he's dead." He didn't answer.

Leo repeated the question.

Mr. Looby considered. "He must be a newcomer, has heard about the accident, and has come to gloat. What a dimwit."

Leo was perplexed. "Am I mistaken? I thought John worked here."

120

"Well, he did work here," finally the man said quietly, eyes cast down.

"Oh," said Leo. "Well, I'm his cousin from Nebraska, and we just got to Martin. Actually, all we need to know is where the Kemps live. They don't know we came. We want to surprise them."

Mr. Looby shook his head to clear it. He now knew he had misinterpreted the young man's stance. What should he do? He couldn't say, "Your cousin is dead."

Finally he muttered, "They live near here. I'll get in my car and lead the way." He paused, and then continued. "I should warn you, though, there has been--an accident."

"An accident? What kind of accident?"

"I shouldn't be the one to tell you. Just follow me."

When they reached the Kemp place, they found the yard full of neighbors and friends. Many were weeping. Mr. Looby stepped out of his car. The confused Millers looked at him expectantly, all traces of excitement and delight gone from their faces.

"It's young John," Looby said, tears moistening his eyes. "The kids often swim at the dam. There was an accident today. The news isn't good."

"What happened?" Millie spoke insistently. "How bad is he hurt?"

"Bad," said Mr. Looby. "Really bad."

"Surely not--he can't be--I hope he's not--"

Mr. Looby nodded his head affirmatively. "I hate to tell you--but yes--he's passed on. He's--left us."

"You mean--dead." She could scarcely say the word.

Mr. Looby nodded as Millie leaped from the car and dashed for the house.

No one knows for sure why John Kemp died. Family members always say he drowned.

Years later, Bill Looby said, "There was no autopsy, so we will never know. Perhaps he did drown. In my own mind, I wonder if perhaps he had a heat stroke. All of us were miserably hot because it was a sweltering day, and that spring-fed pond was cold. When he plunged in, perhaps the instant change in temperature caused him to have a stroke.

"For a long time I felt guilty for his death. If only I hadn't gone over the hill--but finally I had to accept the fact that I had done all I could, even if it wasn't enough to save his life."

Baby Buggy Brakes
Told by Albena Kramer, Atkinson. 1941.

One day I took my youngest brother, Fred Dobrovolny, to Bailin's Grocery with me. As we approached the store, we noticed a baby buggy parked on the sidewalk by the door. Fred was about four or five years old, and was already interested in mechanical things. He gave the buggy a small push, but it failed to respond.

"It has brakes," he informed me. "That's neat. I want to stay out here and look at the brakes."

"No," I said. "You have to come inside. I told Mom I'd keep an eye on you."

In the store, I relayed my order to the clerk. After he had listed all the groceries in his charge book, he began to collect them. In those days the clerks, rather than the customers, collected the groceries from the shelves.

Suddenly I noticed Fred was gone and began to look for him. After traversing the aisles in the store, I decided he must have gone outside. I was worried. It wasn't safe for a small country boy to be outside on the streets by himself. I hurried to the door.

There he was, flat on his back under the baby buggy. He was examining the mechanism for the brakes.

Frozen Face
Told by Henry Dobrovolny, Atkinson.

"I usually don't tell this story," said Henry Dobrovolny, "because I'm afraid people won't believe it. Since we have better ways of hauling hay, it is hard for folks to realize how tough it was to feed cattle during the depths of winter before we had tractors with cabs. Lots of winters, most ranchers froze their faces.

"One year my brother, Jay, didn't go to town for the Fourth of July celebration. He stayed home because of deep scabs on his face. He knew people would ask what had happened, and he was embarrassed to admit that, during the winter, he had frozen his face so badly that he still had scabs in July. Who would believe him?"

Harry's Outhouse
Early 40s

A man whom we will call Harry was especially indignant if, on Halloween, his privy was upset. This fact encouraged the neighborhood tricksters to be sure to include that particular prank along with other acts of revelry. One year when Harry vowed he was going to be on guard in order to foil any toilet-tipping activity in his particular backyard, a pair of young fellows, Chet and Doug, came a few nights in advance of the holiday. The following morning when the earliest riser in Harry's house hurried toward the "little house out back," she found it lying on its side.

After righting the building, Harry appeared at the lumberyard.

"I'm tired of having my privy upset!" he grumbled. "A man has more important things to do this time of the year than to be faced with an extra job like resetting his privy. I'm going to put a post beside it and wire the building to the post with some good, strong wire." He bought the supplies that he needed and departed.

Word of his plan reached the ears of the mischief-makers. "Does he think we don't know how to use a pair of wire cutters?" scoffed Chet.

"He most likely assumes that we wouldn't ordinarily have wire cutters along," said Doug. "But now that we are forewarned, we'll be sure to be prepared. My dad has cutters that will slice a wire in two like snapping a toothpick!"

On Halloween night, the boys waited until the wee hours of the morning, after which they sneaked down the alley, approaching Harry's outhouse from the rear.

"Go!" whispered Chet. Hunching low, they ran to the back of the little building. Simultaneously, they dropped into a three or four foot hole. Too late, they realized that Harry was the one to have the last laugh. When he had set up his privy, he had placed it in front of the hole that was ordinarily located under the toilet seat!

The teller of this tale did not say whether the boys managed to clean their shoes or whether they simply buried them!

Walt Jones' Mules on the Rakes
Told by Kenneth Jones, Atkinson.

Walt Jones (Kenneth's father) kept some mules and enjoyed working them. One summer his father-in-law, Eugene Sanford, was helping Joneses hay and was driving four head of mules on a three-rake-hitch. The mules were young and spirited, and in discussing the problems of placing newly trained mules on the rakes, Walt remarked:

"At least if mules run away, they have the good sense to stop when they come to a fence. They aren't like horses, who go through fences and tear up everything."

Later in the day, Eugene stepped down from the seat of the machine to examine a rake that was malfunctioning. Just then a horsefly buzzed under the bellies of the mules and startled them into action. Eugene ran to the side so that he got out of the way of the broad machine, but in so doing he lost the lines. The mules pounded away, the rake teeth snapping wildly up and down.

Just as Walt had predicted, when they came to a closed gate, they stopped. They were dead still for all of a second. Then off they ran again, hooves thundering. When they broke through the closed gate, the two outside sets of rakes stayed in the fence, one on either side. The rake hitch popped and splintered. The middle rake went through the gate, but one wheel rim was bent almost to the axle.

Catching the mules was only a part of solving the dilemma, for it took a week to repair the rakes, build a new rake hitch, construct a gate, and repair the fence.

The Horses and the Grooming Shears
Told by David Meister, DuBois. 1938.

When I was eleven years old, my father went to a farm auction and bought a spirited team of lightweight horses. They were broken to ride as well as to the harness. At the same sale, he bought some grooming shears.

In size and appearance, the horses were well matched, a beautiful sorrel color with white stars on their foreheads. Their flowing manes were of mixed hues ranging from gold to strawberry. They were a handsome pair and their names, King and Queen, fit them perfectly.

One day my father hitched the team to a stalk cutter and set me to work in the cornfield. Since corn was picked by hand, the stalks were left standing. The cutter cut them down and pulverized them so the field could be prepared for a new crop. Nearby, Dad was disking with four horses.

Because King and Queen were spirited and I was inexperienced, they ran away. Not knowing what else to do, I jumped off the machine, tumbling over and over as I landed. The horses ran for a half-mile with my father in pursuit. Finally one of them got astraddle the tongue, and Dad caught them. He brought them back to the field, held them steady until I got positioned on the seat, and started us over. This time I was more watchful, and all went well.

I loved those horses and liked to fool around with them the same as a child plays with a pet. One day when I was brushing King, I decided to trim his mane. It was fine for Queen to have long tresses, but King was a "boy." He should have short hair.

I got the grooming shears and went to work. It was harder than I thought to cut the thick, coarse hair, but I worked manfully. Finally the entire mane and forelock were gone.

Dad wasn't happy when he saw my choppy handiwork and scolded me severely. He did eventually recover his good humor and in later years, he teased me about it.

My sister, Jean, taught a rural school about three miles from home. She rode King to school. The first day, she got to school fine, but in the evening when she prepared to come home, the impatient horse pulled away from her. He left her standing in the schoolyard and galloped home with an empty saddle.

The second day of school, she was more watchful. Managing to get herself into the saddle, she was whisked home at a fast pace. When they got to the barn, she wasn't able to stop the horse. He galloped straight inside and she was scraped off his back by the low door.

Years later during the Korean War, I went to the Navy. Since Queen had died, Dad decided to sell King. When I found out about it, I was devastated. How could he sell that docile, aging animal?

Eventually, I got over it the same as Dad had recovered when I cut King's mane.

The Hen in the Sand
Told by Mary (Krobot) Hytrek, Stuart. Late 1930s.

During years when the sand cherries grew in the Sandhills near Dora Lake, people came from miles around to pick them. One day Mary Krobot bridled a horse, put a bucket on each arm, and carried a third bucket in hand. The other hand was needed to hold the reins.

"I didn't have a saddle," she reported later. "We kids always rode bareback."

She urged the horse down the road. It happened that an old hen, half buried in the sand beside the road, was dusting herself. Just as the horse approached, the hen fluffed out her dust-laden feathers and gave a mighty shake. The startled horse shied suddenly.

There was a great clang and rattle of the three buckets as Mary landed on the ground. The horse galloped away from the sudden racket, but being a well-trained animal, he didn't run far. After Mary caught him, she led him into the ditch so she could stand on higher ground to remount. She continued her journey to the hills where the sand cherries grew.

The Parachuting Cat
Told by Don Krysl, Stuart. About 1937.

When I was about fourteen, I had a good friend named Charles Siegel. His hobby was airplanes. In those years, we rarely saw airplanes go over, and we had never seen one on the ground. But Charley read volumes about planes and parachutes. After he told me how a parachute worked, we decided to construct one.

"We need a big piece of light weight cloth," he said.

We sneaked a bed sheet out of the house along with a ball of string the folks ordinarily used to tie homemade bologna.

Hours later, our product was finished. A cat volunteered his services by being stupid enough to be caught. He was properly attached. I tucked him under one arm while I climbed to the top of the barn. Charley followed carrying the parachute. We inched ourselves to the peak and dropped the cat and sheet.

We never ascertained whether the failure was due to human error, or mechanical breakdown, but we do know the chute did not open. The cat hit the earth with a dull thud. The parachute followed, empty and rope-like. The parachute did nothing at all to lessen the cat's fall, and did very little to hamper his speed on the ground.

With no appreciation for adventure or for scientific knowledge, the ungrateful cat ran under the corncrib. He added theft to his other shortcomings by taking the sheet with him. After several hours of belly whopping, stick poking, and clod throwing, we finally retrieved the sheet.

It was almost as good as new, since we were willing to overlook some dark stains and a few jagged holes. We sneaked it into the laundry hamper. On Monday, which was "wash day", my older sisters grumbled darkly about what we boys did to the sheet, but they knew us well enough so they didn't expect us to tell. We lived up to their expectations.

Sheep Tales
The 1930s and 40s.

John Laible had an old ram that was inclined to be ornery. John enjoyed teasing the animal, causing the ram to reciprocate by butting him. One day when he was carrying two buckets of slop to the pigs, the ram butted him from behind. John ended up in the pig trough with the slop.

"After we moved to town," said Don Putnam "we had a sheep, but we couldn't keep it in town. So I kept it at my sister-in-law's place. That rascal would eat anything. When it came to getting into things, he was as bad as a goat.

"One day my brother-in-law changed the oil in his car. He drained it into a pan and slid it out. After he had replaced the oil plug, he crawled out. He was surprised to see the sheep drinking the used oil.

"Boy! Did she ever get sick! We thought she would die. She lost all her wool and was completely bare. She did pull through, though."

"My grandparents had a big yard and had sheep in it," said Joan (Steinhauser) Dobrovolny. "We kids were supposed to watch them so they didn't go into the orchard because they'd eat the young fruit trees. At best, it was a tiresome job, and at worst, it was frightening.

"Sometimes when we tried to drive them back from the orchard, they got stubborn and didn't pay any attention to our yelling and rattling of sticks. Other times, they turned on us and drove us back. Let me tell you, you can run mighty fast if an old ram is breathing down your neck.

"Grandpa's yard seemed bigger than ever. I was bumped in the back more than once by that old ram."

Pet Pigs
Told by Maxine (Kuta) Osentowski. York.

We had two runt pigs that could be saved only if they were hand fed. My parents, Frank and Josie Kuta, farmers near Loup City, kept them in a small A-house and bottle-fed them. Since kids in those days had to manufacture their own playthings, we soon adopted them as our special pets and each day crawled into the A-house to play with them.

They quickly became our most beloved toys. I recall that we carried them around and gave them any scraps of food we could find. When they got old enough to eat from a pan, we turned them out of the A-house, and they followed us like puppies. On washdays, we used the rinse water from the laundry tubs to give them baths.

One day our father went to the pasture to fix fence. The pigs followed him. It was a blistering hot day, and they got so overheated that one of them died in the field. Dad picked up the other one and brought him home. We nursed him tenderly, but he also died.

"After all the special care we gave those two pigs," said Dad, "they had to die. There went our profits."

Worse still, in our small minds, was the loss of our pets--our playmates--our toys.

We attended a country school on Dead Horse Creek located northeast of Loup City. The creek was so named because in early times, probably in the 1800s, several dead horses were found there. They had been killed in a raging blizzard.

Our school had no pump and no well. We carried our drinking water to school each Monday in syrup buckets. Each Friday after school, we emptied our buckets and took them home. There were gopher holes in the ground around the school, and we hoped that some day we could have enough water left to drown out a gopher. Of course it never happened. Our tiny trickle of water scarcely dampened the soil.

They quickly became our most beloved TOYS.

Maxine

The Bees by the Fence
Told by John Ziska III. About 1937.

The threshing machine was making its way from farm to farm, and was scheduled to arrive at the Jim Ziska place in the afternoon. Grandfather John called the boys, Gene and John.

"You boys wait on the west side of the orchard," he told them. "The minute you see the threshing machine in the distance, come and tell us. That way we can get the horses hitched to the wagons."

It was important to keep the machine busy every minute since other farms were waiting for it, and no one could predict when a hailstorm might come and ruin the grain not yet threshed.

The boys waited--and waited. It was a hot, boring job. At last the machine, creeping along like some huge dinosaur, was sighted in the far distance.

Gene, being older, led the dash to the house. When they reached the orchard fence, he leaped to the top of one of his grandfather's beehives, jumped the fence, and kept running. John, seeing how easily his brother had crossed the fence, did likewise.

You can guess what happened. The disturbed bees spilled out of the hive, not quite fast enough to catch Gene, but at exactly the right moment to attack John. Their sinister buzzing and sharp stings pursued the screaming boy across the orchard and to the house.

Their mother, Theresa, pulled the stingers from his arms, back, and neck. One must have hit a gland, for his neck quickly began to swell. Theresa called a doctor.

"Give the boy all the hot lemonade he can drink," instructed the doctor.

His swollen neck grew so large he looked as if he had no neck at all. Everyone was concerned lest his throat swell shut, causing him to smother.

"I watched over him all night," said Theresa, "and after a couple days, was enormously relieved when the swelling began to go down."

Walking Barrels
Told by Marva (Moore) Teter, Holdrege. 1930s-40s.

When I was a child, not having toys wasn't much of a problem to us because we didn't expect any. It didn't take much to keep us content. It seems like we always could find some way to entertain ourselves. One thing we did was roll tires or barrel hoops or barrels.

In those days, barrels were easy to come by. Whiskey and other drinks came to the saloons in barrels and were sold over the bar by the pitcher or the drink. Motor oil came to filling stations in them. Some foods such as sugar cookies, pickles, vinegar, oyster crackers, and hard candy came to the grocery stores in barrels. Sauerkraut was made in them. Seed grains, or nails, or bolts might be stored in them.

Sometimes animals were watered in half barrels. Anyway, usually there were extra barrels around the farmstead.

Thus rolling barrels was one way of entertaining ourselves. We learned to stand on them and roll them with our feet. We called it "walking barrels." We walked them all over the yard and finally began walking them up and down the cellar. We could spend most of the day at it. I don't recall that any of us ever got hurt falling off them. Like most kids, we were nimble enough to land on our feet if we fell.

From Horses to Tractors
Told by Jerlene Neilsen, Stromsburg. 1937.

In 1937 my father-in-law, Hans Neilsen, bought his first tractor, a 1936 John Deere B, from a dealer in Stromsburg named Jim Branting. He traded three horses for it. After using it for four or five years, it broke down and he traded it back for another B, this time a 1935. It, like the first one, was on steel, but he later put rubber tires on it.

Eventually, Kermit Hulgren bought the '36 tractor to farm his forty acres. In 1992, he told my husband Morris, "This was your father's first tractor. It is now 55 years old. Would you like to buy it back?"

Morris wanted it, and paid many times its original price. He uses it on a grain elevator. It is easy to start and always runs.

Sliding on the Cellar Door
Told by John Ziska III, Atkinson. Early 1940s.

When we were kids, sometimes we used the cellar door for a slide. One day when I was six or seven, I got a long sliver in my backside. My mother tried to extract it, but it was rotted wood and was deeply embedded.

"I'm going to have to take him to the doctor," Mom told the hired girl, Laverne Hall.

I hated to hear those words. The overworked doctors, Douglas and McKee, took care of a wide area surrounding Atkinson. Neither of them had time for providing a relaxed atmosphere for young patients. I had never found a trip to the doctor to be pleasant.

"Oh, Mom," I begged. "Won't you try again? I'll hold really still. I don't want to go to the doctor."

"Well, the sliver is deep, and every time I manage to dig in and get hold of the end, it breaks off. I just don't have the heart to keep digging for it."

"Let me try, Theresa," said Laverne. "I got a little experience when I was taking nurse's training."

Laverne laid me over her lap. It took a long time, but she finally, piece by piece, got the sliver out. She complimented me on how quiet and patient I was.

"I knew what was in store for me if you couldn't remove it," I said. "I didn't want to go to the doctor."

Binding Grain
Told by Ray Kramer, Stuart. Late 1930s.

August Kramer owned a threshing machine and did custom threshing for the rural Stuart-Atkinson area. One year Frankie Kaup called on the telephone.

"My binder broke down. I'm in a hurry to get our grain bound and in shocks because we're starting to hay. In fact, I have a man mowing alfalfa right now. Can you come and finish binding for us?"

August promised to send a couple of his boys, Ray and Eugene, and his binder. The boys spent the rest of the day binding Kaup's grain. Frankie begged them to continue into the night to finish the job, and they agreed.

Gene, about 14 or 15, was on the tractor, and Ray, four years his senior, was riding the binder. The tractor had lights in back as well as the front in order to accommodate night work. The boys got so tired they were afraid they would fall asleep. They shouted back and forth in an attempt to stay alert.

They worked all night. Toward morning Wilfred Kaup came to the field.

"I have only a small patch of oats," he told them. "I'd sure be glad if you fellows would cut it when you finish here. That way, we can get it shocked later in the day and be ready to hay tomorrow."

It was after lunch when the boys finished at Wilfred's place. They got home about 2:00 PM and immediately fell into bed.

Binding Grain

John Thompson and his son, Roy.

Courtesy of Grace Thompson and Frank Palmer.

A Startling Incident on the Thresher
Told by Ray Kramer, Stuart. 1940 or 41.

August Kramer and his son Ray were threshing grain at the home of a bachelor, Tom Allen, south of Stuart. Tom had driven to the yard to unload a wagon box full of grain. He was gone longer than expected.

Finally, John Krysl, who was unloading bundles into the thresher, said, "Someone better go check on Tom. He should have been back before this."

Ray got into the Model T flivver they used to run errands around the machine, and drove to Allen's yard. The wagon was nowhere in sight, but its tracks went through the yard. Ray followed them, and they led into a grove of trees.

The horses had proceeded into the grove until the wagon caught between two trees. There they stopped and stood patiently. Tom was lying on the top of the load of grain.

"Tom!" yelled Ray as he climbed out of the car.

Tom didn't move. Ray hurried to the wagon and stepped to the footboard on the side. He grabbed Tom by the bib of his well-worn overalls, and shook him.

"Tom! Wake up!"

Tom's floppy hat rolled to the side, but he didn't move. Slowly realization crept over Ray. Tom was dead. Ray picked up the hat and placed it over the expressionless face to shade it from the bright sun.

He hurried back to the thresher and told the others, after which he shut down the machine. Several of the men piled onto the Model T and went to the farmstead. August stayed with the thresher. Some of the men unhooked Tom's horses while the others carried the body into the house. They laid it on the bed and called one of his relatives.

Then because of the urgency of the harvest, the men returned to the field. August, uneasy about the delay, had restarted the machine and was single-handedly threshing grain.

At this time in Ray's life, Europe was embroiled in a fierce conflict, but the United States was determined to stay out of war. Between 1938, and the end of 1941, Hitler took over more than 14 countries: Austria, Czechoslovakia, Poland, Norway, Denmark, Netherlands, Belgium, France,

Italy, Hungary, Rumania, Bulgaria, Yugoslavia, Greece, and some of the countries in North Africa.

After the attack on Pearl Harbor, Ray, like most youths his age, soon was in the army.

Friction in Europe
Told by Francis Soukup, North Bend. Late 1930s.

Before World War II, my grandfather, Pioneer John Dobrovolny, Fremont, would bend forward to put an ear near the large speaker of the radio.

"I don't like it," he'd say. "It isn't good. Something bad is going to happen!"

People in general were, of course, dismayed by Hitler's antics in Europe and North Africa. However, they were intent on pulling their lives together after the Depression. Furthermore, they were determined to stay out of war.

Words such as these, voiced by the grandparents, were descriptive of the attitudes at the time:

"Europe always has had its wars. Our sons went over there 20 years ago and helped them straighten out their mess. That war (World War 1) was supposed to be the 'War to End All Wars.' The World Court was to settle disputes after that. But what can we do if there are countries that won't listen to the World Court?

"I say, let's stay out of it. One reason we came over here was to get away from the endless wars. So let them fight over there if they want to. We've got our own business to attend to."

This line of thinking was the reason we were unprepared for war when it was thrust upon us by the attack on Pearl Harbor.

Dobrovolny Brothers John, Tom, and Fred.

Vaclav Krysl

John Ziska

Many of the now elderly pioneers lived to see the beginning of World War II. Mainly, their grandsons, many of whom were then teenagers, fought it.

World War II Graffiti

    An inspector named Kilroy signed his name on the machine parts he examined. When the GIs saw his repeated signature, they began to quip, "Kilroy was here!" Eventually, they started scribbling it on any flat surface. It became synonymous with, "Americans were here!" Kilroy and the American troops spread over five of the seven continents.

Chapter 4

World War II

Mainly, it was the grandchildren of the pioneers who fought World War II. For the first time, young women took jobs outside the home.

Massacre at Lidice
Told by Georgia Rice and Olga Peterson. 1942.

Why were 199 men, the entire adult male population of Lidice in Czechoslovakia, lined up and shot? Why were the 196 women sent to a concentration camp? Why were more than a hundred children either sent to death camps or else given to German families to be "re-educated"? What horrible crime had the citizens of the little town committed? The truth of the matter was, they had committed no crime.

Historians say World War II began in 1939 when Hitler's armies attacked Poland. However, months before, Hitler had already overrun and had occupied Czechoslovakia. He appointed a tyrannical Nazi, Reinhardt Heydrich, to oversee these newly acquired lands.

Heydrich, trained by the vicious Gestapo, ruled with an iron fist. He immediately rounded up the Jews in the area and also the Czech people in leadership positions. They were killed or sent to concentration camps. After three years, Czechs exiled in England plotted Heydrich's assassination, an action that took place north of Prague on May 27, 1942. The wounded Heydrich died on June 4.

An untrue report that people in Lidice were sheltering the assassins reached Hitler's ears.

"Erase the entire town from the face of the earth!" ordered the angry Hitler.

Five days later, Nazis entered the town. They shot the men, whisked the women to concentration camps, and killed the children, or resettled them in German homes. After the people were destroyed, buildings were dynamited and bulldozers cleared them away.

Heydrich's assassins were found a week later hiding in a church at the edge of Prague. After a shoot-out with the Gestapo, they committed suicide.

Now there is a monument and a museum in honor of the people who once inhabited Lidice. In the museum are pictures of the victims and an account, taken from the extensive files of the Nazis, of how each died, oftentimes including gruesome details. Also from Nazi records are accounts of the problems of the children who were resettled in Nazi homes.

After the war, residents in the area were not willing to let Hitler have the last word. With the help of people from England, a town was built nearby which has been named New Lidice.

Aboard Ship at Pearl Harbor!
By Kenneth Hill, Fairbury. Dec. 7, 1941.

Kenneth Hill, Fairbury, was stationed on the *USS Pennsylvania* at Pearl Harbor on the day of the attack. He says that now more than sixty years later, the hair still stands on his arms and neck when he thinks about it. He was serving as a mess cook and was preparing Sunday breakfast. He went below deck to get some supplies, and presently noticed soldiers rushing up and down the ladders. He thought it was a drill.

When he looked out of a porthole and saw two hangars explode, he realized it was an attack. He hurried to his battle station, which was high on the mainmast. He helped control a gun turret. From his high position, he had a good view, actually a better view than he would have preferred. One picture seared into his memory is of the *USS Arizona* as it sank.

The Japanese fighter planes skimmed low over his head, and he says he will never forget the sinister smiles on the pilot's faces.

Pearl Harbor and After
By Darrell Blair, York, Later, CA. Dec. 7, 1941.

I had been in the Navy for about a year and a half before the Japanese attack on Pearl Harbor. I was on the *USS Northampton*, which was classed as a heavy cruiser. It had nine 9-inch guns, six forward and three aft, and also 5-inch guns on the sides, along with 29mm and 40mm guns for antiaircraft protection. There were about 950 officers and men on board.

We were operating in the area of the Hawaiian Islands. In late November, we delivered some planes to Wake Island, and on the return trip, remained at sea for gunnery practice. We were scheduled to be in Pearl Harbor on December 6th. Luckily, we were delayed because of a minor refueling accident, and were stalled at sea while repairs were made.

On December 7, when the Japanese attacked Pearl Harbor, we were about 50 miles out. When we returned the next day, we passed between burning ships surrounded by flaming facilities.

We took on stores and fuel and left the next day to patrol north of Pearl Harbor. During those uncertain days, it was reported that a total of twenty torpedoes were fired at us. The *Northampton* was one of the few ships that had sonar, and when it picked up a submarine on sonar, the destroyers dropped depth charges.

In January 1942, we went to the Marshall Islands. This was the first offensive action against the Japanese. Our fleet included the carrier *Enterprise*, the cruisers, *Northampton, Chester, Pensacola,* and *Salt Lake City*, and about four destroyers. Admiral Halsey was in charge of operations.

We shelled the island of Wotje, sank some ships, and shelled their installations. As we returned to Pearl Harbor, we tied broomsticks to our smokestack to signify a "clean sweep."

The Japanese conquests during the early months of the war were astonishing. They took over island after island as well as parts of China and countries in Southeastern Asia.

During March, we made raids on the island of Marcus, and also raided Wake Island, which had been taken over by the enemy. Finally in April we were encouraged when we began to see additional ships arriving from the States.

The first gleam of hope for the Americans came in the form of the raid on Tokyo led by Jimmy Doolittle. It so happened that the *Northampton* had a part in it. When we left Pearl Harbor after refueling, we thought something big was about to happen, for we had picked up some newsmen and cameramen.

After we sailed north for a couple days, we met a convoy that was escorting the carrier, *Hornet*. We could see B-25s sitting on the flight deck. When we were told that we were going to sail within 500 miles of Japan and were going to bomb Tokyo, a great cheer arose. It seems morbid, but you can hardly imagine what they did at Pearl Harbor. Also there was continued destruction in the countries and islands they were taking.

As we went west, we hit rough seas. On April 18, we ran into two Japanese fishing boats. We were afraid they might have sent a radio message announcing our presence, and thus Admiral Halsey decided to launch the aircraft early. This action would run the airplanes short of fuel.

We were on the starboard side and watched the B-25s take off. The pictures later released on the news were all taken from our ship. One of the cameramen was Rosenthau, the man who later became famous for his picture of the raising of the flag on Iwo Jima.

After dropping their bombs, the pilots had to continue onward to China, which was then friendly territory. The Japanese apprehended some of those who ran out of fuel. Three pilots were beheaded. Others made it to China, and later returned to the United States.

After the raid, Tokyo Rose, the famous Japanese disc jockey, announced that they had sunk the "Gray Ghost." That happened to be the nickname of our ship, the *Northampton*. Also the newspapers reported we had been sunk. Dad hid the article from my mother, waiting for confirmation from the navy. Of course, it never came.

While the actual bombing of Tokyo was not that damaging, it played a huge part in the American war effort. The Japanese were stunned that the enemy had managed to get close enough to bombard them. Thereafter, they kept more planes and ships at home to forestall future attacks. Also, they stepped up their efforts to expand their front to the point where they were spread too thin, which was an advantage to the U. S.

We returned to Pearl Harbor to a big reception. Cheering people were standing in the harbor entrance. Then the end of the month (April) we sailed to the South Pacific where we engaged the Japanese in the Battle of Coral Sea, May 7-8, 1942. We lost the aircraft carrier *Lexington*, but their losses were greater.

Following the battle, we, along with the *Enterprise* and the *Yorktown*, returned to Pearl Harbor to take on supplies.

By this time, our intelligence had cracked the Japanese code, and we learned that the enemy was headed to attack the Aleutian Islands as well as Midway. Midway, so named because it is in the middle of the Pacific between Asia and the USA, could be used as an advance base in their move to attack our continental west coast. They hoped our fleet, unaware of their plans against Midway, would rush toward Alaska. Thus they would have a clear field in their move against Midway.

Our ships, the Japanese presumed, would be in the wide expanse of ocean between the Aleutians and Midway, and could be easily destroyed. Thanks to our cryptographers, we knew the position of the Japanese fleet, but they didn't know ours. Besides their four aircraft carriers, they had cruisers, and destroyers, along with troop transports. They assumed they had everything they needed to take and occupy Midway.

At the time, Admiral Halsey was in a Pearl Harbor hospital with a severe case of shingles. An officer on our ship, Rear Admiral Raymond A. Spruance, was placed in charge of the operations. (I saw him many times. It so happens he later became Chief of Staff in Washington.) Also, he deployed 25 fleet submarines, commanded by Rear Admiral Robert H. English, around Midway.

The Battle of Midway, later marked as the turning point in the Pacific War, lasted four days, from June 4th to 7th. During all that time, the air was full of bombers and fighter planes and the fires from the burning ships shot into the sky and were reflected in the ocean waters. The Japanese lost their four carriers, which happened to be the same ones that transported the aircraft for the attack on Pearl Harbor. They also lost a battleship and several cruisers as well as most of their experienced pilots. We lost the aircraft carrier *Yorktown* and the destroyer *Hammond*. It was a smashing defeat for the Japanese fleet.

For the next six weeks we were on sea patrol west of Hawaii. In August we sailed for the South Pacific and were in the area of the New Hebrides Islands. On a beautiful Sunday morning in mid August, we ran into some submarines. The aircraft carrier *Wasp* was hit by several torpedoes and sank.

On October 26 we were in the Battle of Santa Cruz. The aircraft carrier *Hornet* was caught in a coordinated dive-bomber and torpedo plane attack and was so badly damaged that she had to be abandoned. We attempted unsuccessfully to sink the burning ship with torpedoes. Finally, two more Japanese torpedoes hit her and she sank. It so happens the personnel on our ship witnessed the sinking of all the aircraft carriers lost during the four years of the Pacific War. What a distinction!

The *Enterprise* was hit by bombs, but managed to stay afloat. Since the *Hornet* had been abandoned, many of her airplanes landed on the deck of the *Enterprise*. The *Porter* was hit by a torpedo and had to be abandoned.

Despite our heavy losses, there were circumstances in our favor. The Battle of Santa Cruz had effectively absorbed the attention of the enemy with the result that there was time for the reinforcement of American troops on Guadalcanal.

The Invasion of Guadalcanal had started in early August. When I first heard about it, I wondered where it was. I had always been interested in geography, but I couldn't recall any canal named Guadal. I was surprised to know it was an island.

We were soon to find out that many islands were not charted on maps because the Japanese government was secretive about them and very careful about whom they allowed into their ports. One of the islands, Truk, was their main base. It was, to them, similar to our Pearl Harbor.

For about a month we operated in and out of the New Hebrides Islands and the Santa Cruz Islands. On November 29th we headed northwest to meet the Japanese task force that was coming down to reinforce their troops on Guadalcanal. We called it the Tokyo Express. They would start at Bouganville and come south with troop transports, battle ships, cruisers, and destroyers.

My battle station was the after engine room. There we cared for the generators, keeping the voltage balanced. However, that night I was transferred to the forward part of the ship to the intercommunication room.

We started firing about 11:30 PM, and ceased firing about 11:45. The battle seemed to be over. Then we got hit by two torpedoes in the after engine room. The ship immediately listed to port.

My chief, MacRae, muttered, "Now what are we going to do?"

I said, "Mac, I think we are going for a swim."

We were about ten miles off the coast of Guadalcanal. Soon afterward, we received word to come topside. When we got on the quarterdeck, we began looking for life jackets. The ship was burning aft with flames going up several hundred feet. Ammunition was exploding, and our ship looked like a Fourth of July celebration.

On that particular night, my friend from high school days, Jack Brittenham, was on Guadalcanal, and he watched the battle at sea. The next morning he heard the *Northampton* was sunk. He knew I was on the ship.

I found a lifejacket and put it on. They were kapok jackets, and we were aware that some of them were defective. We were worried, of course, whether or not they would hold us up. It was around midnight and was dark out, but the flames on the ship lit the ocean.

There was a ship about half a mile away, and it turned its searchlight on us. We were sure shells would be coming our direction since we had previously been instructed that if a ship turned lights on us, it would be a Japanese ship, and we should open fire.

Of course, we weren't able to fire, which was a good thing. We found out later it was one of our destroyers that was checking to see how we were.

The order was given for us to abandon ship. We put cargo net over the side of the ship, took off our shoes, and climbed down to the water. We were immensely relieved to find the life jackets held us up.

We had managed to get one life raft off, but it was immediately filled. Claude Becker and I decided to join the hundreds of others who were swimming toward Guadalcanal. Thankfully, the water was warm.

Then out of the darkness a ship came toward us. We thought for sure we had made it. We would be picked up. Then we heard bells on board, signaling all to man their battle stations. Japanese bombers were coming, and thus they had to leave us.

It was a disappointment because we knew of times when swimming sailors were attacked by sharks. However, we did our best to remain hopeful, and we called encouragement back and forth to each other.

After several hours, the destroyer *Fletcher* returned and started picking us up. The sailors dropped cargo nets for us to climb, but we were tired and our wet clothes were heavy. Sailors and Marines came down the nets to meet us, and they helped us to the top.

You can imagine what a relief it was for me to plant my two feet on the deck. The next morning I ran into one of my officer friends.

He was surprised to see me. Since the torpedoes had hit in the after engine room, all hands there had been killed. What good fortune for me that I had been transferred to the intercommunication room that night.

We proceeded on the destroyer *Fletcher* to Espiritu Santo. There we boarded the cruiser *Honolulu*. They gave us shoes, which were a blessed relief because those steel decks were scorching hot even though we had our socks on. They fed us and then put us on the troop transport, *Barnett*. A destroyer escorted us back to San Francisco. We arrived on December 21.

It was a treat to hear Bing Crosby singing "White Christmas." While we were in the South Pacific, Tokyo Rose provided the music, and it wasn't Bing Crosby! Also we were surprised to see Lucky Strike cigarettes in red packages because before they had been in green.

We were outfitted with new clothes and given a 30-day leave. My girl friend, Roseann Klundt, had grown up in the Lushton, Nebraska, area, but now she was working in Oakland, California. I picked her up and we went to Reno. I was age 20, and she was 18.

On January 3, 1943, we were married in York, Nebraska.

After my leave the latter part of January, I was sent to Newport News, Virginia, where we watched our ship, the *USS Mobile*, as it was being finished. She was commissioned the latter part of March, and we took her out on the Atlantic for her initial sail. We cruised up to Portland, Maine, after which we returned her to the shipyard for adjustments.

We next sailed her down to the Caribbean, through the Panama Canal, and then to San Francisco. Since we were there for a few days, I went to a movie. On the newsreel I saw my old ship, the *Northampton*, which by now had been on the ocean bottom for six months. The media was always late in putting out casualties, but it was a good thing. During the first part of the war, we were poorly equipped and were taking a discouraging beating.

Our raids on the enemy continued. We shelled the islands of Marcus, Tarawa, Wake, Bougainville, and the Marshall Islands. During the invasion of Tarawa, we bombarded it for a whole day before our Marines went in. The first wave of Marines made it, but the men in the second wave were cut down. We soon experienced the terrible sight of dead Marines floating by the ship.

When we finished shelling Tarawa, you wouldn't think anyone on the island could be alive. The trees looked as if someone had mowed them down with a sickle. But the Japanese were well dug in, and were determined to keep fighting.

On January 1, 1944, we began the invasion of the Marshall Islands. Also we raided Truk, the Japanese equivalent of Pearl Harbor. Now with our superior equipment, we had the enemy on the run although there would be many more battles. Even when losing, the Japanese were trained to fight to the death rather than to surrender.

Some of the other islands we shelled were Saipan, Tinian, Guam, Iwo Jima, Peleliu, Yap, Hollandia, and some islands that weren't listed in geography books. Also there were many more raids on the Philippines before the actual invasion.

While we were shelling Wake Island, October 1943, Roseann, who had remained in York, gave birth to our first child, Dennis. At the time the war ended, I was involved in action near the Philippine Islands.

I was discharged from the Navy on August 14, 1946, about a year after the end of the war.

On the Enterprise
Told by Lawrence Hamik, Stuart.

I joined the crew of the aircraft carrier *Enterprise* in November of 1942, but still there was time for me to participate in 14 of the 20 major battles in which that ship was involved. In between those battles, there were dozens of lesser encounters and shellings. I could write a book!

But here I will relate a couple of our more unusual incidents. The first occurred when we were invading the heavily fortified island of Truk. The Japanese regularly operated out of Truk, and our battleships needed to shell its airbase. However, the mountains along the shore protected it. So we lowered our guns and blew the tops off the mountains. That was quite a feat.

Another time, June 1943, we spotted the Japanese fleet west of the Mariana Islands. We took after them. The result was the First Battle of the Philippine Sea. The fighting was prolonged, and we lost a large number of planes. Some were shot down, and others ran out of fuel.

I was on the flight deck. One plane had suffered a minor wreck coming in, and we had just managed to clear it off. Then another plane approached. The signal officer was guiding it. Suddenly, the landing officer dived into a net at the side. About that time, the landing lights went out. The signal officer had seen a meatball (Japan's Rising Sun emblem) on the plane, and had realized it was the enemy. It apparently needed a place to land and had followed our planes in.

Of course, it couldn't land without lights, and it veered to the side. Our radar followed it for several seconds, and then the image of the plane disappeared. Most likely it dived into the sea.

We turned on the lights and continued to land our returning planes. Then we patrolled the sea to pick up as many men as possible from the airplanes that had run out of fuel.

On October 24-25, during the Second Battle of the Philippines, we wiped out most of the Japanese fleet, including their aircraft carriers. The playing field was narrowing, but we still had a lot of fighting to do.

North Africa and Italy
Told by Paul Waller, York. 1941-45.

In September of 1941, a few months before the United States entered the war, I was drafted into the army. My pay was $21 a month. In June of 1942, it was increased to $50 and overseas pay was $60, actually two dollars a day! My term was supposed to be one year, but after Pearl Harbor I was required to stay for the duration of the war, which was four years.

After training in Maryland, I was sent overseas in October of 1942, leaving from the Brooklyn Navy Yards. We were in a 64-ship convoy. There were 6000 men on our ship, and none of us knew where we were going. We zigzagged across the ocean, changing course every 11 minutes so the Nazi U-boats couldn't get a good shot at us. Sometimes the sea was so rough that one moment we could see all the ships and the next we dived down off a wave and couldn't see any.

Paul
Waller

We landed in North Africa at Casablanca and I was assigned to the Fifth Army. When I was issued only thirty rounds of ammunition for my rifle, I told an officer that it didn't seem like enough.

"If you need more, you can get it off a dead soldier," he grumbled. I never did like that officer afterward.

During the three months we were in Casablanca, Roosevelt and Churchill had their famous meeting there. Of course, we didn't see them because of heavy security.

I was a welder. Our unit repaired stalled tanks and damaged weapons. We removed them from battle areas to safer quarters to work on them. Then they were returned to the fellows on the front line. We were on the move. We never used cots, but always slept on the ground. Water was scarce in North Africa, and our company was issued a gallon of water a day per man, which was for drinking as well as for washing. I didn't have a shower from November in 1942, until April of 1943.

Once when we were in Tunisia, we found a grape winery, and after filling our five-gallon buckets with wine, we took them back to the company. During the resulting party, we got the "dog robber" drunk. He was a fellow chosen by the officers to run errands and wait on them. We GIs were called "dogs," and the dog robber was so named because he took the best of everything away from the dogs to give to the officers.

After he was drunk, we persuaded him he shouldn't be waiting on the officers. Rather, they should be waiting on him. When the officers called for another round of wine, he threw rocks at them. He got fired and had to go to work like the rest of us.

The Allies were forcing the Axis troops back, but often Hitler's brutal rule over his forces forbade retreat. On one hill in North Africa, the Italians in a pillbox were chained to their guns. That was one way to make sure they stayed at their posts and fought to the death. Oh, that Hitler! He was crazy.

Tunis fell on May 7, 1943, and a quarter million German and Italian troops were taken prisoner. In July we invaded Sicily. Our unit ordinarily would have been behind the invasion forces, but we had a fire in our salvage yard where there was a field of tanks, half-tracks, trucks, artillery pieces, and a lot of ammunition. That fire delayed us for ten days.

When it was time for us to go, we got on LST boats and departed for Sicily. I was terribly seasick because of the choppy waters, but it got calmer when we neared land. We went ashore the second or third night. Paratroopers were landing in the vicinity of the front line. Unfortunately, both the Nazis and the Allies were shooting at them.

From that time, Italian women could often be seen in dresses made of parachute silk.

After some rough fighting in Sicily, the main enemy was ousted and we pulled back to prepare to invade Italy. We landed at Salerno, and immediately a plane began to dive bomb us. Anti-aircraft fire knocked it down.

Of course, our infantrymen had landed ahead of us. When they saw our trucks climbing up the beaches, they thought it was tanks coming to give them a hand. They were disappointed when they found out it was trucks.

I recall one night when we had a meeting, and the captain asked two fellows to go across a river and bring back a German soldier. Intelligence wanted to talk to an enemy. The captain finished by saying, "If the prisoner is too badly damaged, you'll be sent back to get another."

We were close to Pompeii and Mount Vesuvius. We had some time on our hands because we were waiting for our supply line to catch up. We climbed up and looked down in the crater. It puffed out ashes every seven minutes. The next spring, 1944, it exploded, and lava ran down the sides, but by then we had moved on.

Once when I was going toward the front to bring back a jeep that needed repairs, a GI on the outpost said to me, "Would you like to see me draw fire?"

"No!" I insisted. "I don't want to see you draw fire!"

"I will anyway," he answered. He backed his jeep around the corner. Immediately, mortar shells came whizzing by and landed down in the valley.

We were on alert one day, and something hit me in the pant leg. I mistakenly thought it was someone in our unit trying to startle me, and I turned around.

"You guys cut out the horseplay!" I said and added some rough terms. When we got back to our quarters, I found a bullet had gone through my pant leg. Luckily, it had missed hitting me.

Another time, a fellow from the front came back. He laughed at us and told us that we in the rear area had it easy. About that time a shell came in, knocked him down, and blew his foot off above the ankle. He didn't realize his foot was gone until he tried to get up.

We discovered many of the Italians were glad to be captured because they were usually sent to prison camps in the United States. There they got accommodations that beat those in Germany or Italy. One prisoner who was brought to the stockade, quipped, "I'll see you in New York City!"

The Italians were tired of being bombed and of having their youths killed in war. They blamed Mussolini and were ready to oust him and make a deal with the Allies. But the Germans held areas in Italy that included Rome, and Hitler was in no mood to give up.

Mountain heights, chasms, and swampy lowlands hampered the advance of the allies. To make conditions worse, the Germans destroyed mountain roads, bridges, and, indeed, entire cities. Freezing cold rivers wound back and forth between the mountains, and hampered movement. The Germans, using deep holes covered with snow fences, designed effective tank traps.

As the Germans were shoved out of Naples, they blew up everything as they went and mined many of the buildings. When the Allies arrived, they quickly made the most necessary repairs. One day they turned the electricity on just as we were going to a building for our rations. Over a hundred soldiers were blown up. One soldier who was on guard out in the street was knocked down by the blast and the stock of his M1 rifle was blown off. When we got to him, he was in a daze, and was woozy for some time afterward. It's amazing he wasn't dead.

One big problem I recall was at Monte Casino where there was a tall, beautiful monastery on a hillside. I think it was December of '43. There were tunnels under the monastery and also under the town where the enemy was holed up. The Allies didn't want to damage the monastery but were having difficulty clearing the enemy out of those tunnels.

In January of 1944 the Allies landed on Italy's west coast and the Anzio campaign began. The next month the allies finally received permission from the politicians to bomb Monte Casino. Sadly the old monastery was left in ruins. The fighting was intense, and it took us until June to reach Rome.

Once I got a stomach problem and was in the hospital in a town nearby. A squad of planes came over and bombed the area. There was an Asian Indian soldier called a Gerka in the hospital. He pointed up.

"Americans?" he questioned.

"Yeah," I answered.

He shook his head. I interpreted his actions to mean that it was stupid for the Americans to mistakenly bomb territory they already occupied. Of course, in such a confusing business as war, mistakes were made plenty of times.

The Gerka from India were night fighters on the Allied side. They each carried a large, curved knife about sixteen inches long. They were really handy with them. They could slice a person in two with one swing.

We reached Rome in June of 1944, where we had to wait for our supplies to catch up. We saw damage to the Coliseum, and worse still, many dead Germans on a hill north of the city.

I had a Catholic friend, and he persuaded me to go with him to the Vatican to see the pope. There was a huge celebration of some kind. I don't know if it was a holy day or if it was because Rome had been freed from the Nazis.

The courtyards around St. Peters were packed with people. The Pope was moved about in a chair carried by four members of the Swiss Guard. People were crowded together like books in a bookcase, and so we didn't get near him, but we were able to see him.

When we were stationed near Florence, five or six of us went up in the Leaning Tower of Pisa. We were allowed to go as high as a big platform, after which we were supposed to go back down. But we had a yen to ring the bell at the top. We climbed on up, and the wild ringing of the bell was surely heard all over the city.

I was told that years before, it was decided the tower was leaning too much. American engineers were hired to pump cement under it to stabilize it.

In the spring of 1945 we started for the Po Valley. I helped put the first floating Bailey bridge across it. It was amazing. When the heavy tanks went over, the tracks would dip right down to the water, showing us that our engineers knew exactly what they were doing.

After crossing the Po, we moved so quickly that we caught up with the retreating Germans, for they had run out of gas. As the war in Europe wound toward a finish, we got more and more German prisoners. I had two German fellows working for me in the welding shop. They were good blacksmiths.

We wondered what would happen next. Would we be sent to the Pacific to help with the Invasion of Japan? How long would the Japanese hold on?

When the European War was finally over, I was in the hospital with a bad case of boils. We figured we had traveled a winding 1200 miles from Casablanca to Brenner Pass, and I tell you, some of those were hard miles. But we were lucky. Some companies went from 160 men down to 35. We had done better than that, but I recall a day when we lost six men. Some of them were wounded rather than being killed, however.

I had been overseas long enough so I had accumulated 117 points, and thus was one of the first to head for home. On July 3, 1945, I boarded a plane at Pisa, flew to Africa, then Venezuela, and finally to Ft. Lauderdale, Florida. I went by train to St. Louis where I received my discharge papers on July 10. I hitchhiked from there to Bonne Terre, Missouri, where my folks lived. They didn't know I was on the way home.

I walked in at noon, and found them feeding a threshing crew. They were all stunned. I got a lot of attention that day, I'll tell you! After the threshers went back to the field, I ate with the women. They thought I was sick because I didn't eat very much. I wasn't used to such rich food.

I stayed home for a while, but my uncle in Carthage, Missouri, wanted me to work for him in his cold storage company. In September, I started at 60 cents an hour. While there, I met Bonnie Woods. We were married in May of 1947. Knowing all about the hardships of the depression and the war, and both being accustomed to hard work, we were prepared for a good life.

Chinese Balloon Signals
Told by Dean Clawson, Lincoln.

I was in the army and was fighting in the China-Burma-India sector. I had recently been sent to Kumming, China, located in the central part of the country. I was told the Chinese used balloons floating on strings to signal the approach of Japanese planes.

One ball meant the Japanese were coming. Two balls meant they were close. Three meant take cover. Once when I was going to breakfast, I noticed one ball was up. I waited to see if any more would be added, and when no more appeared, I continued to the mess hall.

As we sat at breakfast, bombs began to fall. Everyone ran for the trenches. Since I was new, I was the last man out of the mess hall and was confused about where the trenches were located. I finally saw a trench nearby and dove into it.

Luckily, the next bomb fell on the other side of us. When it was all over, I climbed out. I was covered with garbage. I had jumped into the hole used to discard the scraps from the mess hall.

My buddies gave me a hard time. As you can imagine, I learned where the trenches were after that.

I was a medical supply officer, and much of the time I was stationed at New Delhi. While I was there, General Stillwell came in every few weeks for medical supplies.

I recall the first time he came in. He ordered a generous supply of toilet tissue and paregoric, a medicine for treating diarrhea and abdominal pains. Both articles were in great demand because of hot, humid weather and poor sanitation.

North Platte Canteen
Told by John "Gene" Slattery, North Platte.

Patriotism ran high during the World War II years. When I heard people talking about the North Platte Canteen, an organization that met the troop trains that passed through and treated the soldiers on board to homemade goodies, I wanted to help. At age nine, I didn't cook or bake, but I watched for a way to earn some money to donate to the cause.

I had three pet goats that were a terrible nuisance. My mother was upset when they got into the garden, but when they ate the small cherry trees, she scolded:

"This is too much. Those goats have to go."

My father, Ben Slattery, attended sales at the livestock market each week, and I sometimes accompanied him.

"Can we sell the goats at the sale barn?" I asked. "Then I can donate the money to the Canteen."

"That's a great idea," he said. "I suggest you take only one the first day. I think they'll bring more money if you split them up."

Sale day arrived, and after loading one of the goats into Dad's old truck, we headed for town. When it was time to sell the goat, the auctioneer asked me to stand, and he told the crowd about my plan to help the Canteen. That first goat brought only about ten dollars, for everyone knew what a nuisance a goat can be. But I was proud to have some money for the canteen.

The next week we sold the second goat, and the third week, the last one. At a later time when we were in the sale barn, someone shouted, "Did you bring a goat?"

"No," I answered. "We don't have any more."

"What? No goats? Now what you gonna sell?"

A voice called from the other side of the sale barn. "He'll have to sell the shirt off his back." The crowd laughed, and then began to cheer.

I glanced questioningly at my dad. He nodded, and I quickly pulled my shirt off and held it up. The auctioneer, his face as serious as if he were selling a prize bull, began to take bids on the shirt. The first person to buy it donated it back and it was sold again.

Thus the game was born. Mr. Harshfeld ran a clothing store, and he told me he'd give me a new shirt any time we wanted to go to the sale. The J.C. Penney Store did likewise. I continued to donate the "shirt off my back" at sale after sale, and raised almost a thousand dollars for the Canteen.

The North Platte Canteen began shortly after Japan bombed Pearl Harbor. One day Rae Wilson, a North Platte woman, and her friends, waited on the cobblestone platform near the depot for a troop train. Rae's brother was to pass through, and the women, arms loaded with cookies, candy, and cakes, wanted to treat the young servicemen in her brother's unit. However, the troop train that stopped that day carried soldiers from Kansas rather than the ones the ladies expected.

Disappointment was short lived, for the good women happily passed the goodies to the appreciative Kansas servicemen. The women then decided to meet every troop train that stopped in North Platte and pass treats. Word spread, and soon women all over Central and Western Nebraska were baking for the project.

The canteen served all passing soldiers each day for four and a half years. It was an amazing feat, considering that the population of Western and Central Nebraska is sparse and that rationing of gas and grocery items was a drawback.

Now the depot has been demolished, but the railroad has erected a monument in honor of the canteen.

Untold Story
By Ben Burch, O'Neill.

When Ben Burch married into the extended family, a new relative thought she could easily obtain a few gripping stories from him. It was known that Ben had been shot down in the Southeastern Asian jungles. Under that circumstance, most fliers perished.

Ben had survived a long walk out, but only with severe privations. She approached him and asked how he had managed to survive.

He looked at the floor for awhile, then answered quietly: "If you want to know what the Chinese Wall looks like, I will tell you. If you want to know what it was like to

159

fly over the Hump, I'll also tell you. But I won't tell how we managed to survive the jungle.

"In the first place, since you have had no such experience, you couldn't understand no matter how hard I tried to explain. A person who is exhausted and starving will do things that you, standing here, would never believe. I survived. That is all. I won't talk about the particulars."

First Lieutenant Lawrence Kramer
From The Atkinson Graphic & from Lawrence Kramer.

Lawrence Kramer is modest about his part in the war, and whenever asked, says he didn't do much. He was a bombardier in an airplane which was a part of the famed Bomber Barons of the B-24 Liberators, and he completed 45 successful missions. They operated in the Southwest Pacific sector, much of the time stationed in the Solomon Islands.

"We flew a mission about every third day," said Lawrence. "On other days some of us would prowl around in the jungle near the camp. It was interesting to observe the natives. A work detail went out daily to dig yams or gather coconuts, bananas, or berries. The detail consisted of about 20 women and two men, one man at the front and one at the rear. The men each carried a long spear."

Lawrence grinned. "I don't know if the spears were to keep the women or the GIs in line. As the women walked along balancing baskets on their heads, they chanted a song. It sounded like the same thing over and over, but not in unison. To me it was like the cries of a gaggle of geese."

Lawrence went on to say, "Clothing was not a main concern of the natives. The men wore only a brief 'jock strap' which didn't do a very good job of concealment. The women wore a skirt, but no top. The Navy was of the opinion that the women should be more properly clad. They issued them T-shirts. That was fine for a day or two, but apparently, it didn't coincide with the women's idea of style. They soon appeared with two large holes cut in the front, each in a position to show what the navy had meant to conceal.

"Always at our pre-flight briefings, the weather was discussed. The reports were not reliable, and could be the exact opposite of what they should have been. Probably, since the reports came from occupied areas, the Japanese did their best to confuse us.

Lawrence Kramer

This man swore me into the American Legion 1950-51?

"Usually we flew our own ship, but one time another crew used it. On that mission, I loaned my flight suit to the bombardier. It so happened he was killed that day. It gave me cause to think, but of course we were in danger on all flights, so there was always cause to think. There were occasions when we limped home on two engines.

"Unlike most of the crew, after the bombs were dumped, I could relax a little. The gunners continued to watch for enemy fighters, the pilot had to fly, and the navigator was responsible for guiding us home. But mostly my job was done.

"Sometimes on the way home, I practiced piloting the plane. In the event the pilot and copilot were wounded, it would be good if others in the crew could fly. So I took rudimentary flying lessons, probably also listening to Tokyo Rose on the radio. She repeatedly advised us to go home to our loved ones, and told us of the great progress made by the Japanese forces.

"We saw plenty of water. Sometimes we flew for hours without seeing a bit of land, not even a tiny island. The south Pacific is an enormous expanse."

The *Atkinson Graphic* reported that one of Lawrence's mission involved 15 flying hours, which up to that time was the longest mission ever flown by a B-24. On that particular trip, the Barons raided Japanese gas and oil refineries on the southeast corner of Borneo.

The squadron regularly destroyed power plants, island fortresses, shore installations, shipping centers, and barracks. Lawrence was awarded the air medal with six oak leaf clusters, the Distinguished Unit Citation, and the Southwest Theater Ribbon with four bronze stars given for participation in four successful major campaigns.

Yet Lawrence says he didn't do much in the war. It is a term heard from other men who were in combat. They are speaking in a broader sense. They imply that it was the young men who lost their lives who really gave to the effort.

Under every cross in the national cemeteries is someone who will never marry, have children, or live to a ripe old age. They are the ones who really gave all. Better than anyone else, the veterans recognize that fact.

A Paratrooper on D-Day
John Bouska, Atkinson. June 6, 1944.

I was a paratrooper and was in the group of soldiers in the famous photo of Eisenhower talking to the paratroopers before the D-Day takeoff. Our group was named Pathfinders. We were to land behind coastal fortifications and send light signals to planes carrying the main paratroopers so as to guide their flight.

We took off shortly after midnight in the early morning of June 5th. However, the invasion was postponed because of bad weather, and we were called back. The next morning Gen. Eisenhower decided to proceed with the attack in spite of continuing winds.

When we reached Normandy, there was a barrage of flak coming up, and the plane crew ordered us out before we had reached the drop zone. First the red light came on, telling us to be ready, followed by the green light, which meant, "Go!"

We each had so much gear that it was a tight squeeze to get out. In addition to our signal equipment, helmet, parachute, reserve chute, and life preserver, we also had a gas mask, rifle, jump knife, cartridge belt, first aid kit, blanket, grenades, canteen, and food rations.

Having come down in the wrong place, we didn't set up our signal system with the result that some paratroopers didn't know where to land. Paratroopers descended everywhere: on housetops, in forests, fields, and towns. Some came down among German forces, and were immediately shot.

When I hit the ground, I heard someone about 50 yards away. I grabbed a hand grenade. I gave the password. No answer. I pulled the pin on the grenade and was ready to wheel it. I paused to give the password again, and this time there was a reply.

I was relieved, but also tense because I had almost hurled the grenade at one of our own men. It was my First Lieutenant. I had a hard time in the dark getting the pin back in the grenade.

We moved forward in the dark, and in a little while we came to a bunch of Germans.

"Am-ees! Am-ees!" they shouted.

We retreated fast, thankful it was still dark which helped us evade them. A couple days later, we came upon a soldier who was mortally wounded. We bent over him. The soldier pointed at the lieutenant's gun, then at his own head.

As the lieutenant reached for something, my own blood froze. Surely he wouldn't respond to the young man's plea. Of course, he didn't. Rather he gave him a shot of morphine to deaden the pain. The soldier soon died of his injuries.

When we started across a road, we sighted more Germans. We ran over a rise, found a body of water, and dived in. I lost my gun and some of my other supplies, but we escaped. Afterward, the lieutenant gave me his side arm.

Later we came upon a couple more paratroopers, and all of us hid in some tall, thick hedgerows. We were exhausted from days of constant vigilance, and I fell asleep. After dark the lieutenant, so I was told later, said that he and another fellow were going to check out a nearby meadow, but I didn't hear him. Later I awoke and heard someone approaching. I grabbed my gun and fired. Luckily, the shell froze in the gun because it was the returning lieutenant.

In the next day or two, we got across the field and back to our main outfit. We were taken to England where we rested and waited for our next jump.

PURPLE HEART -- John Bouska shows the Purple Heart he received in Europe in 1944. Bouska was one of the first 24 American soldiers to reach Normandy on D-Day.

Atkinson native on beach hours before D-Day begins

Courtesy of Atkinson Graphic

I was in Holland when I got wounded. It was a daytime jump, and we had no opposition when we landed. The Dutch people came out and grabbed our parachutes. With a shortage of consumer goods, the silk in the parachutes was in demand. On the third day when we were holding a railroad dike, some Germans rushed out of a building across the road, shooting as they came. About thirty of our men were either wounded or killed.

The next morning I was lying next to a railroad track, shooting at the advancing Germans. An enemy bullet hit the track and deflected. It struck me in the neck. The lieutenant got wounded the same day, and we were taken back to England.

A few months after Germany surrendered, we were sent home where we figured we would be retrained to fight in the Pacific. In the middle of the Atlantic crossing, a welcome announcement informed us that the Japanese had surrendered. The war was over.

D-Day Plus One
Told by Denzel McClatchey, York. June 7, 1944.

Our pent up energy was ready to explode. I was among the tens of thousands of soldiers waiting aboard the ships off the coast of England for the largest invasion in the history of the world. I had an additional reason to be impatient, for I had a young wife, Marjorie, back in Nebraska. I was anxious for the war to proceed to its end so I could get back to her

For security reasons, all contact between us and the rest of the world had been cut off. We could neither send nor receive messages. I knew Marjorie would be worried when she didn't hear from me.

We had been married about a year and a half, but we had been apart most of that time. We had planned our wedding for July of 1942, a time when I expected to get home on furlough. You can imagine our disappointment when my furlough was cancelled. Instead, I was sent to an embarkation point at Fort Slocum, New York. While my outfit waited to be sent overseas, Marjorie and I decided perhaps our unit would be detained long enough for her to come to Fort Slocum, and we could be married there.

She arrived and we made quick preparations. While we were getting flowers for the wedding, I asked the florist if he knew anyone who had a room we could rent. They provided us with a bedroom in their own home. We were married in the fort chapel on November 22, 1942. For a couple weeks, all my off-duty hours were spent in that little rented room.

Since it was obvious that our outfit would soon be moved, I thought it prudent to get Marjorie on her way home before I left. As you can imagine, our good-byes were not easy. She returned to Nebraska in mid December, and our outfit shipped out by train on December 29, 1942, to Halifax, Nova Scotia. We waited there in a bitterly cold warehouse for the ship to be loaded. The temperature was -30 degrees.

Finally we boarded Capetown Castle, a small British ship, and headed toward England. Our trip was unbelievably miserable. The weather was so cold that the pipes on the ship froze, with the result that we had no running water. Everyone was seasick, and the food was terrible. I recall that once we were served tripe, an item most of us had never heard of. The very idea of eating it multiplied our digestive problems.

We were each given one blanket and assigned a hammock. Since it was cold, we slept in all our clothes, including our coats and shoes. At first, every time we tried to turn over in our hammocks, we got dumped onto the floor.

As we proceeded south, the weather warmed so the water pipes thawed. Some of them had split, and once thawed, the water flooded the floors. The seas were rough, and we were forced to hold onto stationary objects in order to move around. We weren't allowed on deck for fear we'd be washed overboard. It was a relief to reach England.

We were split up and I was assigned to join the 115th Regimental Headquarters where I received additional training in communications. Later our company was transferred south into the Cornwall District near the English Channel where we received training in offensive action. By late spring we found ourselves waiting aboard ship for the big invasion.

Officially, we hadn't heard a word about an invasion, but anyone who was not a total idiot knew that something big was about to happen in the immediate future. We waited restlessly, packed together like worms in a bait can. Among men in their late teens, patience is a trait that is in short supply.

Denzel (right) and a friend in London

If I remember correctly, we started across the channel in the early morning on the fifth of June. The skies were overcast and the seas were rough. The invasion was called off because of weather so unfavorable that the ground forces would have no air cover.

The waiting continued. Often people in difficult situations say they live one day at a time. For us, a mass of energetic young fellows existing in a state of inactivity, we lived one minute at a time.

On the morning of the sixth, we again moved out to sea. We had no idea where we were headed, but later we learned that we were a part of the Omaha Beach landing, located on the shore of Nazi-occupied France, If I recall correctly, there were five landing sites, Omaha Beach, Utah Beach, and also Gold, Juno, and Sword Beaches.

The water was rough, but the sky had cleared enough for the planes to fly. Battleships stood offshore and blasted the defenses set up by the Germans. Paratroopers, dropped inland, approached the barricaded guns from behind, and attempted to destroy any missed by the airplanes.

The first wave of infantry, consisting of about 1500 men was loaded onto the landing craft and sent toward the shore. Luckily for me, I was among the men who remained aboard the ship, for nearly all of those who first attempted to land were wiped out. Omaha Beach became a place of slaughter. I have heard we lost about 5000 men that day. Bodies floated in the sea.

Finally on the second day, a time referred to as D-Day plus One, another wave of soldiers, mostly Americans, English, and Canadians, were sent down the rope ladders into the landing crafts. I am told about 28,500 men were involved in the invasion that day. We of the 29th Division were among them. The boats moved toward shore, and when we reached a place where the water was about waist deep, the sergeant shouted.

"Everybody out! Everybody out!"

We jumped into the water, and with guns held high above our heads, headed for Nazi-occupied territory. The noise was deafening. Bullets slapped the water on every side, and again, many of the men were killed before they gained the beach. Others were wounded, but were able to proceed.

When we neared land, a brow of hills that rose from the beach protected us. Those of us who had gained the shore unharmed lay on the sand among the injured and dead. I was glad that Marjorie had no way of seeing where I was.

The action in an invasion is best left to your imagination. To see one person killed is a shocking experience; to see a drove of people torn to shreds is indescribable. If you've been in a similar situation, you don't need an explanation. If you haven't been, I can't tell you because there aren't words to describe the sounds, the sights, the smells, and the jarring explosions that knock you down and momentarily seem to stop your heart.

All the radiomen who had gone ashore the day before had been killed which meant we had no communication and thus no leadership. I was in the signal corps, which was responsible for setting up new communication lines, but for the time being, it was impossible to proceed. Except for occasions when we left the crowded beach to help wounded soldiers get ashore, we lay on the sand and waited. We harbored confused feelings--anyway, I know I did--but none of us voiced what we were thinking.

Gunfire came from a well-barricaded bunker behind a bluff. The bombardment from our battle ships had gone farther inland and had failed to destroy it. Now with Allied soldiers on the coast and no communication lines set up, it was difficult for our ships to know where to aim the guns. We were pinned down for fifteen or twenty hours before the demolition company came in and blew up the German bunker.

Allied tanks were put ashore, and the heavily armed advance crews went ahead. We finally were able to crawl forward on our bellies. The communications department was crucial to the operation, and as soon as we got organized, we began sending and receiving messages. After we established a beachhead, we at last had a foothold in German Occupied France.

In the area of Saint Lo, there were well-hidden German bunkers. At night, a huge gun on rails was driven out of hiding to bombard us. Before dawn, this railroad cannon was returned to its hiding place. Finally, since the Allies couldn't pinpoint the location of the bunker, they decided to bomb the area. After dropping leaflets to warn civilians to vacate the city, thousands of planes swept overhead and bombed the entire Saint Lo vicinity.

When we foot soldiers came near it, we went around it, for it was one huge pile of rubble. Later I talked to a couple of fellows who had gone through Saint Lo. They said there wasn't a building standing and that the stench was indescribable.

Our advance was steady, for now the Nazis were retreating. Occasionally a group of enemy soldiers would find a protected area where they could make a counter attack. Those of us in the signal corps were prime targets since disrupting communications was a main objective. Also, because of the radio and telephone equipment we transported, we were not as heavily armed.

Chow time was not remarkable, for we had small tins of food known by such names as K rations and C rations. I do remember that our favorite meal was beans and bacon. Most often we ended up with something else, perhaps even our least favorite, which was hash.

After about thirty days, our weary unit was pulled back for R&R (rest and recuperation.) During that time we could take a bath, shave, do our laundry, and get our mail. We read the Stars and Stripes, played cards, and wrote letters. I had a fistful of mail from Marjorie, which I read and reread.

After we were back on the Front Line and were proceeding beyond Saint Lo, some of us got separated from our company. There was a fork in the road, and we took the wrong branch. We came to a small town and entered it. There was a sizeable Catholic Church there and some nuns walking down the street. After passing beyond the town, we decided we were on the wrong road and retraced our steps. Again we walked through the little town. We followed the other trail and soon came to our company.

The sergeant asked, "Where have you been?"

"We took the wrong fork in the road and came to a little town. We couldn't find you so we came back and took the other trail."

"You're lucky to get back," said the sergeant. "We haven't taken that town yet!"

Later when we returned to take the town, there was a sniper hidden in the church tower. He kept picking off our men. I don't know why he didn't shoot us when we went through the first two times, but perhaps he wasn't in place yet. Maybe it was our earlier appearance that alerted the Germans that they should set up a defense because this time, we had to fight to enter the town.

One day I was on a switchboard in a foxhole when I discovered that we had lost contact. I was in charge and sent three men in a jeep to check the communication line. After waiting for some time and getting no results, I sent three more men out. None of them returned.

Next, two fellows and I got in a third jeep and proceeded down the curving, hedge-lined trail until we came upon the other jeeps. Four of the six men were lying dead in and around their vehicles. When bullets began whizzing by, I hit the brakes. We managed to tumble out of our jeep and take refuge behind it.

Bullets were coming underneath the vehicle and one of them caught me in the calf of my leg. We held onto the back of the jeep anyplace we could and pulled our feet up. Finally a German tank came around a bend, guns blazing. One of my men, Paul Zory, got hit in the thigh and fell to the ground. We knew the tank could smash us like toads on a road.

"This is it, fellows!" I said. "We can die or we can surrender. Let's raise our hands and hope they'll stop shooting." The Germans accepted our surrender. It was July 18, 1944. I knew it would be a sad day for Marjorie when she got the telegram that I was missing in action.

We were ordered to follow the tank back behind German lines. Soon we were joined by one of the men from the second jeep I had sent out, for he had been taken prisoner also. Later we found out a man from the first jeep, Bill Mallick, managed to escape and return to the American lines.

Since our captors were retreating, they were disorganized and were short of food. They had been separated from their food wagon, a huge soup kettle mounted on wheels and pulled by horses.

You can believe, I'm sure, that not much in the way of nourishment came in the direction of the prisoners. They marched us during the day and bedded us down in a shed or barn during the night. It was good it was summer, for we had no blankets.

We helped Paul Zory, our injured buddy, all we could. We called him "Pop" since he was more than twice our age. We chided him constantly about what he was doing in the middle of a war when he could have stayed home in Syracuse, New York, for he was too old for the draft.

The bullet had gone through his thigh, making a hole about the size of a pencil. The Germans instructed the French to give us some bandages to dress his wound, and we did the best we could to keep it covered. I also bandaged my wound, but it was less severe, and it didn't inhibit my ability to get around. However, Paul couldn't walk unaided those first days, and we took turns walking beside him and helping him.

The French sympathized with us since they hated living under Nazi rule. The Germans had taken over France in June of 1940, which meant the French had been squirming under Hitler's boot heel for four years. Assisting us would have been considered a crime for which they could have been shot. There were times when a Frenchman sneaked a bit of food to us, but he had to be mighty careful.

The Germans retreated through France, a tip of Holland, and into Germany, taking us along with them. The Americans and other Allies were on our heels all the time. We found out what Hitler's troops had been enduring, for we, along with them, were under constant attack by the Allies.

From August 24th to 28th, we were locked in boxcars. During that time, we received no food or water. The summer heat made our thirst almost unbearable. At that time the Germans were moving the inmates from one camp to another, and there were about four trainloads of us. The boxcars heated up in the summer sun, and we thought we would surely bake to death.

Our mouths were so parched that we didn't try to talk much. We stood in silence, nursing our dry scratchy eyes, and every once in awhile, lifting our heads to see if all the others were still breathing the heavy, hot air. We were packed tightly, but there was enough space to allow a few at a time to sit down on their haunches.

We were left in the railroad yards even though the Germans knew the train stations would be attacked. Bombs began falling at noon. As they exploded around us, shrapnel flew through the sides of the boxcars. We lay down, even though some men were on top of others. The concussion from the explosions threatened to derail the boxcars. Those frightful raids did take our minds off our terrible hunger and thirst, however. Finally we were unloaded and we continued our march, tramping wearily along on hot, aching feet.

During one Allied attack, we were put in horse drawn wagons and moved back from the line. We came to a wooded area and as we were passing through it, planes began to strafe us. Everyone, guards and prisoners, jumped out and took cover.

At such times, we prisoners tried to stay together, hoping to escape. But we were handicapped because the Germans knew the territory and we didn't. In a short while, they always managed to round us up.

Mostly the Germans used horses for ambulances and also to transport their war materials and food. However, sometimes they forced us to carry their wounded, their ammunition, and their supplies. We knew that such forced labor was against the Geneva Convention, but since they were the ones with the guns, we didn't argue.

After we entered Germany there was an excessive amount of hatred directed at us. They seemed to have forgotten that it was Hitler, their leader, who had begun the war and who was persisting in continuing it. Sometimes we were stoned or spit upon or threatened with clubs or hoes or axes.

While we were in the Bavarian sector, one of the German guards flew into a rage because the Allies had bombed the railroads through their town. He lunged at us, striking first one and then another with the butt of his rifle.

We knew better than to fight back, for it would then give the guards a reason to open fire on us.

Later when we were in a camp about 30 miles from Munich, we were loaded in boxcars, and sent to that city. There we were forced to rebuild the railroad, which had been bombed by the Allies. By this time, fall had turned to winter, and it was a miserably cold day. We had no warm clothes and no gloves. Our hands were numb with cold from handling the iron rails and the tools. All the while, the Nazis urged us on, cursing, prodding, and threatening us with the ever-present guard dogs. Late that night we were returned to our barracks.

Some of the younger guards prodded us with bayonets. We figured they wanted us to run so they would have an excuse to shoot us. Frightening as it was, we stood our ground and took the prodding.

Also, some English-speaking Germans acted as spies. They dressed in American uniforms and mingled among us. We had to be careful what we said when anyone we didn't know was present.

The camp was so crowded that some of us volunteered to work for the local farmers. We were the lucky ones, for we got more food.

During the winter while there wasn't fieldwork to do, the farm where I worked ran a brickyard. I helped with the baking. There were about six huge ovens. We put the green bricks in the ovens where they baked for several days. Meanwhile, we got another batch of bricks ready. After the baking was completed, the ovens cooled for several days before the bricks could be removed. Then we used padded gloves to restack them outside the ovens, and the entire process was repeated.

There were about twenty people working there, both men and women. The women mostly worked at forming the bricks. The men and women lived and worked in separate quarters. Most of them were forced labor from countries that Germany had conquered. I particularly remember some Belgians, Ukrainians, Frenchmen, and an Italian.

Most of the time while I was on the farm, I got three small meals a day. An exception was when any of the prisoners complained they were ill. Then all of us were denied food and water. We soon learned to bear our illnesses in silence.

Usually we had cooked cereal for breakfast, and soup and rye bread for lunch and supper. The soup might have kohlrabi, potatoes, or dried beans in it. Sometimes there were bits of horsemeat included. We received only small portions of food, but we knew it was more than the prisoners in the camp were receiving.

Since all of us were young fellows, we had immense appetites and couldn't believe we could live on such a small amount of food. When we had a chance, we swiped potatoes from the storage pits and hid them in our pockets. In the evening we sliced them with our pocketknives and laid them directly on the top of the little stove in our bunkhouse. When we figured they had baked through, we scraped them off the stovetop and ate them.

Some of the guards were fairly decent men, though they always referred to us in foul, degrading terms. One fellow, however, was especially cruel. He seemed to enjoy slugging us with the butt of his gun or pricking us with the tip of his bayonet.

One of our fellow prisoners told us that when we were liberated, he meant to take the weapons away from that brutal guard.

"I will blast him to kingdom come with his own gun," he vowed.

The brickyard was closed on Sundays. If the weather was nice, we often sat outside in the sun. An old guard gave us a dog-eared deck of cards, and we sometimes played card games. He shared what little food he had with us. He had a son who had been taken prisoner by the Allies and was being held in the United States. We couldn't converse very well, but could understand that he was worried about whether his son in the U.S. prison had adequate food. We reassured him, telling him that our country rationed food, but there were plenty of basic food items so that no one had to go hungry.

We worked in the brickyard all winter. A French forced laborer on a nearby farm was allowed more freedom than we were. Also, he had access to the war news, which he sometimes reported to us. We were encouraged when we learned the Allied forces were progressing. We rejoiced when American planes began flying over.

Later when the front was near, the Frenchman slipped over to talk to the American troops, telling them where we were being held. By that time, the war was ending, for we were in the part of Germany that was last to be taken.

Early one morning we were overjoyed to see American GIs coming up the road. They first approached the guards who, knowing that the war was ending, calmly handed over their guns. We dashed outside and jubilantly piled onto our countrymen. Our first words were, "Do you have any food?"

"Nothing but these blasted K and C rations," a soldier answered. To us, the rations were a feast!

The prisoner who was intent on killing the brutal guard, hurried to the man's quarters. The fellow was in bed, and the American was able to grab his gun. The elderly guard, clad only in his underwear, looked so pathetic that the GI hadn't the heart to shoot him. He walked out, taking the gun with him.

By this time, the Nazis were giving up by the thousands, and the Americans at the front were overwhelmed with the number of German prisoners to be processed. The major told us they needed to continue to push ahead, but we ex-prisoners were supposed to move back and eventually go to Le Havre, France. He gave us some rations and told us we were on our own.

We proceeded down a road, hardly able to believe we were free and had food in our possession. In a short time we met a long line of German soldiers who wanted to surrender. Having no idea what to do with them, we left them standing there. We headed toward Munich, which by then was in the hands of the Americans.

When we met some German trucks, we stopped them and took one of the trucks. Even though we were weak and exhausted, we could now hope to make some headway. We roared down the road, jubilant that we had wheels underneath.

Eventually we were stopped by American MPs and told to get off the road. An American convoy was advancing, and we were in the way. I steered the truck so far to the side of the road that we slipped into the ditch. We abandoned the vehicle and proceeded on foot.

In Munich there was confusion, but the Americans found a room for us. After several days we caught a plane ride to Le Havre where we cleaned up and got new uniforms. About that time the war was over. We were put on a ship for the United States. When we neared New York, there was a dense fog. The ships in the convoy were ordered to different docks.

Suddenly there was a huge crash, which made the whole ship shake. In the heavy fog, a boat had hit us, had knocked off one of our gun turrets, and had put a big dent in the side of the ship.

"Oh, boy!" I thought. "We've lived through an invasion, a war, and an enemy prison! Now we are going to sink on our own shore!" But the ship limped into a dock and we were unloaded.

I don't remember the name of the camp we entered, but it was nearly empty. In an effort to bring the fighting men home quickly, the partially trained men had been sent overseas as replacements. Since the war was over, no new recruits were taken in.

"You're on your own," said the officer in charge. "Choose your own quarters."

First of all, I wanted to call Marjorie, but there was a drove of men waiting at the telephones. I took a long shower, got clean clothes, and shaved. Men were still piled at the telephone booths. I went to supper, and after that, the crowd at the phones had dwindled. I got in line.

From camp to our hometowns, we rode ordinary Pullman cars. Marjorie and I met in Lincoln and returned to York. I was home for a month, then sent to Hot Springs, Arkansas. Since the company records had been destroyed at the time of my capture, I needed to be reinstated so that I could get my ratings, my combat ribbons, and also be eligible for back pay. I was short a few points of being eligible for discharge, so had to remain a few weeks in camp. Once I was finally discharged, I hitchhiked to Lincoln where Marge picked me up. We have spent almost every day of the last fifty-seven years together.

American Tanks, D-Day Plus Two
Told by Edward R. Oliva, Milligan. June, 1944.

We were a part of the huge D-Day Invasion, but everyone didn't go ashore on the first day. Because of the long wait aboard ship, I'm confused about which day after D-Day our crew went in. Perhaps it was about the third day. But the waiting on board, packed among other anxious soldiers, seemed endless. Time closed around us and seemed to freeze us in endless space.

Then in the black of night, we were on our way toward shore. After being hauled on a landing craft to a point where it ran aground, we splashed into the sea aboard a snorkel, a tank equipped to move in water as well as on land. After releasing its load, the landing craft was again afloat and headed back to the ship. We took off for the shores of France as fast as possible, hoping to get to the beach embankments before we were shot. Due to an error, we landed closer than planned to where the Germans were entrenched.

Some GIs were digging foxholes, and in the darkness, one fellow was shoveling dirt out of his hole and onto another fellow. The second GI made a few choice remarks, advising his buddy to pay attention to where his dirt was landing. The Germans were close enough to hear and opened fire on us.

The French farms were small, perhaps eight or ten acres each. Tall ridges of dirt with hedgerows planted along the tops divided them. Openings in the ridges formed passageways, but they often were mined.

Once we tried to put a bulldozer on the front of a tank and force ourselves through the ridges, but we weren't very successful. The Allies lost numerous tanks, but our tank remained undamaged.

For a week or two, we were unable to make much headway. Then American airplanes poured over and dropped bombs in advance of us. After that we began to go forward, sometimes even using the roads. But it was important not to outrun our supply line, because tanks that ran out of gas were sitting ducks for the enemy.

After a couple weeks, we went through Saint Lo. It was in a shambles and most of the buildings were afire. Smoke choked us, and embers dropped around us as we went through. We can be grateful none of the battles were fought on American ground.

One day we ran over a mine, and when it exploded, it blew one of the tracks off our tank. All of us escaped serious injury, but did spend some time in the hospital. It wasn't unusual to have a tank knocked out. I knew one fellow who lost five tanks. Each time he was reassigned to another. Then on the sixth, he was killed.

We fought our way across France into Belgium, and finally into the western edge of Germany. The Air Force preceded us with fighter planes that blanketed the sky like flocks of migrating birds. Wave after wave rolled over us. God bless those planes! They cleared the way, but there was still plenty of fighting to do, especially in clearing the enemy from buildings in the towns. It was during this time that we had our tank destroyed and one of our crewmen killed.

We were going through a valley where there were houses on both sides. Someone in one of the houses waited for us to pass and then fired a bazooka at us. In addition to the man killed, all of us were wounded except the driver. My injuries were flesh wounds in my face and legs and were bloody, but I was not incapacitated.

One fellow, a man called the loader because of his job, lost his eyesight, and the Lieutenant had a piece of shrapnel in a lung. With the driver and me helping the seriously wounded, we leaped from the tank and took refuge in the basement of a house. We had side arms, and I had a Thompson machine gun.

We remained in the basement until dark, staying on guard and doing what we could to care for the wounded. We heard a vehicle approaching. By the sound, we knew it was an American half-track, but it was too dark to see it. Was it really safe for us to show ourselves? The driver and I took the chance and went out.

We were relieved to see that the men in the half-track were American medics. They loaded the wounded and took us all to a hospital. Since my wounds were not serious, the medical team patched me up rather quickly.

In mid-December a frightful blizzard moved across Europe. The storm was an event that Hitler had been waiting for. He had mobilized English-speaking Germans, had dressed them in American uniforms, and had given them American weapons. Then, under cover of darkness and the storm, these special troops infiltrated our lines. The Nazis pushed across Luxembourg and into Belgium, making a huge bulge in the front line.

This last ditch effort by the Germans came to be known as the infamous Battle of the Bulge. They threw every effort into this huge counter-attack, hoping to push to the sea, and thus divide the Allies. I was assigned to another tank, and on Christmas Day, 1945, I joined the Battle of the Bulge.

Bad weather, the confusion because of enemies dressed in our own uniforms, and the sheer force of Hitler's desperate attempt pushed the Allies back.

For some reason that I will never understand, I had a most blessed piece of good luck. One of my former officers, a man now promoted to major, came to our tank in mid January.

"Ed," he said. "You're going home."

"What, Sir?" I said. Surely I had misunderstood him. Who gets sent home from the middle of battle?

But it was true. I was to get a thirty-day furlough in the States. My feelings were ones of elation for myself and of dismay for the good friends I was leaving behind.

When I left the tank, I rode in a jeep through a French village where the Germans were shelling. We piled out and crawled under a truck. Later we noticed we had made the worst possible choice, because the truck was loaded with ammunition. Miraculously, none of the shells or the shrapnel hit it. I decided Someone was looking out for us.

During my month of leave, the Allies retook the ground in the Bulge, and the front stretched in a relatively straight line from the North Sea to the Mediterranean. Another big push got the Allies across the barricaded Rhine River and into the heart of Germany.

It so happened the army put out a new point system, and I had enough points to keep me from being again sent overseas. In a few more months, the Allies reached the bunkers where Hitler and his officials were barricaded. The German leaders, including Hitler, committed suicide, and the war in Europe was over.

We looked west, though, with deep concern. We assumed we were going to continue fighting the Japanese for a long time before they could be driven to surrender. They were sworn to fight to their deaths, and they were deeply entrenched, especially in their home islands. We thought the war was only half over. Horrible as the atomic bomb was, it brought the fighting to an end, and I'm sure, saved many more lives than it took.

The Battle of the Bulge
Told by Woody Gilg, Atkinson. 1944.

I was drafted into the armed forces in September of 1941, about three months before the bombing of Pearl Harbor. I spent the first three years of the war training other infantry- men in the use of mortars. Then in August of 1944, roughly two months after D-Day, I joined the Allied forces in Europe.

I landed in France, and as we moved through France and into Luxembourg, some buildings were still burning from previous fighting. At that time, the Germans were in retreat, and we were on their heels. After I was at the front for a month, I was pulled back. It was then that, in the middle of a great blizzard, the Germans made the huge counter attack that came to be known as the Battle of the Bulge.

I recall that Allied officers needed every truck they could lay their hands on in order to transport ammunition to the front. I was on a supply truck that was loaded with such items as clothing, shoes, soap, razors, and the like. In the middle of the night we were told to unload it in order to free the truck. We set the entire load off in a residential area.

"What are we supposed to do with all that stuff?" asked a man who lived nearby.

"Whatever you want," we told him. "It's yours." It must have been a windfall for them, for they were suffering from a shortage of such supplies.

Later, our unit was sent toward Bastogne. There the Allies, under the command of General McAuliffe, had been surrounded by the enemy. It was at this time that the Nazis demanded that the Americans surrender and got McAuliffe's famous one-word answer: "Nuts!"

The Germans didn't understand the American slang expression. McAuliffe rephrased his answer, using less than polite terms, and the Nazis then got the message. Later, the weather cleared enough for Allied planes to give support. After about a month of fierce fighting, the huge bulge in the line was pushed back, and a few weeks later, Americans were crossing the Rhine River into the heart of Germany. Our Division was the first to cross.

The Battle of the Bulge had been costly in lives on both sides. It was the greatest single battle fought by any American army. It happened that at one time I was stationed near a collection point for bodies, both German and Allied. It was a chilling sight, especially for new replacements that were arriving. At one time, our unit of more than 200 men was down to 52.

I saw more war than I ever want to see again. But I'm glad to have served--I wouldn't have it any other way.

The Ledo Road
By Midge Bender, about husband, Frederick. 1944.

When my husband, Frederick Bender, was in India and was working on the Ledo Road, some Chinese soldiers were working on the project along with the American men.

Chinese officers were overseeing the Chinese men. The Japanese had cut off the Burma Road farther south. The Ledo Road was being built from Ledo, India, into Burma to reconnect with the Burma Road. Since the Japanese had control of the Indo-China coast and some of the Chinese coast as well, the Burma Road was necessary for transportation.

Much of the road was built on mountainsides. One day a Chinese soldier lost control of a piece of heavy road equipment. He managed to jump clear of it just as it plunged down the mountain.

Imagine what a shock it was to Frederick, a 21-year-old American soldier, to see the Chinese officer pull his gun and shoot the unfortunate soldier dead. The huge machine was a valuable piece of equipment that would be difficult to replace, but shooting the man didn't make replacing it any easier.

In addition to the mountains in that area, there were also steamy jungles. Many soldiers got malaria as well as jungle rot, a disease that mostly attacked the legs and feet. The skin rotted away, leaving huge, running sores. Some people carried deep scars all their lives

In the CBI Sector, the men slept under mosquito netting in an effort to limit the number of people who contacted malaria. One night Lt. Bender was awakened by a rustling noise. He snapped on his flashlight and saw a poisonous snake on top of his mosquito netting. Four poles supported the airy fabric, and the ends were firmly tucked under his blanket.

He had a gun under his pillow. He pulled it out and shot the snake.

At that time, the common people in China didn't have flush toilets. They used yokes over their shoulders with a bucket on each end to carry the human excrement out into the fields for fertilizer. The soldiers were cautioned not to eat fresh garden produce because one could get amoebic dysentery from it.

One fellow who had amoebic dysentery thought he got it from drinking something called Jing Bow Juice. It was a locally made alcoholic beverage. Jing bow means "air raid." It was said if you drank the juice, you didn't have to worry about anything--not even the air raids.

Underground Activities
The names of people are fictitious in order to protect the identity of the participants.

A college student, Ann, said:

"One day when some of us were goofing around on-line, we decided to see what information we could find concerning our family names. Among the bits of information I discovered when I entered our family name, let us say it was Bender, was that during World War II my grandparents, Celia and Dan, worked underground in their country. They were on a list as members of a group credited with saving more than a hundred Jews. I had never heard either of them speak of being in the underground."

After thinking about these people for a few days, a listener decided to contact the grandmother, Celia, by telephone. She now lived in the USA. When he told her about the list on the Internet, she gasped.

"Where did anyone get that information? Such things should be forgotten. No good can come of talking about it, and neither Dan nor I have ever mentioned it. Countries are small in that area, and loyalties are mixed. We still have relatives over there."

"To belong to an underground organization in an occupied country at that time was a heroic thing to do," he said. "You had children. If you had been caught, your entire family would have been destroyed."

"Oh, we were scared, but we were young and daring. We did it because it seemed to be the right thing. I wouldn't have the nerve now, but at that time, all of Europe was in such deep trouble. But I can't figure how anyone found out about it."

185

"Did you live in a town or in the country?"

"We lived on a farm. We traveled with horses and wagon or buggy. We didn't have a car--few people in Europe did at that time.

"The Allies used to fly over our farm in the night and drop ammunition and guns. The men, including Dan, went out and picked them up. Of course, it was necessary to get the parachutes out of sight as soon as possible so the Germans wouldn't see them. Everything had to be well hidden.

"Like many European countries, our country was occupied early in the war--before the USA entered the fight. A few months after the German's took over, they made a sudden sweep of the country and arrested every policeman they could find. The idea was to strip the country of leadership and power. At the time, two policemen in a nearby town were off duty, and thus weren't picked up. The Underground protected them. For a while, we hid them at our farm in our upstairs.

"Everything was rationed and there was a great shortage of all civilian products. We didn't have enough bedding. We went to the neighbors and borrowed some blankets. We said some of our cousins were visiting. I don't know if they believed us, but they didn't say anything. Eventually, we got better equipped, and were able to help fleeing Jews.

"About the only way the underground could make a difference in the war was by sabotage or by passing information to the Allies. I recall that one evening two German servicemen came to our door and asked for food. It was not an uncommon happening. Like servicemen everywhere, they got tired of army rations.

"They were friendly, pleasant young fellows. I served them some meat and bread and made some coffee. We called it coffee, but actually it was made of parched grain. Also, we had milk, which was popular with all the soldiers.

"I couldn't understand them, but Dan knew several languages, and he was able to talk with them.

"They explained that they appreciated getting some extra food under their belts because they were going on a long march to the seashore. They were to embark on a ship in a certain small port under the cover of darkness. They had no idea they were giving military information directly to the Underground.

"Later, I felt terrible when I heard the ship was torpedoed. What a dreadful waste of young lives. It was right to fight against Hitler and his savage ways, but horrible that so many lives had to be lost."

"I am reminded," said her listener, "that we were told over and over, 'Loose lips sink great ships.' There were numerous enemy spies here in the USA searching out bits of information that would be useful to the Axis powers."

"You can be sure there were," Celia said. "And don't kid yourself! There still are spies here."

"Well, probably so."

"I would add one more thing. Most people say that the happiest day of their lives was their wedding day, or when their first child was born. But my happiest day was the day my native land was freed!"

The New Yorker and the Cow
Told by Ted Dick, Hastings. 1944.

For security reasons, servicemen were not allowed to have cameras overseas. However, I had purchased one in New York, and had sneaked it to Europe. Since my job was to deliver supplies, I drove a truck. I wrapped the camera in oiled rifle paper and wired it to the under side of the hood of my truck.

I took hundreds of photos, including pictures of D-Day. However the rolls of exposed film lay in a box for about half a century before I had pictures made. By then the film was so crisp it took special handling to develop it. How those pictures did revive my memories of the war!

. One picture taken in France shows two men experimenting with milking a cow. Since one fellow was from New York City, the animal was an oddity to him. Bryce Hanna of York, Nebraska, was explaining the process. After snapping the picture, the last on the roll, I went into a nearby barn to get my backpack to reload the camera. The barn was attached to the house, a common arrangement in that area.

Bryce Hanna, York, showed a New Yorker about a cow...

Courtesy of Ted Dick

While I was in the barn, an explosion rocked the building. I carefully peeked out the door and saw that I had taken the last picture for which those two would ever pose. One of them had stepped on a mine, which had killed both men and the cow. I would have been with them if I hadn't gone to reload my camera.

Trina's Baby
By Erik, an immigrant to America. 1943.

Trina was "forced labor." The Nazi enemy had taken her from her home in Russia. At the time of this event she was kitchen help on a farm in Austria. I was a Polish youth who was masquerading as a German and was working in the fields on the same farm. I am not giving my actual name because of the nature of my story, but it is a true happening.

In 1939, shortly before the Germans attacked Poland, Hitler had made a treaty with Russia. The idea was to pretend friendship in order to keep Russia from going to the aid of Poland. Among other articles in the treaty was an item in which Hitler said Polish people were unacceptable, and anyone who chose to kill a Polish man, woman, or child could do so without fear of prosecution.

Another reason for posing as a German was that I could get more ration stamps. Food was painfully short, and Polish people received less food and fewer essential items than did the Germans.

As time went by, Trina and I fell in love and soon decided to marry. I went to a German official in order to get a marriage license.

"You can't marry a Russian girl without special permission from Berlin," I was told.

My heart sank. If the marriage must be approved by Hitler or one of his henchmen, I felt application was useless, for they were striving to keep the German nationality "pure". But I decided I must attempt to gain Nazi sanction, and the forms were soon in the mail.

I knew it would not help to admit I was Polish. A union that would produce Russian-Polish offspring would be even less acceptable to German authorities.

When our request to marry was denied, we made private vows to each other and lived together anyway. Eventually, Trina gave birth to a baby boy whom we named Bernard. He was a beautiful, good-natured little fellow, and the girls that were employed on the farm enjoyed taking turns caring for him.

The woman who ran the farm (her husband was in the service) tolerated Bernard but otherwise paid no attention to him. Thus, when he was about three months old, one of the hired girls was surprised to see her feeding him something from a bottle.

The woman put the baby in his basket and immediately rinsed the bottle. In a short while, the infant began to scream. Trina, hearing his cries, hurried in from the nearby garden. When she couldn't quiet him, she sent for me to come in from the field.

Immediately, I knew something was wrong because Bernard was usually a quiet, satisfied baby. Our small village didn't have a doctor, but as soon as I heard the baby's screams, I sent to a nearby town for a doctor. Before he arrived, Bernard died.

While Trina and I wept over our lifeless baby, the woman of the house went outside. When she saw the doctor approaching, she told him to return to his office because the child was dead. The doctor left.

I was upset when I found the doctor had departed without examining the baby, but I could do nothing about it. Legally, a half Russian child had no rights. We were positive the woman poisoned the baby, either because she was told to do so by authorities who objected to a German man fathering the baby of a Russian girl, or else because she thought her hired girls spent too much time tending the infant.

Shortly after that, I was sent to a concentration camp for changing jobs without the permission of the authorities. While I was gone, Trina heard I was dead, and she became engaged to another man.

When I returned, Trina wanted to come back to me, but I decided to go my own way. I lived in a displaced persons camp until I got permission to come to America.

Kind-hearted Pilot
Told by Earl Drapal, York.

Charles Brown, a pilot who was a member of the 379th Bomb Group, was flying a B-17 bomber on a mission over Nazi Germany. The plane was hit by anti-aircraft guns both before and after the bombs were dropped, and later Nazi fighter planes attacked it. In an effort to escape the fighters, Charley dove earthward.

As the B-17 plunged down, the fighters pulled away. When Charley tried to pull out of the dive, the plane didn't respond. It seemed it was the end for both plane and crew, four of whom were wounded, but Charley finally managed to pull the nose up and level off.

For a moment, he was flooded with relief. The Plexiglas nose was shot off, there were gapping holes in the sides, three engines were damaged, and the guns were silenced, but miraculously the plane remained in the air. Then he glanced to the side, and the hair stood on the back of his neck. There, flying beside a gapping hole in the B-17, was a German Messerschmitt.

The pilots stared at each other. Charley waited for the burst of gunfire that would end his life and send his badly damaged plane and the crew to the ground. But it didn't come. The German, his eyes still locked on Charley, finally saluted and pulled up and away.

The B-17 crew discussed options. Charley decided he would attempt to get the plane back to England because he felt three of the wounded men were too badly hurt to survive bailing out. The other crewmembers also opted to remain with the craft rather than jump into enemy territory.

The crippled plane, skimming lower and lower over the waves, barely made it back to England. Charley survived the war. Many times he has told this unusual story.

"I wish I could talk to that German pilot," said Charley, decades later. "I'd ask him why he didn't shoot us down."

"Well, I imagine the Germans have a veteran's organization the same as we do," said one of Charley's friends. "Maybe they have a publication similar to our Legion magazine, and if you put an article in it, you might be able to locate him."

Charley thought it worth a try, and actually was able to find the man, Franz Stegler, who had spared his life. After the war Stegler had moved to British Columbia, Canada, where he continues to live. The two men arranged a meeting at a World War II Reunion in Framingham, Massachusetts, with the German pilot coming as a guest.

"I had never seen a plane that was shot so full of holes and still in the air," Stegler told Charley. "I just didn't have the heart to finish shooting you down. I thought if you limped home in that craft, it would be a miracle. Besides, I could see that some of your crew members were wounded."

Charley and Stegler have become friends. The 379th Bomb Group has made him an honorary member.

"He risked his life," said Charley, "for if he'd have been caught sparing us and our helpless craft, he undoubtedly would have been executed."

The Hawaiian Islands
Told by Ray Kramer, York. 1940s.

I was stationed in Oahu from 1942 until 1945. When I arrived, the area was still strewn with the debris from the Pearl Harbor attack. Men constantly were at work on the cleanup.

Also, I saw numerous ships that crippled to the Islands after being torpedoed or bombed and set afire. But I was lucky, because I never saw any enemy action.

Eugene Aman was one of my good buddies. We were really different. I was quiet and serious, but he was outgoing and full of fun. Robert Bunting, another fellow in our unit, was inclined to be a moocher. He mooched everything: gum, candy bars, cigarettes—you name it.

One day, Gene unwrapped a candy bar and carved a tunnel through the center. After filling it with Ex-lax, he rewrapped it. Man! I think he had poked a double dose of the laxative into it.

When we met Bunting, Aman handed him the candy bar. We watched while he wolfed it down. He didn't suspect a thing.

The next day a pale-looking Bunting told us, "Wow! Was I ever sick last night! I was doubled up with cramps, and spent the whole night in the latrine."

Ray Kramer and Eugene Aman Hawaii

There was a goat penned within the compound. We saved tidbits of food such as apple cores, orange peelings, and bread crusts for him. He seemed to relish everything.

Then the guys began testing him to see how many things he really would eat. Poor goat. They fed him everything: paper, cardboard, weeds, buttons, combs, cigarettes, pencils, twigs, cough drops, handkerchiefs, beer, and even sunglasses. He ate it all. I don't know why it didn't kill him.

Purple Heart for an Army Nurse
Told by Irene Olson, Omaha.

I had arrived in the South Pacific in New Guinea to pick up patients. Since I had time before my return flight, I went with friends to a stage show in an outdoor theater. I even remember the name of the show: *Olson and Johnson, Hell's a Poppin'*. After the show some of us went into the mess hall for coffee and pancakes.

I happened to look out and I saw that a plane down the line was burning. Our radar had been discontinued because the island was supposed to be safe from attack. But when someone yelled "Air raid", we all jumped to our feet to crawl under the heavy tables.

I felt a sharp stab in my thigh, and I supposed that in my haste I had whacked it on the edge of the table. After I was underneath, I rubbed my hand over my paining leg, and was surprised to find it was covered with blood. As soon as the raid was over, I was taken to the hospital.

One fellow in the same mess hall happened to be looking out the window. He was decapitated. Some soldiers who were lying on their bunks were killed, also. There were so many wounded that the doctors worked all night. Since my wound was not life threatening, I waited for treatment until the next day.

Finally it was my turn. I had shrapnel in my leg, but luckily it had missed the femur by a half inch. If you had seen the horrible, unimaginable injuries that I have seen, you'd know that mine was minor because it was a flesh wound. After a couple weeks in the hospital, I went back to work, caring for the wounded in transit from New Guinea to Hawaii.

Nurse Clare Olson

Irene's sister, Clare Olson, was also an army nurse. She was stationed on the upper island of the New Hebrides. On the way across the ocean, Clare rode on a French ship. The rudder broke, and the sailors had to steer by hand for a time, a problem that caused them to fall behind the other ships in the convoy.

"We had to remain below deck all the time," said Clare. "Absolutely no light of any kind, not even a spark, was allowed on deck. It was a rule that was easy to enforce, because we were aware that if our position was made known to the enemy, we would be bombed. In any kind of an emergency, there was no one to assist us. Finally the rudder was repaired, and in a few days we caught up to the convoy."

Clare worked grueling hours in a hospital. The islands were relatively safe at that time. However, often at night a single Japanese plane flew over. The sirens would go off and, tired as they were, everyone had to get up, grab a helmet and a canteen, and get in a foxhole.

"We didn't always get in the foxholes because sometimes rats were in them," Clara reported. "People didn't take the lone Jap plane very seriously. We named it, 'Wash Machine Charlie'.

"However, one night the Japanese did drop a bomb. It fell between the airstrip and the Evacuation Hospital where I worked. It killed a cow. On the spot where it fell, someone put up a sign, 'Here lies Bossy.'"

Entering Dachau
Told by Bob Reckling, Crete. 1945.

By the time I went into combat, the lines defining the bulge made by the Nazi counter-attack were being forced back toward Germany. For us, cleaning the enemy out of the towns we encountered was the most dangerous part of the fighting.

I will never forget one town where the buildings were well defended by the Nazis. Retaking the town required house-to-house fighting. I don't care to talk about it because, even though the Allies won in the end, I lost some of the best buddies I ever had there. I would be glad to give back my medals, including the Bronze Star, if I could have those good fellows at my side again.

As we neared Munich, we were told to hold back. The Russians were to be allowed to take that area. Dachau was close, and we moved that direction.

We were told we were going to enter the infamous concentration camp. We assumed we were going to liberate the prisoners held there. As we neared it, the odor was overwhelming. I don't know how the citizens in the area stood it.

Entering the camp was a revolting experience, for thousands of the prisoners had been killed. Boxcars were piled high with the dead waiting to be burned. I saw only one crematory, but however many there were, they couldn't take care of all the bodies that were gassed in the huge showers. As I gazed at those packed train cars, I wondered how many thin, starved bodies it took to fill a boxcar. It was a mind-boggling, sickening sight.

The rear echelon was left to deal with camp problems, and we were sent to an old castle for rest and recuperation. Soon after, the war in Europe ended.

Gene Workhad fun his Dad

Wounded on Negros Island
About Tony Dobrovolny, Atkinson. 1945.

Early in 1945, Pvt. Anton (Tony) D. Dobrovolny went into front line duty on Negros Island, which is one of the central islands of the Philippines. Those days under enemy fire were endless days--more endless, even, than his days in the hay field when he was ten. He was wounded on April 27th after having been on the front line for seventeen days.

Anton D. Dobrovolny

They had been under heavy artillery attack. Then there was a lull in the firing. They waited in the silence, not moving a muscle, knowing a mere tremor in the tall grass where they were hidden would give their position away to the Japanese. The minutes dragged.

One soldier, a new replacement, decided to sneak a quick peek. When he lifted his head, he revealed their position. Enemy shelling resumed, this time on target.

A mortar shell fell nearby, and shrapnel exploded in every direction. One piece went through Tony's left arm and into his lung. Another hit him in the right hip. A third removed a portion of two toes on his left foot. Of course, it was the lung wound that concerned him most.

"So much air was whistling out of the jagged wound that I thought there was no way I could take that much air in through my nose," he later reported. The injured lung collapsed, but he managed to gasp some air into his right one. He was bleeding profusely.

Eventually, Tony received medical aid and was flown to a hospital on Luzon. Whenever he was conscious, he figured his life was hanging by a thin thread that could sever at any moment. He knew he was correct in that assumption when a Catholic priest came through the ward. Tony had listed his religion as Protestant, but the priest stopped at his bed and asked him to repeat some prayers after him. Tony recognized the prayers as those Catholics say when they are in danger of death.

He listened as the priest stopped to greet other patients. At no other bed did he ask a wounded man to repeat the prayer.

"But there was a new drug called penicillin," he said later. "They gave it to me on a regular basis. It was expensive, and I figure I got enough so the price of it could have bought Dad's whole cowherd. But it was all at the expense of our good uncle--the one we call Sam, that is."

When Tony was able, he wrote to his parents, attempting to reassure them. He said his wounds weren't bad. "They got the piece of shrapnel out of my lung right away," he said.

The full truth of the matter was that, while they removed some of the shrapnel, the largest portion was lodged in a place so near his heart it could not be safely removed. He will carry it the rest of his life.

After several muggy months in a Philippine hospital, he was able to return to the USA. He was discharged from the army on September 8, 1945. He moved to Boulder, and using the GI Bill, he enrolled in the University of Colorado. After graduating as a Civil Engineer, he reenlisted in the army during the Korean War. This time he served as an officer and an engineer.

A Wrong Report
Told by Harry Dobrovolny, Ross, ND.

The report that I was dead was obviously untrue, for I was standing there reading it. I had been in the navy since before the war began, and was in most of the major battles in the Pacific. Shortly before the Allies took Manila back from the Japanese, I was wounded in the Philippines.

In addition to being burned on my arms and shoulders, I had shrapnel in the back of my head and a bullet in my neck. I spent a considerable amount of time in hospitals and on hospital ships.

When we were being shipped home to the States, there were some dead soldiers that were sent at the same time. Each body was covered with a blanket on which the person's name was written. For some reason, there was no blanket for one body. The caretakers looked around for something to cover it. They found a blanket and used it.

It happened that it was one of my blankets, and my name was inscribed on it. Thus for a time, my name became attached to that particular body.

One of the guys on our ship credited me with saving his life. We were near Manila and were bombarding the beach. The Japanese, in desperation, began sending Kamikaze planes (suicide planes) at our ship. There were horrible injuries, and the ship was on fire.

When the third Kamikaze hit us, one sailor was overcome with the horror.

"They won't stop until we burn up and sink," he said. "I'm going to jump overboard. I'd rather drown than be burned to a crisp in this blast furnace of a ship."

"Don't do it," I told him. "We still have a chance. They wouldn't be sending Kamikazes unless they were about done for. Hang on. We might make it yet."

I was wounded soon thereafter, and didn't see him for some time. When we next met, he thanked me and said I had saved his life.

Signing the Japanese Surrender Document.
Told by Daryl Ream, Alexandria. 1945.

We were stationed on Luzon and were preparing for the invasion of the main islands of Japan. We partly ignored and partly hid our apprehension, for all knew the invasion would bring about wholesale slaughter on both sides. Then an atomic bomb was dropped. When the first bomb did not persuade the Japanese to surrender, a second was dropped.

The day we heard the Japanese had sued for peace, we were on a ship, practicing how to make an amphibious landing. As soon as we received the report, we were taken back to southern Luzon where we immediately began dismantling our tents and packing our gear. Since the Philippines are near the equator, our jubilation was somewhat subdued by the heat.

We went by truck down the Batangas Peninsula to where a troop ship was anchored. There was no harbor there, so we rode on landing crafts (LCIs) to the ship. Our ship moved up the coast of Luzon where we joined a huge convoy, which was also heading for Japan. There were troop carriers, hospital ships, destroyers, destroyer escorts, freighters, ships of every size and description. They were all loaded with Allied troops or with supplies.

I don't remember how long we were en route to Japan, but perhaps about a week. A convoy travels at the speed of the slowest ship, but I believe the *USS Missouri* was in the lead and moved ahead at a faster pace. It was early morning,

September 2, the day of the signing, when we moved into Tokyo Bay.

Since there was a multitude of GIs, it took several hours for us to climb down the cargo nets into the LCIs, where we waited. The entire bay was swarming with a huge array of LCIs--many hundreds!

As soon as the signing of the surrender document had been completed, the signal corps sent a message, and the multitude of LCIs converged toward the shores of Japan. It was a memorable sight. It reminded me of a busy ant colony with all the ants streaming toward the hill.

In spite of our elation that the war was over, we felt some apprehension as we faced the new situation of disembarking in Japan, the home of our recent enemy. Our boat landed in Yokohama, which is near Tokyo.

When we reached shore, we were met with organized confusion. The first night we stayed in a warehouse, and the second, we stayed in a vacated Japanese army camp. Later we were loaded into trucks and moved to Tokyo.

Because of heavy bombing during previous months, most of the population had left Tokyo and were living in rural areas or in the mountains. Now the roads were filled with a constant stream of walking people who were returning to their homes in the capital city. They, on the whole, found only rubble when they arrived.

I was stationed in Tokyo for more than a year, and acted as postmaster for the 7th Cavalry Regiment.

Refusal to Surrender
From newspaper clippings, 1945-1974

Japanese soldiers were trained to fight to the death rather than to surrender. It was a disgrace to give up. Thus some soldiers who were not killed at the end of fighting remained in hiding on remote islands. They knew nothing of the atomic bomb and could not believe Japan had surrendered. Some of them stayed hidden for ten, twenty, or even thirty years.

Two of the more famous ones were Sgt. Shoichi Yokoi, who remained hidden for 26 years, and Lt. Hiroo Onada, who hid for 30 years.

Yokoi hid on Guam. He ate whatever he could find: coconuts, papaya, fish, snails, and even rodents. He made cloth from the fibers of wild plants and lived in an underground cave. After nearly three decades of hiding, wild game hunters discovered him.

Onoda remained hidden in the Philippines from 1945 until the spring of 1974. At the end of the war, the Allies dropped leaflets announcing the surrender of Japan, but Onoda thought it was propaganda. Besides, he felt he could not return home since obviously, he had not died fighting.

After three decades, he emerged from the jungle. His commanding officer came to the Philippines to reassure him and to encourage him to go home. He returned to Japan.

Lives Lost, Stuart-Atkinson area, World War II
Compiled by Albena Kramer, with the help of past issues of The Atkinson Graphic and also Before Today, a History of Holt County. Heartfelt apologies to the family of anyone whose name is omitted from this list.

To have an idea of the loss of life suffered during World War II, this list is offered. It includes only the area surrounding the two small towns of Stuart (pop. 650) and Atkinson (pop. 1,380.) Names are in alphabetical order.

Arthur Calvin Barthel, Stuart, was killed in action Sept. 11, 1943, aboard the *USS Savannah* near Salerno, Italy.

Dorson Berwin Brainard, Stuart, son of Mr. and Mrs. Fred Brainard, was killed in action in Italy on July 8, 1944.

Gordon Carl Carlisle, son of Mr. and Mrs. Ray Carlisle, Stuart, served in the Atlantic and the Indian Ocean. He was killed in Philadelphia, June 13, 1942.

HIS DAD WAS A BARBER
CUT MY HAIR

Henry K. Deermer, twin brother to Clara (Deermer) Vrooman, Atkinson, was stationed on an ammunition ship, the *USS Serpens*. A Japanese submarine torpedoed it on Jan. 29, 1945. He and his 250 shipmates were all lost.

Clayton J. Deseive, son of Mr. and Mrs. Ed Deseive, died in the service of his country in March 1945.

Howard Dexter, son of Mr. and Mrs. Frank Dexter, Atkinson, died in the service of his country.

Wilson H. Everett died of a heart attack at the Chicago Naval Base on April 19, 1945.

Charles Paul Goldfuss, son of George and Josephine Goldfuss, died on Iwo Jima on Apr. 19, 1945. Also on that day, Ernie Pyle, a popular news reporter, was killed on Iwo Jima. Ernie and Charles were buried in the same cemetery a few graves apart.

Robert Emery Jungman, son of Mr. and Mrs. Francis Jungman, Atkinson, died in France, Nov. 27, 1944.

Joseph Mack, son of Mr. and Mrs. Fred Mack, Atkinson, was killed in a plane crash during the Battle of the Bulge, Dec. 31, 1944.

Ercielle R. Ninas, Stuart, son of Mr. and Mrs. Robert Ninas, was killed in action in France, Aug. 2, 1944.

Robert Miller was killed in service during World War II.

George Francis Schneider, son of Mr. and Mrs. Frank Schneider, Stuart, was wounded at St. Lo, France, and died on Aug. 10, 1944.

Ivan W. Seger, son of Mrs. Eve Seger, Atkinson, died in Germany on Aug. 28, 1945.

Louis Tushla, son of Peter and Susan Tushla, Atkinson, died on the *USS Arizona* in Pearl Harbor on December 7, 1941. His body was never recovered, and neither was that of his brother, Harold, listed next.

Harold Tushla, son of Peter and Susan Tushla, was an airplane pilot and was killed in battle over the Mediterranean Sea near Italy.

Norman Wilson, stepson of Sam Brady, Atkinson, was killed during World War II.

Burtis Wood, Atkinson, was killed in action during World War II.

Harry H. Zahradnecek was killed on Luzon in the Philippines on May 3, 1945.

Prison Guard
Told by Mark Romohr, Gresham. 1946.

After the war, when the Nazi criminals were being tried in Nuremberg for war crimes, I was one of the guards. I was assigned to take the prisoners, one at a time, from their cells to the Palace of Justice where they met with their attorneys.

At the time, there were a total of twenty-one prisoners, including Himmler, who had organized the SS, Heydrich who had been prominent in setting up machinery to eliminate the Jews, Goering who had developed the brutal Gestapo and had created the first concentration camps, and Keitel who had led the purging of the intelligencia in conquered countries.

During the meetings, the prisoners were not restrained, but were closely supervised by guards at all times. I sat beside whichever prisoner I was escorting. Sometimes the meeting might be an hour long, but other times, it might be six or seven hours.

Probably I'd have found the conversation interesting, but they spoke in German and I didn't understand much of it. Sometimes the attorneys left the room, and then I might converse with the prisoners, most of whom spoke some English.

They were men who had committed the most despicable crimes against humanity, and yet they looked and acted like ordinary people. They were intelligent, well-educated, polite, disciplined men, but they had been carried away by their desire to be among those supposedly elite individuals who would some day, they thought, rule the world.

Skunks on the South Place
Told by H.T. (Tom) Dobrovolny, Atkinson. 1944.

Dad [Joe Dobrovolny] was trapping skunks from under the vacant house at the South Place. LeRoy and Tony were both in the service, so I helped Dad all I could on weekends when I was home from high school. One Saturday after we had fed the cows on the South Place, we checked the traps and there was a skunk in one. We always carried a rifle in the pickup, but for some reason, we had come in the car and had no gun.

The skunk was under the window of the bedroom, and strange as it may seem, hadn't yet sprayed the area. We didn't want to stink the house if we could help it.

"I've heard," said Dad, "that skunks can't spray if you lift them by the tail. They have to brace their back legs before thy can eject the scent, and when you hold them by the tail, they aren't in a position to brace their legs."

"I don't know about that," I said doubtfully. "I wouldn't bet on it."

"I know it sounds funny, but various animals have strange habits. For instance, a female wolf won't fight in her own den. I'd heard it many a time, but didn't believe it until a little wiry fellow in South Dakota told me how he crawled into a wolf den and tied a rope on one. The wolf didn't do a thing in her den, but she sure tore things up once they pulled her out."

I felt skeptical, especially about the skunk. I hoped Dad wouldn't tell me to yank the animal up by its tail.

He was studying the situation.

"We ought to lift him suddenly but can't because of the stake in the ground. I'll count and when I say three, I'll grab his tail and you pull the stake."

It worked. Dad soon had the skunk dangling in the air.

"Now what?" I asked. "No gun."

"There's a short-handled spade in the car trunk," he said. "Get it."

I returned, armed with the spade. He was holding the animal at arm's length.

"Whack him hard on the back of the neck with the side of the blade. Hard enough to knock him out and break his neck."

I knew how to kill rabbits that way, but they had a larger skull. I took careful aim at the small, tapered head, and swung. It killed the skunk, but reflexes took over. He sprayed Dad in the face.

Dad cried out, and his hands flew to cover his eyes. It scared the dickens out of me. I took him by the arm and led him, gasping and moaning, to the stock tank. Over and over, he splashed water on his face.

We had some extra clothes in the old house, and since he couldn't open his eyes, I helped him change. We didn't want to stink up the car any more than we had to. When we got home, Mom put several quarts of warm tomato juice in a tub out in the washhouse, and I helped him rub it on his body. It was supposed to absorb the odor, but it didn't help a whole lot. He couldn't see a thing for the rest of the afternoon, and it was days before the odor completely disappeared.

When the story got around the neighborhood, we were the objects of a considerable number of jokes.

The Mules and the Scrap Iron
Told by Joan (Steinhauser) Dobrovolny. Stuart.

During World War II, people were encouraged to collect scrap iron. When Josephine Mlinar taught our school, she took us to a junk pile on a vacant place about a mile away to gather discarded metal objects. The Flannerys owned it, and they gave us permission. Between our school and the junk pile was a pasture owned by Hubert Kohle. A herd of about twenty-five mules grazed there.

On the way we walked on a road that went around the pasture. Once reaching the junk pile, we happily went to work collecting iron articles. We found an old baby buggy with a broken wheel, and we energetically loaded metal pieces into it. Larger articles we carried in our arms. By then excitement, effort, and the hot sun had tired us.

We decided we could save some of our waning energy by cutting across Hubert's pasture. We took turns pushing the rickety, over-loaded baby buggy. Its bent wheel made it lurch with every turn.

Halfway across the pasture, the mules sighted us and came thundering in our wake, braying loudly. We tore off, running as fast as we could push that jerky buggy. When the mules got close, they thundered back and forth behind us, chasing us all the way to the fence.

The din was terrible. Twenty-five braying, galloping mules can make a racket that vibrates both earth and sky. Not one of us ventured into that pasture again.

Fishhook Accident
About John Dobrovolny, Atkinson. 1943.

When John Dobrovolny was ten years old, his father, Joe, took him and his brother, Fred, fishing in Wright's Lake. John got a fishhook caught in the fleshy part of his palm. They walked home where there was a discussion about what to do. In addition to the fact that wartime gas rationing was strict, the roads were exceptionally muddy, and his father, Joe, wasn't sure if they could get to town. To complicate matters, it was a dark night.

Joe examined the injury. Certainly, the barbed hook could not be backed out.

"I know what the doctor will do," said Joe. "He will shove it on through, cut off the barb, and then pull it out backwards."

He debated. Could he, himself, do it and save fighting through eighteen miles of muddy roads? He decided to burn the gas, battle the roads, and have the doctor deal with the fishhook. An older son, Tony, went along.

The worst mud hole was about five miles down the road near Lawrence Pacha's place. They crossed on planks someone had already laid over it.

"The doctor deadened my hand before shoving the hook on through." said John. "Then he did like Dad said. He cut the barb off and pulled the hook out backwards."

The Young Electrician
Told by John Teter, Holdrege. 1940s.

Dad had bought a short wave radio in the early thirties. Then some years later, probably in the early forties, he hauled some calves to the sale. The reason he sold calves was because all the older livestock was mortgaged. He came home with a new radio.

That was good news for me because I got the old radio. I had always been interested in electrical and mechanical things. Now I was excited to have my own radio complete with a microphone so I could hook it up to one of the tubes and talk over it.

I strung fine horsehair wire all about the house. I could broadcast to any room I chose. Once Mother chided me about the wires strung inside the house, but I saw myself as an inventor.

I asked her: "Do you think Thomas Edison's mother complained about the wires he strung in their house?"

One day Mom was having a club meeting at our place. I decided to extend my broadcasting area a little farther. I strung wires from the house to the windmill tower, and then down to the outhouse. I put a speaker in the peak of the tiny roof.

Some of my friends and I observed from a window in the house. Finally our watchfulness paid off. One of the ladies, Esther Zeller, went outside and down the path toward the toilet. We waited until she had gone inside and had closed the door. Then I spoke into the microphone.

"Why, how do you do!"

The door flew open and she spun out of there. She raced around the little building, looking for the culprit who had disturbed her. Once she was satisfied no one was near, she again went inside.

After the door closed, we turned on some music. The door burst open again and out she came. Around the building she went, first one way and then the other. Finally she stomped back to the house.

When she found out who had wired the toilet, I'm told she was amused. Now all these years later, I can't live it down. Every time we go to Bartley, someone is sure to tell about it.

As more people in the neighborhood got newer radios, I acquired more old ones. Also I built a crystal set. My electronic equipment *was* stretching the limits of our home. Finally, it came to my dad's attention that Dave Beeman had an old building down by the creek that he didn't want. Dad tore it down, moved the lumber home, and built a little shop for me. It was about 8 feet by 12, but to me it was a grand building.

One of out neighbors had an electric prod for loading cattle. I began to figure out how I could make one. I used two flashlight batteries wired to a Model T coil and was proud of the results.

Once a year we had to take "the animal" to the pasture to put him with the cows. In those days, it wasn't polite to use a coarse term such as "bull" in the company of women and children. He was called "the animal." On this particular day, Dad was trying to load the animal into our less-than-sturdy homemade trailer.

Dad was pulling on the rope, and Don, my brother who was three years my senior, was pushing and whacking the critter with a board. The stubborn animal braced his feet and wouldn't go. I raced for my shop to get the prod. My legs were really spinning because I was afraid they would get him loaded before I had a chance to try out my fine invention.

I made it in time! I ran up and gave the animal a jab with the prod. He reared up on his hind legs and then ran through the front of the trailer into the back of the car. He took off, dragging Dad on the rope.

"Oh, boy!" I thought. "Dad's gonna kill me now."

But he finally got control of the animal, and led him back to the trailer. I must have tamed him, for he calmly walked in. Dad and Don fixed the front of the trailer and headed for the pasture.

We had a dog that we named Grumpy after one of the dwarves in the Snow White book. He was a light color, yellow I think, but since I'm color blind, I don't know for sure. Grumpy was subject to fits.

Periodically he'd begin yipping and running around the yard in circles. After he looped the house several times, he'd head for the toilet and jump down the hole. It was no easy job to free him. We had to remove the floor, pull him out, and wash him off. Then he'd be fine for a month or two.

Once we were out in the field putting up the electric fence. I suppose we needed to put the cows on the wheat stubble. Our posts and materials were in a horse-drawn wagon. As we worked, our well-trained horses took care of the wagon. When we moved forward, they automatically moved ahead to stay abreast of us.

Suddenly, Grumpy got one of his fits. There wasn't anything else to circle, and so he ran, yipping and yelping, around the team and wagon. The horses were frightened and since no one was in the wagon to control them, they ran away.

They galloped to the end of the field, scattering tools and staples in their wake. Finally the corner of the wagon caught on the fence. They pulled loose and ran all the way to the water tank before they stopped.

This time the dog got over his fit without jumping down the toilet hole.

210

Sunbonnets
Told by John Teter, Holdrege. 1940s.

The Tommy Sammons family lived in our neighborhood. I can't think that I ever heard his wife's name. We simply called her Mrs. Sammons. She and their daughters, Millie Mae and Essie, wore old-fashioned sunbonnets whenever they went outside.

Once we drove by and saw a girl standing in the garden watching us. She didn't make a single move. We finally caught on. It was a realistic scarecrow that was wearing a big sunbonnet. Since it fooled us, it probably fooled the birds, also.

One day during harvest time, Earl Moore and I drove into the Sammons' yard. The door flew open and a girl wearing a bonnet burst out. She was wringing her hands.

"Oh dear! Oh dear!" she wailed. "What're we gonna' do? The milo is hot! The milo is hot!"

The milo had been binned when it contained too much moisture, which had caused it to heat and smoke. It was necessary to haul it to town and sell it.

Boy Meets Girl
John and Marva Teter, Holdrege. 1930s-40s.

When I was a kid, reported John Teter, families went to house dances in the neighborhood. The kids all played outside while the adults danced. I recall one time when two little girls had a couple branches about three or four feet long. They held them by the thicker part and tapped the end with the twigs along on the ground.

"Granddaddy longlegs! Granddaddy longlegs!" they kept chanting. They were giggling, and I thought they were silly. It so happens it was Marva and Donna Moore.

"I remember that," Marva said. "We didn't have much for toys, but we were happy. We had food and a few clothes made from feed sacks. Donna and I wore feed sack clothes

211

to school all the time. That's how we learned to sew--using feed sacks. They took a lot of starching and ironing though."

By the time we were in our early teens, John continued, those two girls looked a lot more attractive to me.

We had just started high school. For some reason, the school had a wiener roast about a mile south of town on the Smith place. On the way back to town, I saw the two Moore girls. I didn't know their first names, so I called out, "Hey Moore! Can I walk with you?"

Marva peeled off and we walked to town. After that we started going places together. I don't know what would have happened if Donna had peeled off to walk with me instead of Marva.

When I was a freshman, I wasn't old enough to have a driver's permit. We got invited to a birthday party for the Burton twins, Merlin and Marian. My brother Don had a date with Goldene Greenlee, so Marva and I went with them. Don drove a 1929 Model A roadster, and Marva and I rode in the rumble seat. It was cold out, so we covered with a quilt.

Once after I got a drivers permit to go to school, Marva and I were parked by the ballpark.

A state patrolman pulled up and parked by the highway. We had to cross that highway to get home. We sat still, hoping he would leave, but he was patient. Finally, after a lengthy wait, we decided we had to go home. I started up, and he immediately stopped me.

"Driver's license, Sonny," he said. How embarrassing to be called Sonny in front of my girlfriend.

"Permit," I answered as I dug in my pocket.

Then we had to listen to a long lecture on driver's permits, but he didn't give me a ticket.

Marva (Moore) Teter continues:

The first time I was impressed by John was when he came to pick me up for MYF (Methodist Youth Fellowship)

212

on a Wednesday evening. I was staying in town with my grandmother while I attended high school. That was more than half a century ago, but I still remember what he wore. He had a nice trouser and sweater outfit, and had a camel colored overcoat. He looked stunningly handsome, and was remarkably polite. I couldn't get him off my mind after that.

Since we were less than a year apart in age, my sister Donna and I had always been playmates and best friends. We followed through with a double wedding on January 29, 1950. I married John Teter and she married Darrel Burke.

John, Marva, Darrel, Donna

A Mexican Rope
Told by Jay Dobrovolny, Atkinson.

I carried a Mexican lariat during the war. At the time, it was difficult to get good rope because of military needs. My rope was 72 feet long, and even though it was lighter than an ordinary lariat, it was guaranteed in Mexico not to break.

I had to be careful, though. When I roped a critter, I tried to keep him from hitting the end of the rope or it would break. That's how good that guarantee was.

My Uncle Fred told me, "You've got to remember those Mexican cattle are light weight in comparison to ours. Our cows are blocky, but theirs are built in the shape of a mosquito. Probably in Mexico the rope was strong enough."

Near Disaster
Told by Marie Kramer, Stuart. 1943.

I shouldn't have done it, and I'm embarrassed to admit that I did. But circumstances piled up that day, and desperate to perform the job set for me, I made an unwise choice.

Did I know how to handle horses? Of course, I would have said. I'd grown up on a ranch and had ridden from childhood.

"Now, don't pull hard on the reins," cautioned my father when I first began to ride. "They are fastened to the bit in the horse's mouth. You pull just a little when you say whoa, as a kind of warning. The only time you pull hard is if the horse starts to buck or run. Then pull as hard as you need to in order to bring him under control."

The horses we kids rode, Paint and Peanuts, were well trained, and needed more encouragement to make them go than to persuade them to stop. We loved our horses and were careful to keep them comfortable.

Dad hired men to work in the hay field, and it was against his principles to have girls work in the same field with hired men. But my sisters-in-law had worked in their family hay crew from the time they were eight or nine years old, all of them handling horses. By now the two older girls had married and had moved away. Only days after I married into the Krysl family, the remaining girl went to Omaha to work in a wartime airplane factory.

Like most ranchers during the war, my new father-in-law, V.J., was short-handed in the field. It seemed I had arrived in the family in the nick of time.

I was given the junior job, that of driving the stacker team. V.J. drove the truck sweep, brother-in-law, Bill, age 17, raked, using a three-horse team, and my new husband Don stacked. Don mowed in the mornings and evenings while Bill helped his mother with the milking chores, sharpened sickles, and helped V.J. with any repair jobs. As for me, I was given no instructions because everyone supposed I knew how to handle horses.

"Keep an eye on this team for awhile," cautioned V.J. as he handed me the lines of the horses, Ted and Ranger. "They've been running free over the winter and are a little frisky. But they'll settle down after a day or two."

I had no trouble getting the horses to pull the loads of hay up the stacker boards and drop them in the stack. But getting them to back up to the stacker was a problem. They just wouldn't back. I shouted at them.

"Back up! Back!"

Half-heartedly they'd take a few steps back then stop. I needed to handle the long, trailing lines with one hand and carry the heavy, iron-tipped double tree with the other. Carrying the double tree was the result of V.J.'s unique method of double-threading the rope in the stacker. When the buck was loaded and going up, the tautness of the rope held the double tree in mid air, but when backing up, it drug on the ground and got in the way of the hind feet of the horses.

By the third day, the team had quieted considerably. I, however, was worn out from pulling on the double tree in an attempt to back the horses. Sweat poured off me, and I was as red as a fire truck. If I'd have pulled on the lines and tightened the bits in the horses' mouths, I'd have gotten results. But oddly it never occurred to me.

After finishing a stack, we moved around a low spot to reposition and stake down the stacker. While we were thus involved, VJ had time to shove five or six heavy loads of slough grass in position to put over the stacker in quick succession once it was set.

I drove one load over, and Don backed the team before he went to the stacker to begin forming the stack butt. The second load went over, but the horses that had backed so easily for Don were not responding to my commands. I tugged at the double tree and yelled.

V.J. was soon in front of the stacker with another load.

"Back up!" he bellowed. "Get that buck down!"

I yanked at the double tree with the frail strength of my one available hand, but it could have been a flea tugging on the traces. It should have occurred to me that one couldn't back horses by yanking on the mechanism that pulls enormous loads.

"Hurry up! We're wasting time!" V.J. boomed.

If only I could pull on the double tree with both hands, I thought, maybe I could get the horses back. But what could I do with those long lines? Exhausted and hurried as I was, I decided to attempt to solve my problem in a grossly unwise way. I flipped the lines into a loose circle from shoulder to shoulder, which released my second hand to pull on the double tree.

Just then Bill and his clattering rakes came swooping around the stacker the outside rake swinging in a noisy arc as he swerved to miss my team.

Ted leaped into the air, laid back his ears, and jumped forward, startling both Ranger and me as he did so. In what must have been one of the fastest and the most fortunate moves in my life, I grabbed the looped lines, ducked my head, and flipped the leather straps off my shoulders.

Now I knew what to do. To control horses you pull on the lines. I dug in my heels, shouted, and hung on as the horses dragged me until the stacker buck hit the top of the stacker arms. The team slowed under the weight of the staked-down stacker, and pawed the ground. Lumber cracked and splintered. Wildly, the horses clawed forward until the heavy stacker was yanked loose from the stakes. By then, V.J. and Bill had closed in from opposite sides and had grabbed the bridle bits of the struggling team.

The near-disaster frightened all of us, and family members to this day shake their heads grimly when they tell the story.

"The worst part of it was," they mutter darkly, "she had the lines around her neck." Possibly when I'm not present, the word "stupid" floats around.

The next year, V.J. changed the stacker mechanism from a double-thread to a single-thread. It made carrying the double tree unnecessary, and also shortened the rope so the horses didn't have to back so far. Even so, I was glad when I graduated from stacker-team-driving to running the rakes, which by then were pulled by a tractor.

When the Fuel Pump Broke
Told by Amelia Kaup, Stuart. 1946.

We were packed in a 1937 Ford, and with eight people in the car, there was not an inch of space to spare. In the front were brother Don, our mother, Anna, and my five-year-old son, Milton. In back were brother Bill, my sister-in-law Marie, sister Tina, and I with my toddler, Danny. It was a hot day, there was no air conditioning, and even though we were accustomed to being crowded, we were anxious for the trip to end. Our mother, unable to stand heat at that point in her life, had a bursting headache, and Marie probably was as uncomfortable as was I, for we both were planning for a new baby later in the summer.

Don decided to shorten the trip by cutting across a large pasture, but when we got in the middle of it, the car motor died. He and Bill got out and lifted the hood. Bill came back and announced the fuel pump had quit.

"Now what?" I asked.

"Well, its about four miles home. If we have to, I can run home and come back with the tractor," said Bill.

"The tractor has no road gear," Mom grumbled. "In this heat, we'll all suffocate before you return."

"Well, Don is thinking. He'll probably figure a solution."

"There's no way a car can run without a fuel pump," Mom stated. "You just as well hoof it for home. But what are we going to do with this hot, fussy child?"

"Just wait," stated Bill. "You know Don. He'll figure something out." We all had confidence in Don's natural mechanical ability, but we were in the middle of nowhere with no tools and no extra parts.

Don had one foot on the front bumper, an elbow on his knee, and his head cupped in his hand. Obviously, he was pondering our plight. Finally he called to Bill. "Look in the trunk. Tell me everything we have back there. Everything."

Bill soon called, "We have two screw drivers, a vice grip wrench, a wheel wrench, some groceries, a diaper bag, a case of pop, a jack, and a spare tire."

"Pass out the pop. We need some empty bottles. Is there anything for a siphon?"

"No. No hoses of any kind."

While we sipped the tepid pop, Don came to the door on the driver's side and opened it. He felt along the gasket on the side of the doorframe, found a frayed place, and dug in his fingers. A ripping sound told us he had found something he needed and was claiming it. It was a small rubber tube meant to make the door airtight.

"Do you have an extra baby bottle nipple?" he asked.

"I have two bottles. This one is nearly empty. You can have the nipple from it," I answered.

Employing the hose, the boys siphoned gas from the gas tank into the pop bottles. Then they put the nipple on one of the bottles, and using a screwdriver, poked a larger hole in the nipple. They put the hose through the hole and into the bottle of gas. Bill sat on a fender, and inserted the other end of the hose into the carburetor. He could lift the bottle to allow the gas to flow, or pinch the hose to slow it down.

After some trial and error, they got the car started. It took more experimentation to figure out how to let air into the bottle so the gas could flow out. We were soon jerking and popping down the pasture trail. Bill had the extra bottles of gas secured someplace between his leg and the hood of the car, and got so good at changing an empty bottle for a full one that he could do it without killing the motor. Several times, though, we had to stop to siphon more gas from the gas tank into the bottles.

One thing I learned that day was what a difference it makes in gas consumption when a driver revs a motor. On solid ground, the gas flowed slowly out of the bottle. However, as soon as we hit a muddy place where we needed more power, the gas gurgled out in huge gulps.

We got home without further mishap.

The Navigator in Dick Shearer's Crew
As told by Pauline Miller. Decades later.

After the World War II book, *Out of Barbed Wire*, was published, Lily Shearer, wife of Dick, searched out the families of Dick's crewmates and sent copies of the book to them. Pauline Miller, the wife of the injured navigator, wrote back to Lily and said her husband had survived. (Dick and his crewmates had shoved him, unconscious, out of the plane before they themselves had baled out over Nazi Germany. Dick did not know if he had survived.)

Miller had been blinded when Plexiglas was blown into his face by an anti aircraft shell. Pauline reported that when the crew shoved him out of the plane, the sudden cold air outside had revived him and he was able to open his parachute.

He was taken prisoner by the Nazis immediately and sent to a hospital. First he was told that he would lose one eye. Then another doctor reviewed his case and said he might save the eye if Miller would give permission for him to try something experimental. The eye, though impaired, was saved.

At this writing, Miller and his wife, Pauline, live in Tennessee.

"He has had a good life," she reported.

Brief flashes from the times:
Hitler gave special preferences to people who possessed the qualities he wished to encourage in the "Super Race" he was attempting to build. German families were encouraged (actually paid) to have as many children as possible. But Hitler especially preferred tall, blonde, blue-eyed parents.

SS members were told to father as many children as possible, especially with fair-skinned women. They were encouraged to look to any occupied country that tended to be peopled by blondes. According to Carol J. Williams of the Los Angeles Times, a program in Norway, called "Lebensborn" produced about 11,000 children who had Nazi fathers.

In *People's Century, 1900-1999,* Godfrey Hodgson reports: "In Warsaw the Germans allowed themselves 2,300 calories a day. The Poles were allowed 900 calories a day [while] the ration for Jews [was] only 183 calories. This was deliberate starvation."

Told by Earl Frieden, Shickley:

In 1944 Robert Witt, age 20, was a member of a 10-man crew that flew out of New Guinea and never returned. About 50 years later, a small piece of wreckage was discovered in a New Guinea jungle. Research traced it to the missing bomber and the crash site was located.

Human remains were gone, but dog tags and aircraft debris identified the plane and the crew.

In April of 1998 relics from Robert Witt and his crewmembers were placed in a common grave in Arlington Cemetery. Chuck Witt of Doniphan and Delbert Witt of Geneva, brothers of Robert, were among the relatives who attended the memorial service.

BABY

Lawrence Kramer children: Susan, Rollin, Greg, Dan.

Back: Larry Skrdla, Shirley Skrdla, Charles Krobot. Front: Don and Ron Skrdla.

Ray Kramer children: Donna, RoseAnn, Pat, Cousin Brenda, Joseph, Ed, Mary Ann.

June and Elva Berryman

BOOMERS

1946

Helen, Patti,
John J. Dvorak

Dick, Lil, and
Mary Lynn Shearer

Denzel McClatchey,
Nancy, and Donna

Herb Tracy with
Mike and Craig

Uncle Tom Maneely with
Doug and Pam

Bob Heine
and
Doug

Don Krysl and Snookie dig out the barn again.

Judy, 2, in the back yard.

Winter of 1948-1949, South of Stuart, Nebraska.

Don, hungry for potatoes, digs out the cellar.

Chapter 5

Baby Boomers and Blizzards

The Grandchildren of the Pioneers were producing a bumper crop of babies. Big bands and jitterbugging were popular. No one was prepared for the repeated blizzards during the last year of the decade.

The Hay Baler and the Airplane
Told by Aloys Kaup, Stuart. Late 1940s.

Several servicemen who had been fliers in WWII had purchased airplanes after they returned to their ranches. They used them to check the cattle and windmills, hunt coyotes (the sport soon became illegal), fly to town to get repairs for machines, and goof around if they could afford the gas.

"We were baling hay on Fennison's quarter," said Aloys Kaup. "Don and Bill Krysl were pitching the hay, I was feeding it into the machine, V.J. Krysl was tying the bales, and a fifth person was piling the 70-pound finished bales. Also it was the duty of the person who piled bales to backwire (insert the baling wires so the one who was tying could grab them and tie.")

One day a neighborhood pilot was flying around, and saw our crew at work. He decided to startle us by diving low over our heads. The noise of the tractor and baler drowned out the drone of the plane, and we were not aware of its approach until it was nearly on us. Startled, Bill and Don threw themselves flat on the stack.

I was the one that nearly met my doom. I was busy and didn't see the plane approaching. It came directly over my head, and the sudden roar and the wind startled me. I lost my balance and fell toward the mouth of the machine. I saved myself by grabbing a lever.

We five men on the baling crew have often recalled the incident. Ordinarily we could appreciate a joke, but not this one. Can you imagine what a man would look like if he fell into a hay baler?

Fish from Denmark
Told by Astrid Willadsen. 1947.

Chris and Astrid Willadsen and their four eldest children came to America from Denmark in 1947. At the time, they were expecting their fifth child. Some of Astrid's uncles and an aunt had come earlier.

A friend in Denmark had relatives in Harlan, Iowa, which was the place the Willadsens were going.

"In America, there aren't any lute fish," said the friend. "Will you take some along for our relatives?" Lute fish are considered a delicacy in Denmark.

"Of course," said the helpful Astrid. She accepted two brown bags of dried fish.

Once on the ship, they stored the fish in their cabin. When they set sail, Astrid immediately became seasick. The strong odor of the fish multiplied her problem.

Chris and the children enjoyed wonderful meals on the ship, but the seasick Astrid could not keep any food down. She felt like she would be immeasurably better if only she didn't have to smell those fish.

The family was on the ship for twelve days, and on the train, along with the fish, for two more.

"When we delivered them," said Astrid, "You may be sure I was glad to see--and smell--the last of them.

"But wait," she continued. "The next day the family invited us to their house for supper. They served the delicacy we had brought from Denmark. Lute Fish! I couldn't eat a thing. I said I hadn't yet recovered from my seasickness, which was, I guess, the truth."

Disappearance at Midnight
Told by Marcella Bigelow, Stuart. 1947.

It was bedtime when Dana Bigelow stood up from the chair by the radio and looked out the open door.

"There's a little breeze," he said to his wife, Marcella. "Let's go see if the windmill is running."

They lived in a large house in Stuart, and Dana, the grandson of the man who had founded the town, mainly dealt in hay and horses. Also, he had some cattle pastured near town. After supper he had checked on them and had found the water tank empty and the windmill motionless in the still, hot air. Now he would sleep better if he could see the mill was pumping.

"Oh, Dana," said Marcella. "I can't go and leave the children. What if one of them happened to wake up?"

"They never wake up this time of night. They won't know we're gone. We'll be back in a moment."

Reluctantly, Marcella accompanied him to the pickup. It was a short drive, and they would soon be back.

The mill was running, but it wasn't pumping. Something was disconnected. Dana took a flashlight, and climbed the tower. He soon returned and rummaged in the pickup box for tools. Marcella concentrated on remaining outwardly calm while she waited.

"The children are all right," she told herself. "Even if one of them wakes up, Marsha can handle the situation for a little while." But she was uneasy. Never before had she left the children home alone.

Nearly an hour had passed before they pulled into their driveway. Bounding from the car, Marcella hurried upstairs to the bed of the youngest. She was startled to see it empty, but soon decided the toddler had awakened and had gotten in bed with one of the older children. However, real terror smashed her in the chest when she found the girls' beds empty, and then also the boys'. She ran down the stairs, hysterical.

She raced wildly from room to room. "They're gone! All of them! They've been kidnapped." she screamed.

Dana caught her by the shoulders. "They've not been kidnapped," he said. "Who would kidnap six children?"

"Somebody did! They wouldn't just disappear by themselves." Marcella pulled herself free and ran sobbing through the house again.

Dana telephoned his mother. The kids weren't there. He called the village office. The night watchman hadn't seen any children, but he now would cruise the streets and look.

Dana collected the terrified Marcella, and they too drove around town. All the houses were dark and quiet. Dana was finding it more difficult to hide his own worry, and Marcella continued to be frantic.

Could the kids be hiding? They returned home and looked behind the furniture and in the closets.

"Maybe the neighbors heard something," sobbed Marcella. She ran to the house next door. Her neighbor answered her knock.

"Oh, Marcella. Calm yourself. The kids are right here, sleeping on the rug."

Marcella's tears did not immediately abate, but now they were tears of relief. The neighbor explained.

Marsha, about twelve, had been awakened by the pickup when her parents had left, and she had arisen to investigate. After finding that both parents were gone, she hurried upstairs and roused the other children.

They decided their parents had left them!

This terrifying thought clouded their sense of perspective. All their childish imperfections rolled through their minds and were magnified. Just this evening they had tumbled about in their beds, and had complained it was too hot to sleep. Now their parents, tired of it all, had left.

Finally the children decided to seek aid from their neighbor, and went next door. The good lady reassured them that their parents would be back. In the meantime, she would take care of them. Have no fear.

She invited them in, gave each a cool drink, and bedded them down on the rug in front of a fan. Cooled by the moving air, the children were soon lulled to sleep by the drone of the fan. The soothing whir also drowned the sounds of the returning parents, making the sleeping household unaware of the frantic search going on outside.

Uncle Freddie and his Old Buggy
Told by Lorene Perez, Colorado. 1940s.

My uncle, Freddie Ziska, was a friend to every child. Also, he was the main lineman for our farmer-owned telephone line located southwest of Atkinson. There were 15 to 18 other families on the line.

Freddie had kept his old horse-drawn buggy even though he had had a car for several decades. Since in many places, the telephone line went across meadows and pastures rather than along the road, a team and buggy was an ideal way to follow the line and look for breaks. Also, it provided a holiday for his children and his nieces and nephews because they considered "going telephoning with Papa (or Uncle Freddie)," to be the ultimate in entertainment.

Carrying a water jug, a lunch basket, and a stick for investigating gopher, rabbit, or badger holes, the children piled into the buggy. Away they went, following the winding telephone line around hills and through valleys. Sometimes the gentle Freddie allowed the children to take turns driving the equally gentle team, Silver and Maude.

Freddie watched for places where the line might be crossed by another line, for broken insulators, or for sagging wires. Wherever there was a problem, he stopped to repair it. The children piled out.

"Hi-ho, Silver!"

"Pow! Puh-pow! I'm Billie the Kid. I robbed the stage coach!"

The children, in a playground that reached from horizon to horizon, cavorted while Freddie repaired the line. In addition to their cop-and-robber games, they investigated animal holes, chased sand puppies (small, swift sand lizards), and raced up and down the hills. The water jugs, sometimes refilled at pasture windmills, were frequently passed from one thirsty child to the next.

I recall when we approached the Nightengale place near Atkinson, Uncle Freddie always sang an old song, one line of which is: "The nightingales are singing." Then he'd launch into other songs, such as "Turkey in the Straw," "Red Wing," or "The Barbara Polka." Sometimes while the horses plodded along, he pulled his mouth harp from his pocket, and played lively tunes.

It was a tired but happy group that arrived home after a day of "going telephoning with Uncle Freddie."

Hay Shed
Told by Marie Kramer, 1946.

When we moved onto our place south of Stuart in 1946, there was an open-faced cattle shed constructed of hay located southwest of the barn. The walls were about eighteen inches or two feet thick. Inside and out, they were made of chicken wire supported by posts, and then stuffed with hay. The roof was constructed of poles and chicken wire with a thick layer of hay on top.

I thought it was an ingenuous affair, a survivor from the past. I hoped I could get some film for my camera sometime soon, and take a picture of it.

I was teaching rural school District 205, and we had moved to our farm over the weekend. Monday when I came home from work, the shed was gone. Don had torn it down, and the hay, posts, and the neatly rolled wire were stacked in three separate piles.

"Don!" I exclaimed. "Why did you tear down that interesting old shed?"

"Interesting!" he answered disdainfully. "It was an eye-sore. I wanted to get it down before anyone saw it. There's plenty of space in the barn for our few cows." Don's parents had neat, well-painted buildings. To him, the hay shed was an embarrassment.

The only other hay shed I remember was one that had been constructed by my Great-Uncle John in the 1890s on the quarter east of Wright's Lake. It tumbled down and blew away, probably in the 1930s.

Bill's 21st Birthday
Told by Don Krysl, Stuart. Aug. 20, 1946.

My brother, Bill, was having a party on his twenty-first birthday. He wanted to include his cousin, Maxine Ziska, as a guest, but the telephone line was down. After church, he and Frank Krobot went to the Ziska place about four miles away to get her.

When they arrived, they saw the Ziskas weren't yet home from church. Bill, always full of mischief, began to plan. He and Frank hid the car behind the trees and went into the house. In those days, rural people had no reason to lock their houses while they were gone.

They decided to hide upstairs. When the family arrived, Sally Goldfuss, a woman who lived with them, went in the house first. Upstairs, Bill stomped on the floor.

"Albert! Mary!" shouted Sally as she ran outside. "Someone's upstairs!"

Albert and Mary went inside, and there was another stomp upstairs. Mary looked puzzled, but Albert's eyes were wide with concern. Then Bill plucked a ball from an upstairs toy box and tossed it down the stair well.

"Oh, you can't fool me!" shouted Mary in a loud voice. "Bill Krysl, you get down here!"

Bill and Frank came down, laughing, of course.

Mary was V.J.'s sister, and she was accustomed to Krysl jokes. In fact, she had played a few herself.

There was a need to prepare plenty of food for a Krysl party, but planning could stop there. Activities seemed to present themselves. Some guests might decide to swim in the swimming hole or to start a horseshoe-pitching contest. On this day, a volleyball game was interrupted when two of the girls got tossed in the horse tank.

Then a group decided to go boat riding on the pond north of the trees. Water was low, probably only about two and a half or three feet deep. Bill and Clarence Hamik took off their shoes and jumped out of the boat.

"Now you're going to get a good ride. We'll give you your money's worth!" said Bill to the girls. The boys began to rock the boat and spin it in circles.

The girls hung on and each did their share of screaming. Suddenly, some young muskrats vacated a rat house, and the boys were distracted long enough to give the girls a moment to consider revenge. Maxine looked in the bottom of the boat for Bill's shoes.

"There they are! Throw them overboard!" said her friend, pointing at a pair of black oxfords. Maxine grabbed the shoes and set them out of the boat.

Later, the boys looked for their shoes, and the girls discovered they had thrown Clarence's shoes overboard instead of Bill's. A search was successful for the shoes were floating on the pond like a pair of small boats.

At dawn on that same day, Bill's brother, Don, had driven into the yard of his parents, V.J. and Anna Krysl. All were in bed except his mother.

"I came to tell you, you have a new granddaughter," he said.

"Really!" she said in surprise. "It's funny Paul didn't call. He usually calls right away. How did you find out?" Amelia, Paul's wife, was her daughter and was waiting for a child, as was Don's wife, Marie. In spite of the doctor's predictions to the contrary, Anna was positive Amelia's child would arrive a month or so before Marie's.

"Paul's aren't the ones to have a new baby," said Don. "It's us. We have a little girl. We named her Judy."

Godfather and **Uncle Bill** on **Judy's** Christening Day

Judy always considered it a singular honor to have arrived on her Uncle Bill's birthday.

Ziska's Chamber Pots
Told by Sally Goldfuss, Stuart. 1940s.

At the time, there was no electrification in our area, and there wouldn't be for another decade. Since we had no indoor plumbing, the "little house out back" was yet a necessity as were the chamber pots under the beds. In the morning when the family members made their usual trips to the outhouse, each took his pot along and emptied it. Then it was placed upside down behind some tall plants in the flower garden.

One evening I was collecting the pots to take them inside. Strangely, they were all right side up, and in the gathering dusk, I could discern that something was inside.

"Mary!" I called. "Come here. What is this? It looks like a couple clods of dirt are in each one. How could that be?"

It took but one glance for Mary to figure it out.

"That Bill Krysl must have been here while we were in town," she said. "Those are clods of horse manure from the corral." Bill was Mary's nephew.

Painted Work Pants
Told by Norman Brown, Lincoln. Late 1940s.

When we were kids, our farm family was poor. We didn't realize we were poor at the time, but later, I knew we had been. Because Mother was good at gardening, canning, baking, churning, soap making, sewing, and could make-do with nearly nothing, we always had food of some sort on the table. At Christmas time, we were each pleased to get an orange and a pair of mittens or socks. We didn't expect more.

We picked corn by hand in those years. At the beginning of the picking season, the weather was reasonably pleasant, but we dreaded those cold, dark, mornings and evenings in the early winter.

We wore bib overalls. They were well worn before we began picking, but when they got thinner, Mother reinforced the legs with material from seed corn sacks. Nowadays, seed corn comes in strong paper bags, but at that time it came in bags of tightly woven material. After she patched our pants, they were much warmer.

When the patches began to wear, we painted the fronts of the legs, using leftover house paint. They were warm, for not a bit of wind came through the material.

In the fall, Mother and Dad drove to Nebraska City and loaded our '34 Chevrolet with apples. We kids couldn't go because the space was needed for apples. When they arrived home, we wrapped the apples individually in squares of newspaper. The apples, stored in the cellar, kept all winter.

For entertainment, we read. Our books were cheap pulp books such as Dick Tracy and Flash Gordon.

If our busy mother ever prepared a dessert for us, she made something we called "crik-pot". It was viewed as a family joke and she'd probably whop me if she were alive and knew I was telling about it. I wonder if the word "crik-pot" could have meant "Quick-pot".

The way I remember it, she put grease in a pan and dumped in some flour. Stirring, she let it brown. Then she added milk, vanilla or cinnamon, and a sweetener such as honey or sugar. We ate it like pudding.

I graduated from high school in 1949. After the corn picking was done the following fall, Dad (J.D. Brown) told me I could stay for the winter if I liked. I could work for my room and board, but he couldn't afford to pay me anything beyond that.

So I took a job shoveling corn at three cents a bushel for Ray Shuck. He contracted with various farmers to shell their corn. He hired two or three young fellows to shovel corn onto the conveyor belt that carried the corn to the sheller. The shelled corn went into trucks and was hauled either to storage buildings or sold.

Shoveling corn all day is hard work. Sometimes, to get a little break, we'd try to shovel fast enough to jam the machine. But if Ray saw a greater volume coming, he'd rev the motor so the machine wouldn't stall.

On March 17, 1950, I joined the Army.

Prince Albert Goes on a Cruise
Told by Don and Bill Krysl, Stuart.

The Tasler brothers loved to joke and tease. One day V.J. Krysl was drilling a well for one of them. In the 1940s the Krysl drilling equipment was mostly manual.

V.J.'s son, Don, turned the water pipe by hand so the drill bit on the end of it would bite down into the ground and loosen the soil below it. The pumps carried the detached soil up with the water that was circulated. V.J. turned the winch that allowed the pipe to settle lower into the earth.

The men had to be attentive in order to keep the pipe from getting stuck in the ground. As the work progressed, V.J. mentioned that his tobacco pipe had burned out. He was anxious to find time to refill it.

One of the Taslers, realizing how dependent V.J. was on his smoking supplies, reached over and slipped the can of Prince Albert tobacco out of his bib overall pocket. They tossed it from one to the other while V.J. worried the lid would fly open, and the tobacco would spill.

Finally, one of them teasingly said, "I'll bet Old Prince Albert would make a good sailor."

He placed the can on a small piece of wood and set it afloat in the swirling water hole that was fed by the returning water from the pumps. It sailed around in endless circles.

V.J. was concerned that his precious tobacco would get wet and thus be spoiled for smoking, but he could not leave his job to retrieve it. It would be hours before the job was completed and he'd be back home where he could get more tobacco.

When the hole was drilled, Don stepped to the water hole and retrieved his dad's tobacco. For the rest of the day, V.J. kept "Prince Albert" in a more secure place.

Blacksmoke's Train Wreck
Told by Willard Emerson, Western NE. 1940s.

Engineer Hess who was in charge of a steam-powered freight train running between North Platte, NE, and Cheyenne, WY, was often called Blacksmoke. He was a mischievous character and liked to provide plenty of work for the firemen who shoveled coal. He made the fire burn hotter and faster by giving it more draft. This action kept the firemen shoveling. It also made smoke spew out the smokestack in a huge, black roll, thus giving the engineer his nickname.

One day another train was stalled on the track. By the time Blacksmoke saw it, it was too late to stop his train. No one likes to be in an accident, but a train wreck is especially bad. In addition to the damage done by many tons of colliding steel, there was the danger that valves and lines be ruptured, allowing steam to spew forth. The furious fire burning in the firebox and the huge boiler of hot water were other dangers.

The anxious crew set the emergency brakes.

"Bale out!" shouted Blacksmoke! "Jump!"

The men needed no further urging. Soon each, unmindful of skinned elbows and sprained ankles, was rolling down the side of the railroad grade. As soon as Blacksmoke stopped tumbling, he jumped up and ran to the edge of the field where a farmer, seeing the desperate action, had stopped his tractor.

"Look! Look there!" Blacksmoke shouted, pointing at the track. "You're gonna see the most horrific wreck you'll ever see in your entire life!"

There was a deafening crash, buckling cars, spewing steam, and rolling volumes of black smoke, but no one was hurt. All had jumped out.

I never heard what regulation was broken or who was blamed for the wreck.

Another Outhouse Story
Told by Melba Dvorak, Atkinson. 1947.

"I need to take a trip down the little path," said Melba Dvorak one day when she and Rudy were visiting the neighbors.

Soon, she came hurrying back to the house, face flushed.

"There's a skunk under the toilet," she gasped. "Just as I sat down, I heard a noise and looked down. There he stood, his tail end pointed toward me in a threatening way. I got out fast!"

The men took the gun and went out. Even though it would cause a terrible stench, they decided to shoot the skunk.

It was good there were plenty of bushes on the place because it was days before the toilet aired out enough so it could be used.

Christmas Storm
Told by Jerlene Nielsen, Stromsburg. 1948.

My mother tried to call us in Oklahoma to tell us not to come home to rural York, Nebraska, because a blizzard was moving in. However, we were already on our way. My father, Jewell Matlock, my sister Luverne, my brother Delbert, and I had gone to Sapulpa, Oklahoma, to visit my grandmother and to bring my Uncle Norman back to Nebraska to spend Christmas with us. The weather in Oklahoma was beautiful, and we departed in shirtsleeves.

We met the storm in Kansas, and temperatures soon dropped to near zero. Dad's Studebaker was beginning to slip and spin which prompted us to stop while the men put chains on the car tires. Our concern deepened when stalled cars began to appear along the road. Passing them was tricky, but with the help of Delbert and Norman and a shovel, we managed to move around them and keep going.

We drove down the middle of the road, more worried about hitting a stalled vehicle or skidding off the shoulder than we were about oncoming traffic since very few moving cars were on the road. The strong wind came through every crack. Only scant warmth from the heater reached the back seat. We had blankets and were using them, but when Luverne complained her feet were cold, I admitted mine were, also.

"Put your feet over this way," said Norman, "and I'll try to rub some warmth into them." He massaged first Luverne's feet and then mine.

A patrolman stopped us in southern Nebraska.

"We are asking all travelers to seek refuge until this storm blows out," he said. "The farther north you go the worse the conditions are. Visibility is dangerously low."

"We live south of York which isn't too much farther," my father told him. "We need to get home for the sake of the livestock. Since I know these roads well, and I have chains on my car, I'd like to proceed."

Reluctantly, the patrolman let us continue. We all strained our eyes into the swirling whiteness, struggling to detect possible vehicles on the road. The drifts got deeper, especially where they piled up near stuck cars. We inched along--shoveled--and inched.

It was an extended, cold, anxious battle, but we made it. Our driveway was lined with cedars on both sides. Even though the storm was in its initial stages, snow was already piling up between the cedars. I don't remember how we got into the yard. Walked, I suppose.

That winter, blizzard followed blizzard, and we couldn't use our driveway until late spring. The two rows of cedars and the space between them were covered with huge drifts. I do recall that the snow was so hard in some places we could drive the tractor over the drifts, even over banks that went over fences and gates.

Rosemary Linder, who later married my brother Maynard Matlock, said her father dug a tunnel through the snow from the house to the barn. Once during the winter, their waterworks froze. They loaded every barrel and cream can they could find into a wagon and hitched up the horses. They had to haul water from the neighbors for the house and the livestock for about a week before they got their own pump thawed out.

Stalled Model A
Told by Marie Kramer, Stuart. 1948.

After church services, we went to the rural home of V.J. and Anna Krysl who were my in-laws. In the early afternoon, it began to snow and temperatures plummeted.

My mother-in-law laid down her playing cards.

"You better get on the road," she told my husband, Don. "It's getting bad out." Her eldest brother, Roman, had been killed at age nine in the Blizzard of 1888.

Don grinned teasingly at his mother. "A bit of wind and snow isn't going to hurt anything. My little jalopy will sail right through. It always does."

"You should get where you're going before things get worse. Go right now or else expect to stay for the night."

"We can't stay the night. We have cows to milk. Besides, the dog is in the house. Deal the cards, Bill."

239

"Sit down, Mom," directed Bill amiably. "We can't quit now when Dad and Don are ahead."

A while later, we prepared to leave.

Bessie in Summer

"Wear Tina's overshoes," Don's mother directed me. "Your flimsy Sunday shoes are worthless in snow."

"I know, but Tina's overshoes are too small."

"You'd better stay all night."

"No," insisted Don, who trusted his car. "I'm positive Old Bessie can get us to the corner north of our place. If we need to, we can run the last half mile."

"With Marie in nylon hose and a Sunday dress?"

"Well, we're probably not going to get stalled. You always like to think of the worst thing that can happen, Mom." Don grinned as he scolded gently.

We warmed a quilt by the wood heater. Then with Judy, age two, rolled snugly inside it, we dashed into the howling storm. Stinging cold engulfed me to the waist as the sharp wind swirled my skirt.

Once inside the car, I said, "Hey! The weather *is* bad. There are sure to be drifts piling up."

"The worst places will be on the roads that run north and south," said Don. "The road past the school is high enough so it won't be drifted yet. The stretch past the Miksch place is an east-west road. That leaves only the last half-mile into our place. We'll make it OK."

The sturdy Model A Ford chugged down the road in second gear. With Don's skillful hand on the wheel, the car exploded drifts into loose snow that joined the blizzard in the air. Sometimes we skidded when we hit a diagonal snowbank, but Don stayed in control.

I heaved a sigh when we turned into our half-mile drive. Don knew every swerve in the trail, every dip between sandy knobs. The car skidded, recovered, nosed down, leaped up, zigzagged, and straightened out. We came to a low, sandy stretch.

The car was still in second gear. Don aimed it at the most advantageous angle and revved the motor to gain momentum. I clung to Judy with one arm and braced against the dashboard with the other. There were no seat belts in those days.

The car snapped through a curve and slowed. Don shifted into low. The car reared onto a drift and stopped dead. I knew any other travel would be on foot, but we were young and it was less than half a mile home.

The blizzard leaped in when Don opened the car door. He plucked the tightly wrapped Judy from my arms, and headed south. I jumped out and gasped as I discovered the snow covered my nearly bare legs almost to my knees. I followed Don, every labored step stirring up a spray of snow that was caught by the fierce wind.

Battling the wind and the deep snow with the bundled Judy in his arms soon had Don panting.

"Give her to me," I shouted above the howl of the storm. "I'm used to toting her around." Thereafter, we took turns carrying her. Our short, snow-hampered steps made the distance seem endless. My hands, feet, and legs quickly became numb.

I was relieved when, panting, we climbed up the north side of the drift that rose over our cellar. Reaching the top, I handed Judy to Don and sat down with nothing between the full length of my numb legs and the snow except my thin nylons. I slid to the ground below. It was a relief to get into the leeway between the cellar and the house. I hurried to the east porch and reached for the doorknob.

I was shocked to find that my hands wouldn't close around the knob. I was disbelieving. How could I have gotten so cold that quickly?

"Open the door!" shouted Don insistently.

I tried again. No luck. My hands were like two flat boards. I put one on either side of the knob and tried to turn it. It wouldn't budge.

"I can't open the door! My hands are dead."

He soon had the door open and we bounded inside.

I set Judy, still swathed in the quilt, on the couch and cautioned her to stay there until we had started the fires. Then I removed my snow-packed shoes and nylons and slid into some bedroom slippers. In the meantime, Don got an armload of kindling from the porch, tossed it in the heater, stuck in several kerosene soaked cobs, piled on some small slabs of wood that had been meant for the kitchen range, and threw in a match. I stood near the warming stove.

Almost immediately my hands and legs began to burn like fire. I moved back from the stove and began patting them gently. They were covered with marbled red and white splotches. I was soon moaning and pacing the floor.

Don looked on with amazement. "It can't be that bad," he told me.

After a few hours, I was able to pretend to feel normal. Apparently my bare legs, feet, and hands had been frostbitten in the relatively short run. They healed in a few weeks but they were subject to chilblains for the rest of the winter.

But this storm was only the beginning. Possibly, that afternoon Old Jack Frost stood looking at us. He might have grinned wryly and said, "You think this is bad? Just wait until you see what else we have planned for you during this winter of 1948-49."

Sudden Storm
Told by Kathleen Miles, Brownlee. 1948-'49.

While I was home from Duchesne College at Christmas time, my sister and I and our boyfriends, Carl Faulhaber and Robert Miles, went to Valentine on New Year's Eve to a movie. We had had some bad storms in November and December, but this last day of 1948 was pleasant. When we came out of the movie, however, it was snowing and blowing.

Visibility was poor, and drifts were forming across the roads. Sometimes we could hit a drift and make it through. Other times the boys got out in the stormy darkness and shoveled. We girls had not worn caps and gloves, and none of us had overshoes.

We got a couple miles beyond where Robert lived and as far as the Carl Faulhaber Ranch. Genevieve and I stayed there, but Robert felt he must get back to the Miles Ranch. Later I learned the car stalled in a deep drift, but they were able to walk the rest of the way.

The telephones were out and we couldn't contact our parents. I knew my mother was wild with worry, but there was no way to let her know I was safe.

After a couple days the weather cleared enough so my dad could travel with a team and sled. Following the road he figured we had taken, he at last came to the cabin where we were and stopped to check. It was a glad reunion both at the time of his appearance and also when we arrived home.

I was concerned about how I would get back to Omaha to my college classes for we were completely snowbound. Finally, my cousin, Dan Higgins, who lived in Ainsworth, came to my aid. He had an airplane. He put skis on it, picked me up, and took me to Omaha. I didn't get home until spring.

I'm sure you believe me when I say that every time our children went somewhere in the winter, I made sure they had plenty of warm clothing along.

Charley Tasler's Trip to Town
Told by Charley Tasler, Atkinson. 1949.

In January, Charley Tasler who lived about fourteen miles southwest of Atkinson, was desperate for a way to feed his cattle. The snow was so deep his tractors were useless. He telephoned Keating Implement and bought a Caterpillar. He also called Leo Kramer and asked him to build a sled with a six by eight foot box.

"My son Charles and I rode horses to town to get the Cat," said Charley. "We left before dawn when the temperature was about 21 degrees below zero. We had warm clothes, but even then, it was mighty fresh out."

Marlie Fetherston and a friend who had been snowed in at Taslers for a few days rode with them. It was a slow trip because the horses broke through in places and had to lunge to get out of the deep snow. Often the drifts were too deep on the roads, and the riders had to hunt their way on higher ground through meadows and pastures. Sometimes they had to take fences down.

After they arrived in Atkinson, they learned that Rudy Dvorak and Jim Ziska were stranded there, and were looking for a way home. The two men joined them in the sled pulled by Tasler's new Cat.

In the box, they hauled mail and groceries for the neighbors and two barrels of diesel oil for the Cat. They tied the horses behind the sled.

Jim sat near the barrels, one of which had a loose bung, and fuel leaked on him. When he arrived home long after dark, he discovered that the seeping fuel had burned his back and shoulders.

Caught in a Blizzard
Told by Dorothy (Koca) Bunker, Milligan. 1949.

My sister, Angeline, who was attending college in Lincoln, was coming home for the weekend. She caught a ride with friends as far as Wilbur. Then she called our parents, Louis and Alice Koca, to come and pick her up.

My husband, Jim, our year-old baby, Letitia, and I lived a mile from my parents, and we were at their house that day.

"Let the baby go with us," said my mother. "She will enjoy the ride."

"I'd rather she didn't go," I replied. "The weather doesn't look that settled."

"I don't think the weather will be a problem," said Mother. "We won't be gone that long." But she respected my wishes and said no more about taking the baby.

By the time they had driven to Wilbur, an ugly blizzard had moved in. They picked up Angeline and quickly headed back. The winds accelerated and soon visibility was down to zero. About halfway home, they stalled and were forced to spend the night in the car.

Worried, we waited at their farm, wondering where they were. The howling wind was thick with snow, preventing us from seeing out. As concerned as we were about them, I can't imagine how frantic we'd have been had they taken the baby. It was a long night. Jim did their chores that evening and again in the morning.

In the stalled car, they had blankets and Angeline was wearing a fur coat, an Alaskan seal garment made by an acquaintance in Lincoln. Even then, she was bitterly cold. They huddled together in an attempt to counteract the frigid wind that edged through every crack in the car body. Periodically, they massaged their feet and hands in an attempt to keep their circulation going.

By morning the storm had let up enough to reveal a farmyard in the distance. My father walked to it and called for help. Of course, he also called us to tell us they were safe.

Sick Baby
Told by Marian Roberts, Atkinson. 1949.

We were living two miles southeast of Atkinson, said Marian Roberts. Fred was employed in town by Frank

Brady, and because of the constant storms and the deep snow, he and our school-age children walked to and from town each day. I was home alone with our two small children, ages 18 months and three years.

We had no telephone and no electricity. Fred kept the wood box full, but since we had an outside hand pump, I had to go out repeatedly for water, and also to visit the toilet out back. The snow was impossibly deep. Drifts were as high as the eaves on the barn.

Our older toddler, Mickey, had a bad cold, so I had the kids sitting on a day bed in the living room where I was doing my best to entertain them. I wasn't aware that the baby, Ron, was sick, but I wanted to keep him, as well as the older one, from getting down on the cold floor.

All at once Ron stiffened and threw his head back. He had gone into convulsions. Being, inexperienced with such a situation, I was so scared I was shaking as badly as he was. I didn't know what to do. I got a quilt, wrapped him in it, and rocked him. I was terrified, knowing there was no way I could get help, no matter how bad the emergency might become.

After he quit convulsing, he went into a deep sleep. Sometimes I couldn't tell whether or not he was breathing. Was he dying? Was he already dead? I was sick with worry. It was a terrible time, but with prayers and home remedies, he did survive.

A Small Girl's Promise
Told by Loretta (McGowan) Teinert, McCool Junction. 1949.

During the winter of '48-'49, my parents ran out of food, and we were living on some of mother's old hens, butchered one by one. Finally, my father, James McGowan, walked to McCool Junction. He planned to get the mail and bring home groceries. He pulled a child's sled on which he loaded a 50-pound sack of flour and a gunnysack with smaller items such as sugar, yeast, coffee, beans, rice, and oatmeal. When he picked up the stranded mail at the post office, he received a nine-day-old telegram informing him that his father in Ireland had passed away. It was, of course, a jarring blow.

I was four years old, and didn't understand what had happened. That evening, I climbed onto Dad's lap and asked why he was sad.

"My father died," he said, "and my relatives in Ireland are sad. I feel bad because I can't go to Ireland to be with them."

I patted his cheek. "Don't worry, Daddy," I told him. "When I get big, I'll take you to Ireland."

While I was a teenager, I worked and saved. I wrapped meat at a grocery, and cleaned in the hospital. By the time I was nineteen, I had saved enough for plane tickets to Ireland for my parents and me.

After the plows, Pet and Barney are put to work.

James McGowan, years later...

Courtesy of Loretta McGowan Teinert

It was a wonderful trip, almost like going to fairyland. Their standard of living was much different from ours, for they still toasted bread over the open hearth and herded sheep in the meadows. They "cut turf" (peat) for fuel.

We had a glorious time. Dad was a new person. He seemed younger and more animated. He danced an Irish jig and laughed with boyhood friends. It was a magical experience for us all.

Angry Calves
Told by Robert Miles, Brownlee. 1949.

Later in the winter, after more bad storms, the fences drifted under, and the cattle could walk over the top of them. The calves penned near the ranch yard got out. After Dick Lovejoy and I hunted for three days, we finally found them near some haystacks.

They were blind because their faces were encrusted in snow from a driving storm. They didn't understand why we were riding close to them and slapping their faces. As soon as we had knocked enough snow off so a critter could see, he'd let out an angry bellow and charge us. We'd get out of the way, but then had to ride back and slap another icy face.

Dick was quite a clown. Waving his red bandana, he pretended to be a bullfighter. The handkerchief was small enough so the calves didn't pay much attention.

After we got the critters de-iced, we were able to drive them over the drifts back to the ranch. We put some posts in the snowbanks and made a temporary fence above the one that was covered by the hard drifts.

Cow on a Pedestal
Told by Morell Ayers, Thedford. 1949.

The Ayers Ranch borders Halsey National Reserve. One day when I was out by the Reserve, I found a critter that had apparently walked in a small circle while it was storming. As the snow fell, he packed it down, but much of the snow that fell around his little circle was whisked away by strong winds. By the time I found him, he was standing on a platform of packed snow about three feet high.

I tried to chase the steer off the mound, but he refused to jump down. I rode my horse back and forth to make a trail, but still he couldn't be persuaded to leap.

Finally, I roped him and dragged him off.

I rode a spirited horse. Usually, if he hadn't been ridden for a day or two, he would try to buck me off. But I really wore him out that winter, riding around in the deep snow. Whenever I got off to do something, he stood still. When I came back, he'd be standing in the very spot where I left him, too tired to move. He didn't even think of bucking.

"What was his name?" someone asked.

"Why, uh--uh--he didn't have a name."

No one smiled or challenged the remark, but all knew the horse had a name. All, too, knew the problem. Morell didn't want to mention the colorful name of his ornery steed in mixed company.

Ranch by the Roadside
Told by June Gilman, Atkinson. 1949.

We lived near Highway 11 about 17 miles south of Atkinson. Since ours was the only ranch close to the road, we became a stopping-off place for people going farther south. Some stayed for a meal and others overnight. We butchered a pig at the beginning of winter, and I ran out of meat before the roads were open again.

One evening we heard a motor in the distance. We looked out and could see lights dipping up and down over the snowdrifts. What vehicle, we wondered, could cross the hills and the drifts so effortlessly?

It was Raymond Garwood on a new Caterpillar tractor. He had been stalled in town. Desperate to get back to his ranch near Swan Lake, he bought a Caterpillar. He and Chris Warden, also from the Swan Lake area, stayed overnight.

The Gene Hansen family were stalled on Highway 11, and stayed at our place. Gene walked home the next day, but his wife and children were with us several days.

I recall that some of the Paddocks stayed with us for a time. Later in the winter when the army came to open roads, we kept army men several nights.

We couldn't get to our haystacks with the tractor and underslung. (An underslung is a large platform on wheels that can move an entire stack of hay.) My husband, Lee, fed the cattle the best he could with a team and sled.

Telephone Call
Told by Dave Haumann, Thedford. 1949.

When the State Road Department in Lincoln was unable to get in touch with one of its employees who was in Thedford, they called me, Dave Haumann, because I worked for the telephone company.

"I've been trying to get in touch with Shorty Parker," said the road official. "Can you get a message to him?"

"We're having a bad storm here," I said. "Shorty doesn't have a telephone, but I probably can get a message to him."

"Just tell him to call me back." He gave a telephone number.

Shorty was staying several blocks away, and the drifts were piled high. Pulling on my coveralls and warmest cap, I stepped into the howling storm. The wind nearly took my breath away, but I braced myself and headed into it. In addition to the sting of the whipping wind and falling snow, there was a terrific ground blizzard.

I struggled to stay on my feet, glad the drifts were solid enough to hold my weight. I pushed forward. Suddenly, one foot broke through the snow, and my entire leg disappeared into a drift. While I struggled to retrieve it, the other leg fell through.

Using my hands and feet together, I finally crept back onto the crusted top layer. In order to distribute my weight on four points instead of two, I crawled on my hands and knees. This put my head near the drifts and allowed the skittering snow to continually slam me in the face. It was a long, miserable three blocks to Shorty's place.

After delivering the message, he and I headed back over the deep snow to my place. I called the Lincoln office and handed the telephone to Shorty.

"We would like to have a photo of Highway 83 south of Thedford on the Dismal River," said the Lincoln man. "Can you drive down and take a picture for us?"

For a moment, Shorty was silent. The Dismal River was about twenty miles away. Finally he answered.

"I'm sorry, but I can't do that. We are in the midst of a paralyzing storm. My car is drifted so deep I can't even tell where it is. The streets look like a mountain range. Not a thing is stirring."

"Oh. I didn't know it was that bad. How did you manage to get to a telephone?"

Shorty laughed. "Well, I certainly didn't drive my car. This may be hard for you to believe, but I came most of the way on my hands and knees."

A Trip for Supplies
Told by Robert Schrup, Burwell. 1949.

I was discharged from the military in the summer of 1946, and my wife, Bernice, and I began setting up our ranch. When the blizzards of '48-'49 hit, I hadn't yet been able to afford a tractor. I was hauling hay with a steel-wheeled hayrack and a team of horses. I struggled long hours every day, but the drifting snow was winning the battle. It was especially deep around the haystacks. Sometimes it balled up on the wheels of the wagon and had to be chopped off. Other times the horses got stuck and we had to shovel them out. It was an exhausting mess.

When aid came to this area in the form of a "hay lift," I asked for some bales to be dropped from an airplane. It was a great help. I put them in the haymow and used them sparingly.

Even though we had stocked up on groceries for the winter, we were running out of everything. Worse still, Bernice's uncle, Art Scherzberg, who lived two miles back of us, was a diabetic and was low on insulin. It was late winter, and we knew the main highways had been opened, but our problem was getting to them.

A neighbor who lived about four miles away, Lee Johnson, had a little jeep, and he decided we should attempt a trip to town. He picked up a fellow from the Fred White place, and they managed to get to our ranch by hunting their way on high ground, shoveling, and following trails packed from hauling hay.

I managed to give the cattle a wagonload of hay, and got another load on for the next day. I unhitched the horses, Pearl and Polly, and turned them around toward the hayrack so they could eat from the load.

We couldn't go the usual way to Burwell, which was southeast of us, because the road was still closed. However, we managed to fight our way to Highway 183, which was about six miles west of us. We went to Taylor and then to Burwell. With three of us, there were two to push and to shovel whenever we got stalled in the drifts.

When we arrived in Burwell, we hurried to get supplies loaded. Lee Johnson filled the jeep with coal. I filled a cream can with fuel oil and tied it to the bumper in front. (We mostly burned wood, but used an oil-burning heater in emergencies when we couldn't manage to get in enough wood.) We stacked groceries and bundles of mail in every corner.

The sky was beginning to darken when we headed home. The wind was rising, and we knew our tracks would soon drift shut. Shortly after we left the highway, the little jeep slid off the road and high centered. There was a ranch about half a mile away, and Lee walked there and called my wife.

We couldn't shovel out the jeep in the pitch-blackness of night, so Lee and I walked to our ranch, arriving in the early morning. I had the insulin in an inner pocket so it wouldn't freeze. Once home, I fed the team some grain while Bernice set out some food for us. Then we ate and took a few brief winks of sleep before dawn.

I walked behind my horses all the way back to the jeep. The weather was so cold the jeep wouldn't start-- wouldn't even offer. But the horses had been working hard all winter, and when I gave the command, they squatted low, and yanked it out. We pulled it about half a mile, but it wouldn't start.

There was an old building beside the road, and I knew there was some lathe in it. We got some, and I soaked one end of a slat in the gas tank and set it afire. We held it under the manifold of the jeep. When we got it warmed up, it started.

By then it was about 10 AM. It took Lee Johnson until 4 PM to get the four miles from our house to his. I tell you, that trip was an exhausting hassle. In addition, we were behind with our feeding.

After I fed, I got on my saddle horse, Lady, and set out to take the insulin to Bernice's uncle. It was only two miles, but we had to wander around on high ground because in the lower areas, the snow was too deep for the horse. Even then, the going was tough. Sometimes she walked on top of the snow, but other times she broke through. Then she'd have to scramble until she managed to get on top again.

It was late when I got home, and I was glad to grab a bite of food and fall into bed.

The Load of Grain
Told by Alice Dubry, Thedford. 1949.

We were living at Broken Bow during the Blizzards of '49. My folks lived about seven miles north and had been snowed in for some weeks. They were low on groceries, but worse yet, they ran out of feed for the animals. They needed a load of grain. We had a grain truck, so as soon as Highway 183 was open, we called the folks.

"We can get out on 183, I told them, but how will we get to your place from the main road?"

"Reed and I will plow a trail across high ground from our turn-off to the ranch," said my father, Lloyd Hamilton.

It was a good thing we left early. The highway had been plowed for one-way car traffic, but the snow was deep, and our truck box was too wide. Progress was slow because it was necessary to scrape off the sides of the drifts in order for the truck to get through.

We were glad when we saw my dad and Reed, coming to meet us with the tractor. They helped with the shovel work. Even then, it took a long time to get to their place. By the time the grain was unloaded, the winds had come up and the roads were blowing. It was too late in the day for us to fight our way back.

We were snowed in for some days before the roads were again opened, but at least Dad had grain to help out with feeding problems.

Sledding Hay
Told by Bill Krysl, Stuart. 1949

Bill Krysl said, "Earlier, we had made a box about 10' by 10' to haul bluegrass seed. Now, Dad put runners on it. Early one morning, Brother Leo came with his team and sled to our place and borrowed our larger sled to go to Crawford's. There, he stabled his horses and hooked Crawford's four-horse team to our sled. He and Crawford hunted their way across the prairie toward Stuart, choosing higher ground in order to avoid the deepest drifts.

"Mom had called the store for groceries. Leo came home in the night, bringing mail and groceries for the closer neighbors.

"Usually, I hauled hay with a hayrack," continued Bill. "But now the snow was too deep which meant I had only that 10'x10' sled. Of course, I had to make repeated trips to the meadow. It was hard on the horses to fight the drifts.

"One good thing was that we were able to keep the telephone lines working. We had a party line with about twelve or fifteen families on it. The phones wouldn't ring, but we could talk and be heard by any neighbor who happened to come to his phone.

"At first, we'd often pick up the phone to see if anyone was on the line. Then we could tell the two people who were talking to help us watch for our relatives and tell them we would come on the line at a given time. Eventually, people worked it out so each family had a specific time to talk. Everyone soon knew the schedule. It worked better than you would suppose.

"Each family was responsible for keeping the line repaired from their place to the next farm. I can still see Dad. If the phone went dead, he'd toss a wire stretcher over his shoulder and walk north through the trees and across the pond to look for breaks in the line."

Judy Krysl,
waiting for Grandma
to come on the
PARTY LINE.

V.J.Krysl
considers digging
out the **PASTURE
GATE** far below him.
He decides to
build a temporary
fence on top
of the snow.

Imaginary Friends
Stuart & Atkinson. 1949.

Judy Krysl was about two and a half years old when she acquired an imaginary friend named Catalina. Is it any wonder, since she had been shut in the house all winter because of the successive blizzards? Catalina was involved in all of Judy's activities.

Judy's mother welcomed the little newcomer and treated her the same as she did Judy, dressing, washing, combing and feeding both. Usually Judy's father was equally cooperative, reacting quickly when Judy's alarmed cry signaled that he had sat on Catalina or stepped on her invisible toys. He was especially good at helping Catalina clean up her plate.

On a Sunday morning in the spring, it was raining, and the family made a dash for the pickup as they prepared to depart for church. Once in the vehicle, Judy was tearful. Her daddy, who had carried her to the car, had failed to bring Catalina.

"She wants to stay inside during this downpour," said Don. "She will be warm and dry."

"No, she is dressed for church. She wants to come. Besides, she's too little to stay by herself," wailed Judy.

"Of course, she's too little," said the mother, knowing how concerned the child would be all day without Catalina. "I'll run back and get her." She put a newspaper over her head, and ran back to get the little friend.

Catalina, minding Judy's instructions, was well behaved in church. On the way home, they stopped at Don's parent's farm.

The mother-in-law, upon hearing about Catalina, chided the young mother for participating in the fantasy.

"You shouldn't waste time monkeying around on a Sunday morning, especially when roads are muddy. You need all the time possible to get to church. If you'd ignore her little games, she'd soon forget them."

Catalina stayed until the days warmed. Then Judy and her dog played outside with tricycle, wagon, cats, baby chicks, doll, swing, and all the usual things that interest farm children. Catalina had served her purpose, and slowly faded away.

In telling this story over the years, the family found that other children of their acquaintance also had imaginary friends. A fellow named Hellagoda shared Mark Serbousek's playtime for several weeks. One day Mark wanted to go downtown to get some glue to mend a toy airplane. His mother wouldn't let him go, so he sent Hellagoda. Mark waited and waited, but Hellagoda never came back. He must have gotten lost.

Mike Krysl, Ken and Charlene's son, had a companion named Mawchy who shared Mike's home and toys.

Chuck Krysl named his tiny friend Little Lou. He sat in the palm of Chuck's hand and had soft conversations with him. One day Little Lou was on the floor, and Chuck's mother, Theresa, stepped on him. Sadly, little Lou didn't survive. Chuck was heart-broken.

Danger at the Dam
Told by John Dobrovolny, Atkinson. 1949.

After school on hot days some of us students from St. Joseph's went to the dam west of Atkinson to cool off. There was no swimming pool in town, and few of us were good swimmers. But we could dog paddle a little, and we appreciated an hour of splashing and clowning.

Because the huge drifts of the '48-'49 winter had melted, the Elkhorn River was out of its banks. There was a swift current in the channel, but the flooded meadows along the river were shallow enough to be safe for beginning swimmers. I usually paddled around until I grew tired, then put my feet down until I caught my breath.

At one such time, I lowered my feet and suddenly realized I was in deep water. When it closed over my head, I knew I had swum into the deep channel of the river. I pawed to the surface and struggled toward the shore, but the current was strong and I lacked experience in dealing with such a situation. I went down again. After repeating the process several times, I realized, even though I was near the underwater shelf, I was caught in a deep current that I could not negotiate. I called for help.

My cousin, John Ziska, came to my aid and pulled me to the safety of the underwater bank. Without his assistance, I'm sure I'd have drowned.

It was a couple weeks later. Ed Ziska, John's brother, and I had been to the old gravel pit and were walking back to town. We met our friends, Marvin Farewell and Harold Klinger.

"Are there any girls out there?" asked Klinger. "Marvin doesn't have his bathing suit along."

"Here," I said, "Use mine."

2001

John Dobrovolny and John Ziska

Ed and I were still in the western part of town when the fire whistle went off. Immediately, we were concerned and paused to see which way the fire trucks would go. When they went west, we turned and ran that direction also.

By the time we got to the gravel pit, a rescue operation was underway, looking for two boys who had disappeared under the water. Doctor McKee, one of Atkinson's elderly doctors, was among the onlookers.

"If they find them right away, Doc, can the boys possibly be saved?" asked a bystander.

"No," said the doctor, "They've been under too long."

The bodies of Harold Klinger and Marvin Farewell, the latter wearing my swimming trunks, were recovered that evening. It was a sobering event, made worse for me because I had nearly drowned earlier in the month. Atkinson soon began planning a city swimming pool.

More '48-49 Comments

"Gee whillikers!" exclaimed Ralph Ries, Atkinson. "That was some winter. It started snowing in the fall and never quit. Some people didn't have Christmas until spring."

Ralph couldn't get around with his tractor. He hooked a team to a steel-wheeled wagon and hauled hay to his cows with it. Because of the many trips he made, he packed the snow. When more snow fell, it was packed on top of the old. Finally he had a trail about four feet high.

Ralph's sister, Henrietta, was teaching school in District 89. The school was closed a good part of the winter.

John Steinhauser of Stuart died early in '49. Snowplows got the road opened to the cemetery, but the drifts in the cemetery were too huge. The coffin bearers struggled from the gate to the gravesite, stumbling through the snow, often sliding the coffin on the top of the drifts.

"That was our worst winter," said Harvey Evans of Ogallala. "A lot of cattle were lost that year, and many got frozen feet, couldn't walk, and had to be sold. We sold about 60 head and lost about the same number. Cattle piled in fence corners, drifted in, and froze or smothered. One rancher lost 300 head, but I won't give his name. People are embarrassed to lose that many. It makes them seem like poor cattlemen, but that wasn't the case."

"My tractor was helpless," said Frank Stanek who lived south of Atkinson. "I fed 200 head of cattle the best I could, using horses and a wagon box mounted on two logs for runners. I made as many trips as the length of the day allowed, and the horses and I all wore ourselves out. And you can bet, not a single cow was overfed!

"I had a good team. Their names were Blue and Daisy. Boy, did I ever appreciate them. They saved my cowherd."

Mrs. Pete Ramold died in January. The church service was held on schedule, but the roads to the cemetery couldn't be opened. The undertaker stored the body for about a week or ten days to give the road crew time to open a route.

Gus Obermire, Stuart, stated: "I put tractor wheels on a truck to carry mail. I still couldn't get through my entire mail route. That was one bad winter."

The drift in Greenfields' yard was so high it reached the eaves of the barn and swooped down on the other side. Since he was afraid of heights, Lawrence carefully crept up the side of the drift and peeked over to see how much snow was piled in front of the barn.

When the picture taken by his wife came back, she entitled it, "Where, oh where have my little cows gone?"

...he was
afraid
of
HEIGHTS...

Pete Weber was working at the sale barn southeast of Atkinson. One day they started shoveling the snow off the road, hoping to get to town. They shoveled all day without much headway. The next day they got up and found the trail was blown full. They started over. It took them two weeks to get the road open. It was open a short time, and then new snow and more wind closed it again.

Theresa (Laible) Krysl, Atkinson, who was a junior in high school, remembers she got to school only two days during January. Finally, her dad took her to town with a team and wagon and she boarded with the George Penry family. Her parents had no phone, so she wasn't able to call home. She remembers being distressingly homesick.

Joan (Steinhauser) Dobrovolny was in high school. The class play was scheduled for November 18, 1948, which was the date of the first big storm that winter. At noon the play was postponed. Because of successive storms, they weren't able to have it until spring.

A huge drift went up and over Steinhauser's grove and yard. There was no way to get a vehicle out. Joan climbed over the drifts and down to the highway where DeWayne or Hazel Lockmon picked her up and took her the two miles to school. If it was storming out, she stayed home and if it began storming while she was in school, she left early. She missed a lot of school that year.

Helen Coufal of Coufal's Market in Stuart said: "Ed had to walk to work all winter. He carried his scoop shovel back and forth because he needed it both places. To protect his face on mornings when the temperature was low, he raised the scoop shovel in front of it.

"If a rescue mission was going to a rural neighborhood, people in that area telephoned for groceries, and we sent them out. We didn't ask any questions or make any comments about being paid at the time. In late spring after the drifts melted, we sent bills. Most people were glad to pay, but some didn't.

"Fifteen years later we were closing our store, and I sent bills out with a note that said, 'It is better to pay your bills in this world than in the next.' Again, some paid, but not all."

The wife of a rancher in northern Nebraska was snowed in town. Snowed in with the rancher was the hired girl. When the Fifth Army rescuers arrived, it was about 4:00 o'clock in the morning.

They could see the underslung with a stack of hay on it. It was completely covered by snow banks. Cattle had climbed on it and were standing on top. Obviously the man needed help to get his underslung out and to get a trail opened to hay. The rescuers knocked on the door.

The man was embarrassed. He didn't want to ruin the hired girl's reputation, or his own, by letting it be known she had been snowed in with him for some time. His goal was to quickly get rid of the rescuers.

"I have plenty of hay, and the cattle are fine," he told them. "We aren't in need of anything."

Ed Krysl said, "It was a terrible winter. Just terrible. When spring arrived, we thought it was finally coming to a close. But at the end of March we got a dreadful spring storm. The snow was fine and the wind so strong a person could hardly breathe. People lost a lot of cattle during that storm. They were weak from the hard winter and they smothered in the fine, blowing snow."

On March 30, the Dohman Brothers, rural Atkinson, went out to rescue some yearlings that were caught in the sudden storm. The men became exhausted, probably from struggling in the deep, heavy snow. Their bodies were later found in a meadow near their home.

Sophie Murphy said, "The first time I saw plastic bags was at the home of my sister-in-law, Amelia Kaup. She had bought them, six-for-$1.00, through a homemaker's program on the radio. She washed them and used them over and over. The six bags lasted for months."

Mid-Century
By Marie Kramer

As we leave the grandchildren of the pioneers in the 1950's, they are teenagers or young adults. The men, home from battle, are trying to catch up for the time lost during the war. Some are attending college on the GI Bill, some are working at various jobs, and still others are trying to get their starts on farms or ranches.

Rural women in Nebraska continue to manage without electricity, which means no refrigeration, no indoor bathroom, no hot water in a faucet, and no electrical appliances. In order to have meat, each morning during warm weather, the rural homemaker continues to kill, pluck, and butcher a chicken or two.

Each day, mothers wash diapers and baby clothes by hand, for the washing machine powered by a gasoline motor is used only once a week, usually on Mondays. Tuesdays are for pressing clothes, and all items except underwear are ironed.

Teenagers, wearing bobby socks and saddle shoes, are jitterbugging. Big band music remains popular. Women deem nylon hosiery a necessity. Harry Truman, who took over when FDR died, is serving a second term. Television sets are beginning to appear. After depressed times and war, the grandchildren of the pioneers are producing the baby boomers.

Unrest in Europe keeps the diplomats on their toes, but mostly ordinary citizens are willing to leave the beginning of the cold war and the Berlin Airlift to those men in charge. People are worrying about what to do in the event of an atomic attack.   Most, however, have no clear idea of the great danger the Soviets are posing to the free world.   ·

This book leaves the grandchildren of the pioneers looking ahead with hope and determination.

Index

MY MOM & DAD
worked
there

268